D0415837

LEE DUNNE

No Time for Innocence

Also by the author

Goodbye to the Hill
A Bed in the Sticks
Paddy Maguire is Dead
Does Your Mother?
Ringleader
Ringmaster
Requiem for Reagan
Hell is Filling Up
The Corpse Wore Grey
Midnight Cabbie
The Day of the Cabbie
The Cabbie Who Came In from the
    Cold
The Virgin Cabbies
The Cabfather
Maggie's Story
Big Al
Harbour Hotel

Non Fiction
Sober Thoughts on Alcoholism

Stage Plays
Goodbye to the Hill
Return to the Hill
Does Your Mother?
Busy Bodies
One Man's Meat
Only the Earth
The Full Shilling
Tough Love
Bless Them All (One-Man Show)

Television
Only the Earth
No Hiding Place
Callan
Vendetta
Troubleshooters
Wednesday Play
Weavers Green

Radio Plays
The Trials of Tommy Tracey
Whatever Happened to You, Mick
    O'Neill?
Tough Love
Aunty Kay
No Hiding Place
The Pot Wallopers
Only the Earth
The Kennedys of Castleross
Harbour Hotel
Konvenience Korner
(comprising 2,000 scripts)

Film
The Pale Faced Girl
Paddy
Wedding Night
Circles
Goodbye to the Hill (optioned)
Do You Remember Bray (optioned)

LEE DUNNE

No Time for Innocence

Gill & Macmillan

Gill & Macmillan Ltd
Hume Avenue, Park West, Dublin 12
with associated companies throughout the world
www.gillmacmillan.ie
© Lee Dunne 2000
0 7171 3110 6
Design by Vermillion
Print origination by Carole Lynch
Printed by ColourBooks Ltd, Dublin

This book is typeset in Sabon 10pt on 15pt.

All rights reserved. No part of this publication may be copied,
reproduced or transmitted in any form or by any means,
without permission of the publishers.

A CIP catalogue record for this book is available
from the British Library.

1 3 5 4 2

LEABHARLANN CHONTAE Longfoirt

L 92. 399| 920 |DUN

For Katy who knows now
For Sarah who doesn't know yet
And for Maura who holds the torch

With thanks to Michael Ryan, Gordon Thomas, George and Laura Pratt

And for Glasser who died too young. RIP.

Some names have been changed in this memoir to protect relatives of those concerned.

Contents

1

Going back so that I could write this story, I've been swamped at times by the flotsam and jetsam of a life that turned into some kind of wild river, with me in there getting soaked to the skin. A river of memories now. Memories like postcards sent to yourself, thrown into a drawer, ink faded, so how accurate, how factual are the pictures you can make out under the hard lamp of your curiosity?

I feel my first words were 'Leave me Ma alone!' I hear a threat in it. And it has to be directed at Da since he felt entitled to put a hand on my mother. Surely there were many baby words before this; just no memory of them. So all I can give you is what comes up on the roller, but I'll do the best I can to hit the bull's-eye of truth because that's all I'm interested in these days.

I'll vouch to a day in 1940 when I was five years old, in a hospital with the little brother, Brendan, and the sister, Rose, to see Ma, frightened because I really had no idea what was going on. Ma is in this big room called a ward after something called an operation. She hardly notices me beyond a squeeze from her hand which is bruised-looking, and in that minute I know I began to believe some of the rumours, the whispers that were going around about her.

Whispers from people like Da and our grand-aunty Kay who spent more time in our flat than she did in her room at number 8 Ranelagh. I'd heard her with her whispering at the door, that it was touch and go whether Katy was going to make it or not. At the time I didn't know exactly what that meant, but there's something about the way these things are acted out that makes you worry. You don't need arithmetic to add up two and two and feel four in your belly.

'All the plumbing had to come out. The baby girl's in heaven, better off with The Man Above than living in this dump. Been through hell, so she has.' Aunty Kay's very words at the door with Mrs Doyle, who loved a good gossip as much as the next person.

Being gabby little me, I kiss Ma and I say, 'I know you've been through hell!' Ma sniffs back a tear and Rose grabs me and makes me stand back. She is twelve going on thirteen going on a very big mouth! It's as if she thinks she's Ma the way she dishes out the orders.

'Just keep your mouth closed and don't bother Ma.' Rose gives me a shake as though I'm badly in need of it. 'Ma's getting better but she's not up to you pair yet!' The puss on her letting you know she'd belt you as quick as she'd look at you. I never really got around to liking Rose.

A minute later she is in tears. I don't know what's going on because I'm looking at an oul' one on her last legs in a bed in the corner. But I'm made up to see Rose upset. Let her keep her shakes to herself.

'A cake, Rose. I sent home a cake!' Ma is so angry you don't have to strain yourself to get it.

'Mammy, Da never brought any cake home,' Rose pleads as though it's all her fault. 'He never even said he was in to see you yesterday.'

'Ah sweet Jesus. The deceitful animal! The woman in the next bed there — she died in the night, God be good to her — she gave me a cake because she couldn't eat it and I gave it to your Da. Take it home to the kids! I said it three times just to make sure. Him and his cursa God mother! Hell is too good for the pair of them!'

I'm wishing that Ma had held onto the cake till we came in ourselves to see her. Cake was something didn't grow on trees, not where we lived. Certainly not at number 162 in the Buildings. At times even bread was scarce on the home front. Fresh bread anyway.

Ma collapsed back on the pillows that day and we had to go so the nurse could look after her. Rose was a bit shell-shocked but she didn't say anything. Rose thought little brothers were for other girls and you could hear Ma coming through when my sister said, 'Little pigs should be seen and not heard!' Rose was a great one for quoting Ma. 'Don't do as I do, do as I say!' was another one she rattled out to us from time to time.

All the same, as much as Rose scared me and ordered me about, much as I hated her at times, she was our rock along with Aunty Kay, the only woman I ever met who couldn't boil potatoes without ruining them.

Ma was laid up, Da had nothing to give us, and, because you were small, nobody considered you beyond your physical needs. They'd talk to each other in front of you as though you were deaf, and they'd spell out some words as though you were totally stupid, and all because you were a kid. So I tried to shut them all out, them and their whispers and gossip and their stupid opinions. I dismissed them by just saying Hail Marys all the time, telling God that all I wanted was for Ma to come back home. I didn't say anything to him about her being hateful sometimes. I just wanted her back in the flat and I didn't care about anything else.

The hospital Ma was in was called St Anne's, more of a converted nursing home really, and it was run by the Sisters of Charity of St Vincent de Paul. I was at school in St Louis Convent up in Rathmines, also run by nuns, nuns who didn't know a lot about charity. But I was taught to read there in no time by a lay teacher, Mrs Reynolds, who said I was a very good boy, bright and well mannered in class. She was the only one in St Louis ever said anything like that. As a matter of fact, I can't remember ever hearing the like of it again! I love her right now because she taught me how to write with a nib. A hero of a woman.

We did get Ma home from St Anne's and she was crying a lot, weeping to herself which was something I'd never seen happen except when she just boiled over in temper. For a while, anyway, herself and Da stopped attacking each other the way they normally did over the least thing, but I didn't like the way we were being put out on the street more and more. You were just told to go out and play, so I'd take Brendan by the hand or heave him into our old pram, which was held together with twine, and shove him up to Palmerston Park or somewhere. I began to hate having to go because I didn't want to leave Ma. It was as if I couldn't trust her any more to be there when I got back to the flat.

Will I ever forget the day Brendan got a bang on the head from a swing in the park? I used to look after him the best I could, but this day he just got out of my sight, and he wandered across the flight path of this swing with a kid on there as though he's trying to get to the moon. Bang! Brendan takes a hit in the head, and he's out like a light. A minute later I'm running down Palmerston Road puffing and moaning in terror that the little wagon is gone for his tea, and that Ma will take my life for letting him get killed by the belt of a swing when I should've been minding him.

Ma only gave me a bit of a slap and that was just to shut me up. The minute she wiped Brendan's face with a damp cloth he woke up, and after a drink of water there wasn't a bother on him, although he had a right duck egg on his forehead. I heard Ma sigh as she said something like, 'It's a weary worrold, brethren, God keep us in it!' I hadn't a notion of what she meant but I nodded like a little oul' fella agreeing with her, which I did all the time even when she was in the wrong.

And she could be in the wrong even when she wasn't aware of it. Da might be reading a paper that was a week old and I might ask him a question about something. Whether he was going to give me an answer or not, Ma would dive in fast with something like, 'Ah leave your Da alone. He's weary looking for work — in the newspaper!'

Even at six or seven years of age I could feel that sort of snotty remark going in like a knife and poor Da, he never managed to let it slide over his shoulder out of harm's way. In a few moments they'd be at it, yelling at each other, while my older brother Michael and I, we'd just try to stay out of the way. Things could fly sometimes. A teapot, crash! Tea leaves all over the wallpaper, which was dead anyway. A hatchet once from Da. I can still see it, stuck in the side of the old wardrobe that was in the room with the two beds and only the length of a cat between them.

Michael was a good-looking young fella, a blond, nearly three and a half years older than me. He looked like a German you'd see in the pictures and he had shoulders as wide as the door of our lav. He also carried a very heavy punch, so I usually made sure there was plenty of space if I was annoying him. Da said he could punch like the Granny Dunne and she was famous for the use of her fists. Aunty Kay adored Michael because he looked like 'a Rogers', which was hers and Ma's side of the family, and by the sound of her, only a step down from the royal family over in England.

If Michael was 'a Rogers' I was certainly 'a Dunne', with the dark hair and pale skin that made me look like my Granny who lived in the Gut, down in Ballsbridge. But I got along all right with Michael, which wasn't bad considering we couldn't escape from each other without going out. A funny thing was that we never talked about the rows between Ma and Da. It was as though, well, if you didn't talk about them they hadn't really happened. Meanwhile we just tried to stay out of the way when the words and the slaps and sometimes the delph was flying around the place.

The rows and the fights were always about money, which, in our place, there wasn't any of. And there was no money because there was no work for Da to go to, just as there was no work for most of the other men in the Buildings, and thousands more all over the city of Dublin, as the Fabulous Forties took to the road.

Ma moaned a lot about Da not working. She moaned to us kids, she moaned to herself in the mirror; she even complained to Aunt Lily, who was Da's youngest sister and my second favourite woman on earth. Lily was a born listener and she never seemed to mind hearing the same moan repeated week in, week out, when she dropped in to see us. She was a darling and I was crazy about her, and she said I was the best-looking young fella in Ireland. Lovely Lily with a heart as big as a wardrobe.

'His bloody pride a course! Cost him two grand jobs!' Ma spat the words out while Lily could somehow look as though she was hearing them for the first time instead of God knows how many. 'His feelin's, if you don't mind! Lord Muck has feelin's and his family starvin' half the time!' Ma starting to puff on one of Lily's cigarettes, only sort of inhaling, like someone uncertain about going the whole hog. 'Fags cost money, so I don't want to get a habit goin' that I can't afford.' Lily smoked all the time like Mrs Doyle upstairs, with the fag like a lodger on her lip except when she was eating or drinking. 'The cursa God, Lily, on the day the British pulled out. I saw the writing on the wall that day and I was right, God help me! The Irish couldn't run a two-seat public convenience, so they couldn't. Paint the postboxes green! Put the street names up in Irish! Dear God, we'll starve altogether without the Brits!'

Ma loved all things English but with Lily you wouldn't know. Lily could sing the birds off the bushes but she didn't say a lot. Except about people she knew.

Ma never drank, even when Lily brought an extra bottle of stout or two. Just as well because whatever few pounds arrived into our lives didn't last long. And sometimes when a couple of pounds would tumble out of a letter from Granny Rogers, now living in Middlesex in England, the money seemed to go very rapidly, though there mightn't be anything to show for it. Once or twice I wondered about this. Where did the money go? Then I'd just remind myself that Ma was usually paying off something or other. Still, it would have been nice if it had meant back rashers in a sandwich or big fat Hafner's sausages, but most mornings it was just porridge, which you couldn't seriously call breakfast.

Breakfast to me would have been the fry-up of rashers-sausages-tomatoes, with two big eggs grinning at you and fried bread and, if you were really jammy, black and white pudding. This seemed like a dream when I was seven or eight years old. The only time I'd seen a meal like that was on the screen in the Prinner or the Stella, on Rathmines Road, so I suppose I was very lucky that I liked porridge. Well, I liked it when there was a bit of sugar to go on it with a drop of cow juice. Da ate his porridge, which he always made himself, with salt over it and a little drop of milk. And he was forever saying how good it was to eat it like that, but he remained on his ownio and we kept the salt for the spuds.

Once a week an egg would turn up and Ma would beat it into a sup of milk. Then she'd dip bread into the mix and fry it to make what she called French Toast. This was great, really tasty, egg and bread combined, fried onto one another softly so you got the taste of the egg, which was delicious to me, and the flavour of the dripping, beefy and strong, delicious. Was it any wonder you were left longing for a whole plateful all to yourself.

There was never enough of it; never enough of anything. Sadly you can only dip so many slices of batch loaf into one egg before you're singing to the deaf. Six kids and a mother and father need a fair bit of grub any day of the week, not forgetting Aunty Kay, though she hardly seemed to eat anything. Food costs money, so if there's no money you'd better tighten your belt, Da used to say, as if that would help you cope with just being plain bloody hungry so much of the time. It's funny to think I had to be in hospital to know what it was like to eat, day after day, without hunger ever joining the company.

I can still see Ma the day she came for me to the hospital at Clonskeagh. I was going home after three weeks of torture, my tonsils taken out no problem, until a septic throat moved in immediately, so that I couldn't swallow a thing for nearly a week, just sipping water and stuff through a straw. Ma held me so tight I thought I'd break, and she wept tears that wet my face. I tried to tell her it was all right, that I was coming home, that I wasn't going to die, and she sobbed and kissed my face as though I really mattered. I wept too, then. When Ma suffered, I couldn't seem to stay out of it. It was as if my heart couldn't hold back.

It was a long walk from Clonskeagh to Mount Pleasant on legs like valve rubber, but I kept my mouth shut. I knew that if Ma had any money we'd have been riding on the 48 bus. Anyway, before we started the journey down Sandford Road to Ranelagh village, we had to drop into the convent at Milltown for a handout from the nuns.

Ma held me with one hand. In the other she carried this half-gallon can. An elderly nun filled the can with soup and bits of meat and potatoes and my mother thanked her, and there was a lot of talk about God in his almighty glory blessing you and yours. I was already fairly anti-nun, thanks to the way you were treated by the ones running St Louis. So the decent woman of a nun in Milltown, for all her generosity and her decency to Ma, had no chance with me.

This was August 1941 and in a few months I was going to be seven. Even so, small kid that I was, I can remember how I felt about some things at that time. That day as we went into our flat, a kitchen where we lived, one bedroom, a scullery and a lavatory, I was glad to be out of the hospital in Clonskeagh and yet I was sad to be back in the Buildings.

To me Mount Pleasant Buildings was like a scab, a huge dry sore on the face of Dublin city. In the house, as we called the flat, the comb was in with the spoons and the knives and the boot polish brush, and you slept three to a bed, and sometimes when someone was home from England I had to sleep with Ma, and you had to wait your turn to go to the lavatory. I didn't like any of this. There was something else too, though I couldn't make up my mind what it was. A long time afterwards I realised it was the sheets on the bed in the hospital. I liked the feeling of the sheets.

A while after I got out of hospital, Da went to England to look for work. He wasn't happy about going because he honestly thought Germany was going to win the war. 'And I don't want to be in England when Jerry invades it!' he said, having some trouble keeping his voice down. But he went. 'Worn down', so he claimed, by Ma's 'drip drip moaning. She's like bleedin' Chinese water torture, wearin' you out, drop by drop!' Da laughed like a dog with a short bark and I remember Ma looking at him as though she really hated him.

When he was gone, she was happier than I had ever seen her. Within a few weeks Da wrote a one-line note with his address on it and he sent some money. And every week after that he posted something, which was a big help to Ma and the rest of us. It was good, seeing Ma happy like, but I couldn't help missing Da, even if he hadn't a word to throw to a dog a lot of the time. Hard to work out how you can like someone who never puts himself out to win you over, but it happens. Of course we were all relieved that he wasn't rowing with Ma and she wasn't threatening to swing for him, or to throw herself into the Grand Canal. Whenever Ma talked about the canal like that, I was scared and I could see fear in Rose too.

Then, just as everything was going along lovely, just as we were getting used to Da not being around, home he comes without a word of warning. Ma went into a blue fit, let me tell you. I heard her wish him dead to Rose, who didn't argue; she hated Da as though he was Oul' Nick himself. Ma wasn't the least bit religious, but I heard her one day, praying, as she washed herself at the sink in the scullery, for him to be taken, his return having left her sort of mindless in her disappointment.

He was hardly in the door from England before he was telling people with no small hint of glee in his manner that 'Germany's bombing the shite out of England, and if you don't mind, I'd prefer to die in my own bed, thank you kindly.'

'Which you probably will do, you spend so much time in it!' Ma's voice was drenched in disgust. Aunt Lily laughed, choking on the John Player, but if Da thought it was funny, you'd never have guessed it from the look on his face.

Da wasn't home a wet day before he was waking Ma up in the night. He woke me up as well because my second eldest brother, Joe, was suddenly home from Middlesex for a few days, so I was sleeping on the sofa bed in the kitchen with my mother.

Da would have needed to be stone deaf not to have heard the Go Away message in Ma's whispering as he came to get into the sofa bed between us. She warned him that he'd wake me. I'm not sure if Da said anything to that, but Ma soon came to understand he wasn't about to take no for an answer.

'You'll waken Leo. Ah for God's sake, Mick, let me get my bitta sleep. Ah sweet Jesus, have you no consideration.'

Da's need meant more to him than any plea Ma could make as he stood there by the sofa bed, in his skin, sort of like a mongrel straining on a leash in the small light of the street lamp through the gable end window.

Finally Ma let him have his way, and I held my breath in case they realised I was awake. He started off sounding as if it was wonderful, as if he was having a great time altogether. Ma was in the opposite camp, moaning and complaining about the lack of consideration, but then she quietened down and after a while it was as though she was content enough with whatever was going on. Not long after this, Da starts making noises that'd have you convinced he's in agony; then a while later they both give some kind of a cry or a groan, and in another minute Da leaves the sofa bed and heads back to the bedroom where Rose has the small bed, and he sleeps with Brendan and Michael, with Big Joe on the floor for the few days he's home. Fair play to Ma, she soon goes back to sleep and all I know is I'm lying there wide awake feeling confused and just a little bit uncomfortable, though I don't know why.

My seventh birthday arrived and you couldn't help noticing that nobody blew a bugle. Only Ma said anything at all to me as she gave me a threepenny Cadbury's chocolate bar. She sent me out on my own then: 'So you can eat it all to yourself.' This was a great present to get at any time. Something that was all yours, something you didn't have to share with anybody. It made you feel important, if only for as long as the chocolate bar lasted.

Christmas came four days after my birthday every year and every year Ma would be out of her mind with worrying about what she'd be able to serve up on the big day. So it's no surprise that the celebration of my arrival into the world four days earlier hardly rates a mention. Like who could compete with Jesus and the Three Wise Men.

Sometimes at Christmas Ma would recall my delivery in 1934. Not because I'd relieved her of a ten pound four ounce bump — it was more to do with what happened because I had squeezed my way into society on the morning of 21 December. To hear Ma tell it, the cupboard was really bare, she was worn out after a very heavy labour with me, her fifth child, and there wasn't a penny piece in the Little Brown Jug! The story goes that because I was due to arrive in or around the same time as Our Lord, a lot of interest in Katy's new baby sprouted up in the hearts of friends she hadn't seen or heard from in donkey's years. Women she had known since they were all girls together, having started work on the same day in Jacob's biscuit factory in Peter Street on the edge of the Liberties in Dublin. Ma often said that her life really began when she got that job. Before that she had been a skivvy and a childminder, but at the age of seventeen she got the call-up from Jacob's and even the 1914–18 war was only in the ha'penny place compared to Ma's first real job.

I heard the story so many times, it's carved into my mind like initials on a tree trunk. How five of her workmates, all married women now, with kids of their own, and all of them living in better circumstances than Katy herself, came to see the newborn baby. Arriving like a team from the St Vincent de Paul society 'with their arms full like the Three Wise Men bearing gifts, and all of them, dear Jesus, very, very welcome!' Nobody could say that sentence like my mother.

The gifts were food and drink and the sort of goodies we got only in our dreams: a big box of biscuits, a large tin of chocolate sweets, a chicken and a shoulder of ham, a shop-bought Christmas pudding, and loads of other stuff, the likes of which the cupboard hadn't harboured since the last time Da worked 'And that wasn't today or yesterday,' Ma would say, giving God and Da a good nudge with the one breath.

Da would leave the room rapidly, taking it as a deliberate reminder that he hadn't measured up in the providing for your family department, which, let's face it, he hadn't. He came back out of the bedroom in his hat and coat and stormed out of the flat, nearly taking the door with him, and you could see that the energy of his going was fuelled by another chapter of the double-barrelled huff, himself and Ma visited on each other from time to time.

Ma's gratitude for the help of her friends turned to the belief that it was a sign God had not forgotten her. But it was more than the generosity of those open-hearted women who could visit us in Mount Pleasant Buildings — Ma was bitterly ashamed of having to live in the flats, of 'having come to this'. She was charged with a sense of pride in her old workmates, 'that they could sit in our flat with the bare floorboards and the few chairs held together with bits of twine, and three of them huddled together on the edge of the oul' sofa bed and not one of them looking down their nose, God bless them anyway'.

Ma and Da were RCs, but the Granny Rogers grandfather had been a Protestant minister over in Manchester. Ma had only a nodding acquaintance with religion, but she went through the motions of going to Mass on Sundays and Holy Days of Obligation. I didn't know about Da because he did what he did on his own. But I never knew of my parents going to church, chapel or meeting, except for a funeral now and again. Even then they would come and go separately. In all the hundreds of times I must have seen my parents leave our flat, I never saw them go out the door together, not once.

One Sunday morning when I was about eight, Da, who was doing a stint in the army to keep the wolf from the door, came and collected me to take me with him to Griffith Barracks, where, much to my mother's relief, he lived for most of the week. We walked up the South Circular Road to the barracks and in the billet, a sort of dormitory he shared with a bunch of other soldiers, he let me run wild.

The other men were all very decent to me. Big rough-and-ready fellas, most of them younger than Da, country blokes on the whole, so Da said. In a matter of minutes the soldiers were letting me play with their rifles. So I had a great time while the men sat around and smoked Woodbines and every so often burst out laughing. I noticed that the men liked my Da and it made me wish that Ma liked him, too. I remember her having a dig about Da being in the army which paid her one pound nineteen shillings a fortnight to feed and clothe her family and keep the Corporation roof over our heads. 'They keep him up there in Griffith Barracks to frighten off the Germans when they invade us.'

Anyway, with one thing and another myself and Da were late for Mass, which meant we weren't going. It didn't cost me a thought. I'd made my First Holy Communion and I'd been to Confession, but I was with Da and he was the boss. Ma had dished out severe instructions before we left the flat earlier. 'No matter what, you be sure you take Leo to Mass, I don't care which church. I'll find out if you don't.'

Da took me roughly by the arm as we came out of the barracks onto the South Circular. I looked up at him as he leaned over me. Under the peak of his green army cap, his eyes looked deadly serious, like little bits of coal, and he said as though he expected me to hear him first time: 'If you ever tell your Ma we missed Mass this morning, I'll break your neck. D'ye hear me, Leo?'

'I won't squeal, Da.' Are you kidding! I was made up to be in on a secret, any secret, but especially one with my own father. 'Where did we go to Mass?' I asked when he let my arm go. 'Which church did we go to?'

We spent a few minutes concocting a story, like a couple of pals who were in trouble, only pulling together to get out of it. Once we had the details of the story worked out, Da was more relaxed but even so he didn't say much unless you asked him a question. I asked so many, he told me to shut up and be quiet. Thanks to Michael calling me Piggy Gabby — meaning I was a pig with a big mouth — I knew I talked a lot. But, all the same, I wished Da would just answer the questions that were burning me up. He knew so much that I wanted to know too. But when Da told you to keep quiet, that was the smart thing to do. Anyway, he'd been great to take me to the barracks in the first place. The only pity was it was the only time we ever did anything together, just the two of us like.

His name was Michael Patrick Dunne and he was born in a tenement room in Turner's Cottages, known as 'The Gut'. Even now I can hardly believe that this single street of run-down, two-storey cottages was just a stone's throw from the Royal Dublin Society in Ballsbridge.

To me the Gut was a great place and the odd time Ma took me down there, when she was again talking to Granny Dunne and seeing her about a possible loan from the Jewman, I willingly dived into the street games with the kids living there and I didn't get in as many fights as I did in our own flats.

The first girl I kissed hung around there, Kitty. We played Hop Scotch a Rue Cock together, hopping across lines into chalk-drawn beds on the foot-path. And Relievio, which was a Try Not to Get Yourself Captured Game, and if you were still playing in the evenings, Spin the Bottle, which was how I first felt my lips touch a girl's.

Granny Dunne was famous or maybe it was notorious. A lot of women admired her for finally throwing her husband down the stairs from their tenement room and, physically, booting him out onto the street, packing him out of her life for all time on account of his drinking. I never knew Granda Dunne, but Ma said he wasn't a bad man at all, but, like her own father, 'he was devoted to drink'.

The Granny loaned money for the Jewman, as the moneylender was called. She also collected the repayments for the same man and sometimes this meant she had to punch somebody hard enough to help him realise that paying back with interest was a very important part of the moneylending business, which was thriving, so Ma said, in the poor areas of the city. Her method of dealing with people who didn't play by the rules was to Hit First — Talk Later. She reared her children, four of them, and she brought them up to be decent people even if they didn't get enough education to be anything more than members of the labouring class.

But the thing that turned Granny Dunne into a local legend was the way she had knocked out two guys in a fist fight after one of them called her illegitimate grandson a little bastard. After that, word travelled that when the Granny hit you, you stayed fucking hit!

She never let anybody forget that her youngest son, Leo, was playing soccer in England for Manchester City, and that he was an Irish International as well, which was a very big deal around Ballsbridge and Ringsend. I got to know a man named Mulvany I delivered milk to on Mount Pleasant Avenue and he told me that he'd played soccer with Mick and Leo, and that my father was a much better player than Leo ever was. I told this to Da, but he was so proud of his young brother that he gave it no houseroom, never said a word in reply.

I met Uncle Leo a few times when he was home for a holiday after the soccer season ended. He was a very tough character, 'Hard as nails and mean with it,' Ma said. I thought he seemed all right, he made no bones about admitting that he'd never managed to win a fight against Da. According to Ma he drank too much and he fancied himself as a lady's man. 'Lily has the only heart in that family. The resta them got swinging bricks.'

I didn't say anything to that. But I thought Granny Dunne was a great oul' one and she was very decent to me whenever I saw her. She never let me out of her sight without giving me a threepenny bit or a tanner, and I liked Fanny too, though Ma said she was a bad-minded woman without a good word to say about anybody. Lily, of course, was my favourite and I was glad Ma had nothing bad to say about her. I'm not saying I'd have argued if she had, but I would have felt like taking Lily's part.

It was just that Ma had a down on Da's side of the family, and it would come out when she sneered at his accent. 'What would you expect from someone from Raytown!' This was an insider's name for Ringsend and Ma included the Gut in this put-down, even though it was way up Shelbourne Road near the Ballsbridge end. Some sort of snob thing, a joke when you considered how we lived, having to scratch from day to day, with Ma often not knowing where the next meal was coming from. But Dublin was kinda like that, everybody seeming to need somebody to look down on.

2

By the time I was twelve years old, I'd been working for nearly four years for Nellie Rafter, who had a milk shop, a dairy, on Mount Pleasant Avenue. I took over the job from Rose and Michael, who'd been doing it for a couple of years. Rose was leaving school, going to work in a factory in Rathmines which made boxes out of cardboard. Michael just couldn't get up in the morning. Well, he could, but the effort that Ma had to put into getting him on his feet was turning her into an oul' one before her time, so I was drafted in because I was an early waker-upper and Brendan was still too young to be sentenced to hard labour.

Nellie Rafter would remind you of a horse because she spent an awful lot of her time looking at the ground. When she wanted to look you in the eye, which wasn't often, she had to throw her upper body backward and up, as if she was rocking on her heels, her eyes like ulcers behind cheap wire-framed glasses. She was a fanatic about time, so Ma said. And that was about right. If you were a minute late, Nellie had all her notions of ladyhood stolen from her by her temper, which could have kept the *Titanic* afloat by melting the icebergs. And right away I could tell she didn't like me. A general splash of hatred seemed to spray off Nellie as though she was a dog out of a river shaking itself. Even St Francis of Assisi, a man who by all accounts kissed lepers, would have had a hard time giving the lips to Nellie, a woman who'd have scared a crocodile if she got to him before half eight in the morning.

'She's a martyr to the piles,' Ma said, as if she cared about the old harebaiter. I knew she was trying to help me give Nellie a break in my mind. Ma wanted me happier than I was sounding after just a few mornings in the job, because the five shillings a week wages that Nellie paid me was very badly needed. This was the sum I was getting for delivering fourteen milk rounds, one morning and afternoon, every day fifty-two weeks of the year. Though to be fair to Nellie, I had Christmas Day off, except for the morning delivery.

I asked Ma to give me some idea what piles were and, fair play to her, she did try, in her own words and in her own delicate way. When she finished I said: 'Sounds like they're varicose veins only up the bum. Would that be right, Ma?' She nodded as though she was happy to close the subject, while I thought to myself that Nellie carried on like a woman who had them on the brain as well as in the other place.

It has to be said that she offered me a cup of tea and two slices of bread every morning as part of the working deal, ordering me, from the off, to consume this collation in the sitting room behind the shop. She had a little countrywoman working for her, washing churns, cleaning the house and the shop. Her name was Rosie, a little darling with a hoppy leg and a moustache like my Granda Rogers in the picture of him that Ma had. Rosie smelled strongly at times, probably because she sucked eucalyptus pastilles every day. She gave me one whenever I'd get them for her from O'Higgins' the chemist next door to the dairy. I never got through one of those sweets but I didn't let on to Rosie.

The first morning Nellie warned me, 'Don't take all mornin' eating your breakfast.' I gave her a smile that didn't work and the minute she left the sitting room, I opened the press and took two more slices of the loaf bread, putting sugar on top of the butter, which was new to me and just the best taste you could imagine. Home-made too, so Rosie told me later, which made it even more worth the stealing.

I shoved the contraband grub up my jersey and headed off on the first of the three trips I would have to make each shift. I was soon drinking two quarts of udder juice daily to go with the sandwich, and the penn'orth of broken biscuits I somehow got my hands on for every afternoon shift. I just added a bit when I was filling each can, so I didn't have to steal from the customers.

This seemed only fair to me when I thought about the wages Nellie lashed out to me on a Saturday morning like a woman with no arms. It was encouragement to steal as far as I was concerned. All right, giving me the milk and bread was decent, especially when I left the flat on an empty gut. I'm not recommending butter sambos and milk, or broken biscuits and milk, as a staple diet, but it's only fair to record that I worked nearly five years at the milk, a lot of that time spent running about in my bare feet, winter and summer, and I was as healthy as a horse.

I never considered myself a dishonest kid but I stole anything that wasn't nailed down. In a way you had to steal and you had to be seen to steal, though not by Ma or Da. If you passed up on something that was there for the taking, the kid who did swipe it made a laugh of you for being thick, or gutless, and your image could take a real battering. Sounds funny now. Image at that age in those circumstances, but if you didn't look after your standing on the street, your life could be more difficult than it already was without any help from anybody.

Most of the stuff I nicked I sold or bartered. Any money I made went to Ma though I always held back a bit for myself. Sometimes she'd give me back a penny or two but more often than not she needed whatever I came up with. I'm talking about the price of a loaf or a pint of milk or a couple of fags since she'd started smoking a few every day. So I parted with my earnings on a very regular basis, though I didn't always do it with a good heart.

The way I saw it, even as an eight-year-old, I had no real interest in religion. 'Honour thy father and thy mother' was something you didn't even have to think about. Whatever the day produced, your parents kept you going till you could look out for yourself, and that had to be respected. Which meant you never spoke ill of your Da, even when he was lousy to you, and you gave your Ma all the help you could. Maybe I was making excuses for the stealing, not that excuses would be any use to me if I ever got caught. Ma laid down a lot of law and the top of her list was: 'Don't ever bring a policeman to this door or you'll know the full meaning of Black and Blue!' So, even though I didn't believe, I prayed the odd time that I wouldn't get nabbed stealing, so that I could sort of obey the Fifth Commandment, if you see what I mean.

The fact that I was a little thief was bothering me something terrible as my first Confession got nearer, because even though you went through a rehearsal with a nun which helped you understand the ritual, this didn't really prepare you for your first encounter with a priest one to one. Lucky me, I found myself in my first confession box with a priest called Father O'Connor, who was a kind man and only gave me three Hail Marys to say for my penance, even though I told him I had started work on the milk round and that I stole milk every day.

Father O'Connor was a nice change after nearly three years of the nuns in St Louis primary school. They wore a black habit with a white front and a crucifix at their chest and they were well scrubbed like polished apples, but, no exaggeration, I never met one nun in that first school of mine who had a heart bigger than a walnut. It was as though they'd been chosen especially to beat and bully five-year-olds who were the children of the poor around our part of Dublin; kids who apparently needed to be forced through fear into some level of submission. I believed this only because the nuns were so nice to the kids who were well off, and you couldn't help noticing how friendly they were with the parents.

Father O'Connor helped me more than he ever knew when he suggested that I say the odd little prayer as a matter of course. This was how I came to acknowledge the Angelus when the church bells rang at noon and six o'clock in the evening. My only other prayer was a request each night, which was supposed to stop you dying before you woke up in the morning.

You made the sign of the Cross with your thumb on your forehead and you said, 'Jesus of Nazareth, King of the Jews, preserve me from a sudden death!' I started it because I liked being alive and I was afraid of dying. By the time I was ten years old with three years of regular reading behind me, and convinced that I was a very smart young fella, I thought that this little nightly prayer was a great stroke on the part of the church, which obviously had all kinds of brains on the team. Once you said the prayer the first time before getting your head down, and you woke up the next morning, you had proof that the plea to Jesus had worked.

The thing I couldn't work out was why Catholics were advised to pray to the King of the Jews to keep them alive till the morning when a lot of them who did wake up wished they were dead. Also you couldn't miss the truth about Catholics and Jews in Dublin. From my experience on the streets and in shops and even at home, it was dead easy to work out that the RCs hated the local Jews; and that included the Jews who had been born in Dublin, on the South Circular Road or in Little Jerusalem, which is what Clanbrassil Street and its tributaries were called.

One day I asked Da why the Dub was so down on the Jews. He said, 'They're far too crafty, and they work day and night and they save every penny so they can be more powerful than we are.' Or words to that effect. I said I'd be willing to work long hours for proper pay, and I claimed that I would have loved to be able to save a bit of money. Da said that was okay, but Jews were different. I asked him how were they different. He said, 'They're all bleedin' foreigners for a start. From Germany and Russia and Christ knows where. They're different to us and they should go back where they came from.'

I said, 'What about the ones that got born here in Dublin?' Da got up from the old kitchen table, giving me a look that would have split a wooden block. He went into the bedroom, and I felt disappointed. Just when we were getting somewhere, he got fed up with me and my questions, and I wondered what was wrong with people working hard, when all the problems himself and Ma had stemmed from him not working at all.

Ma said the Jews were unpopular because the church claimed they had crucified Jesus. I accepted this at the time and it was a lot of years later before I came to understand that the Romans actually did the number on Our Lord. For years I was the Irish guy in the joke who punches the Jew on the jaw, telling him, 'You and your mob, you crucified Jesus.' 'But Paddy, that was two thousand years ago.' 'Never mind that,' says Paddy, 'I only heard about it yesterday!'

One of the things you couldn't get away from was religion and I went to St Louis convent school because that was the only school available to kids with my background. 'High Babies' has a nice sound to it but I was scared and confused by how severe the nuns seemed to be. I remember sitting cross-legged on a polished parquet floor. A fresh-faced young nun is in charge of us. We're playing with a bag of marbles. You sit in a line with some space between you and the kid in front of you. This kid will throw the bag over his head, you are to pick it up and throw it over your head to the child behind you. I'm six years of age and already I am a dreamer. So when the bag lands in my lap, things come to a standstill, because I am not paying attention. The nun in charge smacks me so hard that I scream in terror, falling sideways from the force of the blow.

I don't even know what hit me and then I'm going over to wallop against the floor. Then she is dragging me howling to the lavatory and she stands there promising me a real smack if I don't get my face washed and stop my blubbering.

Day to day this wasn't in the least bit unusual and there was one girl of about six who got her jaw broken because a nun punched her so hard that the child was knocked unconscious. The head nun there was called Sister Scholastica or something like that, and no mouse stirred in and around Rathmines that this lady didn't know about. So she knew what had happened to me and the other girl. And she didn't do a thing about it.

I believed there had to be good nuns somewhere, women devoted to God and all that, but I never met one of them in St Louis. The years there were like a punishment for just being me, and I swore that when I got out I'd never moan again.

As Ma used to say from time to time, 'Innocence, did I ever offend thee!'

Just before I went to St Mary's National School on Richmond Hill, I made my First Holy Communion. The host got stuck to the roof of my mouth as if it was glued to it. I broke into a sweat because we'd been given dire warnings about biting into it or chewing it. This was the body and blood of Jesus, so you can imagine how terrified I was before I somehow managed to swallow it without biting into it and without actually choking to death on it.

It's supposed to be a day you will always remember. I was wearing my first suit and a brand new shirt and tie. They were only mine for the day really because on Monday morning they would have to go into Gibson's pawn office. I felt good in the gear and as soon as I had my picture taken in Jerome's in Henry Street, I was on my way to see my relatives, who were supposed to give you money on the biggest day of your life so far.

Ma had me by one hand and Brendan, who was the quietest young fella you ever met, by the other. We got the bus to Kimmage to see Ma's youngest brother, Uncle Paddy Rogers, who was home on sick leave from the British army. A nice man, he had plenty of time for us kids, and I could hardly breathe as I put his ten-bob note into my pocket. I'd never had so much money in my life before.

Ma had it off me by the time we were on our way to see Aunt Molly in Rathfarnham. I can't pretend I didn't mind because I minded more than words could say, but I knew she needed it to go towards paying for the suit, the shoes and the shirt. Even getting your picture taken in Jerome's photographic studio in Henry Street cost money, and Ma was the person had to find it. Still, I was hoping I'd be left with something at the end of the day.

Aunt Molly lived with her husband, Dick Byrne, in a council cottage above the village of Rathfarnham, at the foothills of the Dublin Mountains. I thought it funny, Dick being such a countryman when he was only born a few miles out of Dublin. He was a quiet fella with a big shy smile and he made the tea that afternoon while we all climbed up the wooden stairs in the two up, two down cottage to see Molly, who was back in bed, laid low once again by the tuberculosis, so Ma said.

I got a huge hug and Molly wept when she gave my suit the once-over, touching my rosette and running her hand gently down my face. It was very upsetting to see her so sad and unwell, but in a minute Dick brought up whiskey along with the tea and Molly drank a glass straight down the hatch, which gave her a lift, and then she was saying she felt grateful she hadn't had any kids in case they'd been born with the TB already installed.

Ma was very quiet and sad-looking on the way back down from Molly's house. All Brendan did was look out the window of the bus so I left him alone.

Then I felt sad myself, asking myself why most people were like that a lot of the time. Today of all days, when I was supposed to have a great time and it wasn't working out like that at all, even though I was picking up a bit of cash. Without knowing I was doing it I squeezed Ma's hand. She turned to look at me, like someone coming out of a sleep, and she had tears in her eyes as she said, 'We're going to lose poor Molly. She's going to be taken from me as sure as God.' I felt like crying myself, but I thought what's the use of that and I gave Ma the half-crown Aunt Molly had slipped into my hand when she was kissing me goodbye. Ma gave it straight back: 'Keep it and say nothing about it. You should be able to keep every penny you get today. Most of it has to go to pay for the suit. Granny Dunne got the money for me from the Jewman and he has to be paid back.'

When we got to Granny Dunne's she gave me two shillings and a bag of broken chocolate. I thought that was great: to give you whatever you were going to get the minute you got in the door. It saved you wondering while you were there, whether or not you were going to get anything.

'Savin' dat for weeks so I was, Leo, for your Holy Communion day,' the Granny said like a woman who knew she had done the right thing. Aunt Lily soon got word that the communion party had arrived, so she came across from the Swastika Laundry where she was a forewoman, and she gave me four shillings. And when she had a bottle of stout going and a fag on her lip, she granted my special request by singing 'I'm Just a Wanderer of the Waste Land', even though it was only four o'clock in the afternoon. Lily could sing any time, and nobody could chant those cowboy songs better than she could. In a while Aunt Fanny came over from her own room in the cottages and she gave me a tanner and a copy of *The Dandy*, which I had left behind over a year ago though Fanny couldn't have known that. Ma said Fanny probably nicked the comic from the newspaper shop.

Fanny's son, Gerry, the young fella Granny knocked the two fellas out over, came in from mooching around the docks at Ringsend. He was so casual about it even though he was only the same age as me. He sounded like a little man and I thought he was great. I liked the feeling of the Dunnes in the Gut. In the most natural way they were definitely closer to one another than the Dunnes in Mount Pleasant, even though they all seemed a bit mad, wild-like. I'd have lived with them in a flash if I could have taken Ma along with me.

By the end of the day Ma had twenty-five shillings and I had the half-crown from Aunt Molly and Granny Dunne's florin, which was a very tidy sum to have all to yourself.

Rose was almost fifteen and there already was talk of her going away to England like the two eldest brothers before her. Joe was living with the Granny Rogers in Middlesex and supposed to be getting married, so I heard without anybody actually telling me. Aunty Kay again gossiping at the door with Mrs Doyle: 'A panic letter, looking for his birth certificate and y'know what that means, a shotgun job!' In the same way I heard that Jimmy the eldest guy was gone off to Australia or somewhere. Not that I cared, about either of them, or them about me.

Granny Rogers had gone to England in 1937, Ma's brother Jim going with her because work was so scarce in Ireland. 'I wanted us all to go at the same time, plenty of work and a decent place to live, education for the kids, but he wouldn't hear of it, he hated my mother so much.'

I was delighted to hear that Rose might be going, even though you had to take some of Aunty Kay's rumours with a grain of salt. Let's put it this way though, I hoped Rose was going, and I wouldn't have minded if she took Michael, too. Not that I had anything against him, but we were all just one great bloody nuisance to each other, and they never tried to hide what they felt about me either.

If they hadn't been there, I'd have had enough grub to eat and I'd have been able to go to the lav without having to get in a queue, or bang on the door because Mickey — my slag name for Michael — was hunched on the pot reading *The Indo* smoking a fag, judging by the smoke creeping under the lav door, unless his guts were smouldering. I mean it, if it hadn't been for Roy Rogers and The Sons of the Pioneers, I'm not sure what I would have done to get by.

The Sons were a singing cowboy band and they were in most of Roy Rogers' pictures, just like George 'Gabby' Hayes. If these were the sons you'd have to wonder what their oul' fellas looked like, because if there was a spring chicken among them they kept him well hidden. Roy usually ran into them as they were singing their latest number. 'Cool Water' was a good one, written by Bob Nolan, the Son with the big chest. Roy wasn't a bad singer, not like Gene Autry, who sang through his hooter.

Somehow, Mondays and Thursdays, I got the money for the Prinner. Over the door were the words 'The Princess Cinema'. For a shilling you could have the best seat in the house; for sixpence if you were a kid. The cheaper seats were eightpence for big people and fourpence for kids. Myself, I always went to the Fourpenny Rush. When I was lucky enough to have a tanner, I'd buy broken biscuits with the extra twopence and munch my way through 'The

Folly an' Upper!' I saw Flash Gordon and Captain Marvel so many times, I knew most of the dialogue by heart.

After Hopalong Cassidy faded, Roy Rogers was King of the Cowboys and his horse Trigger was the smartest horse in the movies. I knew this was right because it said so on the screen just before every Roy picture started. And before long we said Trigger was smarter than Gabby Hayes, who was Roy's devoted sidekick. Trigger could count up to ten by banging his hoof on the ground and we said that Gabby was in trouble once he came to the end of the fingers on one hand! We made no bones about taking someone's character or being cruel, if it earned a cheap laugh.

I have to confess I was crazy about Roy Rogers. He was no Buck Jones, who'd been my first real cinema hero. How I cried my eyes out when Buck burned to death trying to save his horses from a blazing barn. Gene Autry was a big star too, but to me he always looked so chubby, I guessed they probably had to tie his feet in the stirrups to keep him in the saddle.

With Roy it was different. He could knock out six crukes and not even lose his hat. And in the last ten minutes of every picture he always got hit on the head with a bottle or something. Every kid in the picture house would be hoarse from yelling at him to look out for the fella behind him. 'Roy! He's behind you. Jeyzuz! Look out! Duck, Roy. Mind your head!'

But Roy never seemed to hear us for all the shouting and he'd get a right belt on the head and fall on the floor of the shack, and the crukes would tie him up and take off to rob the stagecoach, which was carrying gold or the wages for the miners, but Roy would wake up in about twenty seconds and he'd give a whistle, and good old Trigger would hear it and he'd gallop down the hill and kick the shite out of the shack, and he'd untie the rope knots with his big teeth and Roy'd lep into the saddle and he'd be off like the clappers firing 249 shots out of his six-gun. And I loved every second of it.

Not only was I in the saddle every foot of the way with Roy Rogers. During the following week myself and the other kids in the flats remade the movie in the street and whoever had the boxcart would be the 'Chap'. The 'Chap' was the hero, Roy Rogers. A boxcart was what it sounded like: a box on top of an axle and two wheels. The wheels normally came off some poor woman's pram and with two bits of wood for shafts the stagecoach was ready to roll.

'Yis all can't be cowboys. Summa yis has to be fuckin' Indians!'

Every time the problem was the same, everybody wanted to be Roy Rogers. The Chap chased the stage down the trail (Coffee's Lane), he stopped the runaway horses. The Chap went for his gun; his hand came up like a flash from his hip, first two fingers forward, the thumb cocked, last two fingers folded against the palm like the butt of the gun; and he outdrew the villain every time. 'I'll be the Chap and you must be the cruke and you must go for your gun and I must beat you to the draw!' I got myself a really strong box. I stole an axle and a thick pair of iron wheels from a building site in Ranelagh. And I paid one and sixpence in McCambridge's in Richmond Street for the best pair of shafts ever seen in the Buildings. From then on I was the Chap, but I remember one kid giving me a very rough response when I offered him the part of Sitting Bull.

'Sitting Bull was a great chief, a tremendous warrior,' I cajoled, knowing that no kid could argue with this. 'He was a Prince of the Sioux nation. Like a king among Indians!'

'I don't care if he's the Kinga England,' your man, who is all of seven years old, tells me, two-tone green candles hanging from his nostrils, and then as he turns to leave me for good and all, he assures me with more vehemence than he was entitled to show at his age, 'If he's so great you be him or you can go and fuck yerself.' And he was gone. It was no lie to say you were more likely to be told to go and shite by a seven-year-old than you were by his mother. Though that could happen too, if you didn't mind yourself.

So I had plenty to occupy me but nothing compared to poor Ma, because Brendan was suddenly on his way to Cork Street fever hospital with something called Bull Neck Diphtheria. As if Ma didn't have enough on her plate already and Aunt Molly very sick again with the tuberculosis.

I was washing my face in the scullery when I heard Mrs Doyle giving Aunty Kay the SP — the starting price — on the situation. 'An epidermic of diphtheria', she called it, and though I didn't quite know how she got the word wrong, somehow I knew it wasn't just right. She went on to say that youngsters all over the city were dyin' like flies.

Ma wasn't allowed in to see Brendan. The closest she could get was to look through a window into the sealed ward in the hospital. And the word was that the numbers were getting bigger every day. Finally the hospital announced that it couldn't deal with the huge number of enquiries from people concerned about patients. It came up with the idea of allocating a number to each patient afflicted with the diphtheria, and put a special box in the *Evening Mail* every day. By checking the number, you could find out if your loved one was Critical, Improving or Unchanged, and Ma, like a lot of other mothers I suppose, opened the paper breathing novenas that Brendan was on the mend, or, at least, holding his own for another day.

I'd watch Ma open the *Mail* with dread peeling off her eyes like old wallpaper. 'Condition Unchanged,' she'd say, closing her eyes in relief. 'Oh thank Jesus!' This went on for something like eight or nine weeks, and during all that time, with Brendan far from being out of the woods, Ma seemed to be just an inch away from collapse, without ever going down.

When he finally did come home, I could hardly remember what Brendan looked like. If he recognised me, he gave no sign of it. He was like a little oul' fella, all tucked into himself.

Ma was very relieved to have him home and that made him all right with me, even if my existence didn't matter to him. None of us was close in any way, though Michael and I nearly got there a few times. There were just too many of us in too small a space, though it did get a lot easier after Rose left to join the women's army, the ATS, in England. You had to get out if you wanted to be alone. Which I was doing more and more even when I didn't have a job to do, or I wasn't carryin' the dough for the flicks. I went to the Reading Room in the Carnegie Library in Rathmines and that was where my appetite for reading reared its head.

I was well into reading comics by this time, waiting for every edition of *The Hotspur* and *The Champion* as they appeared. I nicked them from an oul' one I delivered some papers for when I took out the milk. This serious, practising Catholic woman was a newsagent close by the dairy where I worked for Nellie Rafter. She paid me the amazing sum of tenpence a week (this was one twenty-fourth of a pound note) because she reckoned that's all it was worth, since I was passing the doors of her customers anyway. I tell you, this woman made Nellie seem reasonable, a miracle in itself, and I didn't argue with her. But she got fined for her meanness since I stole comics and any fags or bars of chocolate that I could get my hands on.

I wasn't allowed to borrow books from the library because my family didn't own a house, or anything else for that matter, but I was allowed into the Reading Room, where you were free to read any book, once you didn't stuff it up your jersey on the way out. Once I got in there, the stories that fluttered around in my head seemed to find some idea of formation, and even if it was all pie in the sky stuff, the simple act of reading a short story soon became a sanctuary for me.

I was having a pretty good life because, even though I wouldn't have admitted it to anybody, I didn't really care about the things I had to go without. Sure, I moaned some of the time but I didn't mean it. Moaning was a family habit, and I could say the same for most of our neighbours. I knew people who could have moaned for Ireland! I sounded like them, now and again, but I was nowhere near the gold medal class like my Ma and Aunty Kay.

Because I only read what I liked, having given the book a ten-page chance to hook me, I enjoyed myself, which probably helped me love reading as much as I did. I stumbled over words on every other page so I nicked a small dictionary out of a shop in Rathmines. I was very happy to be learning new words and I was convinced I was getting more education in this way than I was in St Mary's National.

Speaking of school, wasn't I lucky that the nuns in St Louis had been such bitches. If I'd hit the new school after three years of kindness, my mind might have snapped under the assault that Mockey Muck and two of his teachers, Durt and Baldhog, made upon it.

I'm not denying we were rough-and-ready kids and that we'd been known to break the rules here and there. But to see a man who weighs twelve or thirteen stone swinging a boy less than half his body weight around a class-room, punching him about the head, slamming him against a partition, and then smacking him open-handed about the face, is enough to turn your stomach. And when you know that if you look crooked, you too could become a punchbag for this teacher who carries the weight of plenty about his frame, terror comes to you on a daily basis, and you will do well to remember your own name at times.

In my eyes Muck should never have been a headmaster, and it seemed to me that a schoolyard full of boys was offensive to his sight. In the years I was forced to stand before him at Assembly five days a week, I never saw anything other than anger and disdain in the way he looked at us.

This was something he had in common with the parish priest, Canon Fleming, who was the boss of the school. This old priest was regularly captured by such anger that you had to wonder was he a madman choking to death in the tight white collar of his calling. He hated sinners, made no sort of allowance for anything you might call wrongdoing. People had to be herded to his confessional because nobody except the local crawthumper types would go near him. If some innocent stranger wandered in to the church and shared something dodgy, meaning some sort of sexual sin, Canon Fleming could usually be heard out on the street. This man could make hell sound so awful that if you went there you might even end up disappointed with it.

3

By the spring of 1945 I was starting to write down some of the little stories that invaded my head. Sometimes, too, poetry would come to me, pages of verse, what you'd call lyric poetry, and in the next few years song lyrics would show up, some of them with a tune or the suggestion of a tune attached.

I began to make notes of things that impressed me or bothered me, and I wrote about people now and then. Odd people and funny people, or others who weren't the full shilling, not normal. I kept notes about films and about film stars who came and went, and I began to fill copybooks with potted biogs of certain writers. I copied down a line or a paragraph when something really struck me in any way.

I enjoyed the Biggles books by Captain W.E. Johns and I loved Jack London, who gave us *Call of the Wild* and the brilliant *Martin Eden*. The stories and poems of Rudyard Kipling made a great impression on my young mind, as did the verse of Robert W. Service with his marvellous ballads of the Yukon and all the romantic notions I had about that from the pictures.

So reading books and seeing lots of motion pictures loom large on the screen of memory, along with the women in my early life: Ma, Aunty Kay, Granny Dunne and Granny Rogers. Then there was Da, with Rose, Michael and the others out on the fringe. As I said, we were not a close family, we did what we had to do together, not a lot more than that. I remember some years later when I was a drinker and coined the line 'Blood is not thicker than Guinness,' I knew it stemmed from the emptiness I felt at not being part of what you could call a real family.

I was still called Leo but I decided to change it by the time I was twelve years old, because I got tired fighting kids who called me Leo the Lion. So I knocked the letter 'o' off the end, and told Ma and the family I wouldn't be answering to the name Leo any more.

'I never wanted you called after Leo in the first place,' Ma assured me. 'Anyway,' she smiled at the visit of a happy memory, 'thanks to your Granny Rogers, Leo was never your real name.'

She remembered Da being so proud of his young brother playing for Manchester City and Ireland that he wouldn't be turned off calling me after him. She had never liked Leo Dunne, 'even if he got his name in the papers for playing football. He was never a nice man and, above all, I wanted you to be a nice person and a decent human being.'

Granny Rogers knew how Ma had hated the idea of me being called Leo. The Granny liked Da about the same as leprosy, and he felt the same way about her. But for all his street smarts he was an innocent soul really; he knew nothing about women, so having no idea his mother-in-law could shaft him, he let her get on with registering my birth.

Years later when I got my birth certificate with my first passport in mind, I had the proof of Granny's duplicity in my hands. Christopher Dunne was the name I had been given. Da never knew it, and he would pass on before I would formalise the change to Lee, the name I had chosen for myself.

I didn't say anything at school about wanting to be called Lee. I didn't say much of anything at school, and if I tried to do my school work as best I could, it had more to do with the fear of what would happen if I didn't, than any wish to be educated by most of the teachers at St Mary's National — especially Roche, who terrifies me.

I'm so anxious to steer clear of him as much as I can, I raise my hand one day and offer to go out and get him ten cigarettes. He smokes, and drinks something from a flat half-bottle which he shoves back into his coat pocket.

'You know where you can get cigarettes!' Roche beckons me to join him at the head of the class, already reaching into the waistcoat pocket of his suit for the money. 'You'd better not be messing.' I leave the classroom knowing that if I have to steal them, I can't come back without the fags. Just as I know that if I can't get them, I just won't come back to school.

I'm talking of the time when World War II — in Ireland we called it 'The Emergency' — had been raging through Europe for almost six years, when even neutral Ireland was living on rations. Even people with money had to go without certain things, like butter, tea and sugar. Cigarettes were also rationed to the extent that they were as valuable as gold dust to some people. Cigarettes rationed in a country where the people who smoked usually did so as if their life depended on it!

So you had shopkeepers, anonymous people you wouldn't even recognise if you saw them out from behind the counter, and suddenly they had a lot of power. Imagine standing behind the counter in your Mickey Mouse shop and a guy comes in badly in need of a smoke. He asks you very politely for ten cigarettes, and you give him a sad little smile while you say 'We haven't got any' even though you have boxes of them stashed under the counter. That's what I was up against when Roche gave me the money for the fags and let me know that if I came back without them my immediate health would take a turn for the worse.

I'd worked out what I was going to do and for a while things went well. I'd go into a shop sniffing back my tears. If there was somebody ahead of you to be served, it was even better because you could throw in a few more sniffles before you had to face the person behind the counter.

'My father is dying,' I'd copy Mickey Rooney being sad. He was a great little actor, very funny at times, but he could be terrific at being sad, too. I'd make myself think Da was on his last legs, using everything I could come up with to help me bring real tears to my eyes without letting one of them fall. 'He's craving for a cigarette.' I'd take a breath — the brave don't cry — 'A Woodbine above all,' I'd say quietly.

As the weeks ran into months, I was having to go further from the neighbourhood in search of cigarettes and my badly needed freedom from Roche. Even I with my leather neck couldn't go back to the same shop. Some days I'd get really lucky, have the fags secure in my possession early and then I could go for a ramble until about three in the afternoon. I had to make tracks back to class after that, and more than once I thought that life would have been perfect if only I'd had a shilling or even a tanner to buy myself something to eat. But I didn't, so I was continually having to take chances by filching things to keep my belly button from kissing my backbone.

Fruit came my way down on the docks, damaged oranges and apples, very quickly put out of their misery by my need to get something into the bread basket. When I had a few pennies life was great altogether, a bag of broken biscuits for a penny, and pinching the odd bottle of milk was part of the daily routine. I used to go to the Liberties a lot, curious of its history of giving lodging to the Huguenots and the Jews from all over Europe, including the Mushatt brothers with their KK (Kill or Kure) soap and all their exotic lotions and potions. The Liberties had a feel that was different, larger if you like, than the regular roadways of my existence. In Dame Street I used to sit down on the footpath while office girls cycled home for their lunch. That way you could see their stocking tops when they cycled by and I have to admit I was early devoted to the top of the leg over the stocking.

Back to school then, back to Roche, with only minutes left before the bell went. One day when I got back to class at about half past three, Roche had me up in front of everybody. He made a game out of asking me questions about the things they'd been learning while I was out. I couldn't even guess at an answer and he made an example of me by giving me twelve of the best, six on each hand, with a cane that really cut into you. I was so humiliated, hating him for doing that to me. In a matter of minutes I would be making the afternoon milk delivery, carrying milk cans with narrow wire handles; gloves weren't a luxury I'd managed to secure for myself.

After the caning from Roche, I told Ma to 'Get me out of that school or I'll kill myself!' I got a smack across the face for my trouble. Ma could be large herself, the drama queen of my life. She knew I was acting the maggot. Suicide? And me in short trousers. She did promise to go and talk to Mr Gallagher who ran Tranquilla National School and I knew that if she could get me a transfer she would. Meanwhile I kept my head down as much as I could in St Mary's, and even going home to the flats didn't seem as bad as usual, now that I knew Ma was trying to get me a move out of there.

The overall image of Mount Pleasant Buildings was a cross between a badly run-down army barracks and a tired prison that had seen better days. It was a three block to the unit affair, each block containing nine flats running to two rooms and a scullery with a cold water tap and a lavatory. Some people thought it was a great place to live and it has to be said there were some very decent people there. There were others who were damaged, broken up by life, so that they could behave very badly from time to time. There was a lot of drunken fighting, some cruelty that went unnoticed, so it's fair to say that we weren't all noble and charitable just because we were what you might call underprivileged.

What I have never forgotten are some of those winter evenings with five or six of us trying to huddle around a one-lung fire in the tiny grate of the cooking range. We had a gas mantle fixed to the wall and what this did was spit out a chilly off-white light that made you look like a zombie. Sometimes when pictures like this present themselves out of memory's misery drawer, you wonder was it really this bad? And you wonder was your sister Rose right when she said, years later, that we didn't go through any barefoot days, that bare feet in Dublin were just a figment of somebody's imagination?

Then you remember the stone bruises gathered during the years without shoes. And you've never forgotten not having any kind of decent coat to keep out the rain and the cold. You remember kidding yourself you were angry on Ma's behalf, flaming because Ma was made to feel so bad for having to send you out barefoot and barebacked. Nothing to do with Ma. It was you, just you, feeling very hard done by, and very angry because of being so hard done by. You know you have never completely rid your mind of the taste, that you taste again and again the feeling of fury that you, yes you, just you and never mind anybody else, that you had to live like this.

But then sometimes you remember as well how good you felt when you actually got a pair of boots, thanks to the Herald Boot Fund. This was a scheme sponsored by the evening newspaper because the number of barefoot kids in Dublin had become a national scandal. Its readers donated money that was used to buy footwear. At one stage Dublin Corporation gave out free boots with the letters CP printed on the soles. The fact that they were Corporation Property made it sound as though you only had a loan of them. Anyway, some of the oul' ones still got them into the pawn office by burning the letters off, rubbing a bit of soap into the damaged area, and getting Big Julie, a well-built local girl who shared herself around, to chat up this pawnbroker, who, according to her, was built like a greyhound, 'All ribs and prick! And a martyr to the diddies!'

I didn't mind going barefoot once the weather wasn't too bad. But when winter came, it was something you could live without. I know for sure I'd have stayed in a lot of mornings if I hadn't needed to hold onto the job with Nellie Rafter.

Dublin in the 1940s. Picture it. Home Sweet Home and the Fire Blackout! The open hallway leads to nine flats and there's a general smell as if something's gone off. The open bin on the left as you went in from the street added to the power of the pong. Sometimes you even got smoke to walk in by, a bit of diversion thanks to someone dumping hot ashes onto old papers and garbage.

The plain concrete hall leads to flats on three levels, and you badly need the light bulb on each floor. The doors are dark green to really brighten the place up. You have lovely dove-grey concrete steps to the two upper floors, and the black iron handrails go well with the iron bars facing the street, in place of a window, on the first and second levels. This may well be the best air-conditioning around. Certainly it helps the flat block stay cool even when there is a foot of snow. And of course, it means that the landings will be kept fairly clean with all that rain coming through the bars.

When you walk towards the flats up Coffee's Lane, it's like a prison there in front of you. Those black iron bars where there should have been windows. The open bin in the entrance hall. Look, we all know that Dublin has a massive job on its hands trying to get people out of the slums, the tenements all over inner Dublin. But I have to wonder why it's so crude, so ugly, so functional with no solitary patch of green, no single blade of grass growing in that entire complex. I guess they felt we didn't need any of that, as though poor meant bovine, and unemployed ensured that you were bereft of any aesthetic sense. And the way they built these places, they felt the same way about privacy. For God's sake, what did people like us need with privacy?

We did need privacy, we didn't need the lack of hot water, the lack of floor covering, the lack of bedclothes, beds and food and cups and saucers and clothing and soap and shampoo and toilet paper and sanitary towels, and whatever else is needed to help people hold on to the God-given dignity that you bring into life with you.

People who won prizes for creating instant slums like the Buildings, didn't they know that birth control was not only a mortal sin but was banned by law? So, most families will be large; they'll need a bit more than one step from the pavement housing. Did anybody care? A few maybe, but there was far from enough caring in the land of saints and scholars for the poor fish who could only dream of getting their dinner every day.

Even today you'd like to forget the awful smells that are spread across the crust of your memory, the smells that lack provides, a sort of metaphysical aroma that pervades the day and the night of the body and the mind, as if it was sprayed on as you came off the assembly line. Are they part and parcel of being born into a situation nobody would volunteer for? Are people who tell you otherwise mad? Is it possible that you choose your mother even though she lived in a Corporation slum that should have been pulled down three weeks before it was erected?

No wonder Ma thinks Ireland is a joke, though not the kind that makes you laugh. She saw it as the kind of joke that causes your anger to rear up on its hind legs, anger that stays with you though mostly you don't let it show. You hide it a lot of the time behind this inbuilt facility you have to make people laugh. It's easier than letting them know how you feel. Anyway, most people are afraid of how you feel, they don't really want to hear it. So you try to keep some of the people happy at least some of the time, but when you lie down at night you're not smiling. You lie there with your brothers and you pray to yourself, in case anyone hears you, Jesus of Nazareth, King of the Jews, preserve me from a sudden death. And you never ask yourself why bother? The question never even arises because you love life and you believe with all your heart that they will not keep you down for ever.

But you could feel things you couldn't say. You felt a connection when you looked up at the sky with all the space that was there between you and the stars on a clear night. You somehow felt part of all that. When you took a breath, God, magical. And you didn't have to earn it. It was yours, given to you by . . . given to you by what? God? What? Maybe the air was God? Always there, always available, unless you turned your back and held your breath until you went blue in the face and passed out.

One of the brothers turns over in the bed and you get an elbow in the kisser or a knee in the crown jewels. This gets rid of the fancy thinking very rapidly and you give him a good dig to get him to move off your bit of the bed. Three lads between the ages of seven and fourteen in the same bed is called crowded. Not crowded if you compared it to this neighbouring family of eighteen and maybe more, not counting the parents who were two of the nicest people living in the whole flat complex. But it was crowded enough for all of us in the gable end flat on the ground floor, so much so that you might find it hard to believe Ma adopting another fella she found trying to get a night's sleep in the entrance hall one night when she was coming in.

This is how Jack Johnson came into our lives, with no objections from anyone except Aunty Kay. She now spent most of every day in our flat. She slept in her room at 8 Ranelagh, and some days she worked cleaning a house up on Sandford Road, but really, she had become a part of our household without anybody knowing exactly how it had happened. She came one day and she stayed talking, and the next day she came back. After that she was just there.

She was put out about Ma taking Jack in off the street, started hinting that my mother was a bit long in the tooth to be getting herself a boyfriend! This wouldn't have surprised anybody who knew Aunty Kay. She was great in her own way, giving Ma part of whatever few bob she earned charladying, but she'd always been bad-minded, so Ma claimed. She was generous to us kids, though, and I liked her, even if she thought the sun shone out of the thing Michael sat on when he was smoking in the lav. So we just laughed at Kay. I never knew what Da thought about the situation; he never confronted Ma about Jack sleeping on the kitchen floor. Da was like a man who had lost his place and didn't know how to find it again. I felt sorry for him because, no matter what, I loved him something desperate, though you couldn't tell him. He'd just scoff at you as if you were a cissy.

Jack looked about twenty and he said his name was Johnson, but some people said later it was Redmond. We never sorted this out one way or the other. I mean, who cared! From the first day he went out and got work, some gardening one day, a day's labouring the next, and when he came in of an evening he gave Ma part of whatever he'd earned. I noticed, when we were sitting around the grate and there was some bit of heat from the fire, that Jack would sit well back, sometimes on the floor. He was naturally polite, with the build of a very strong man, and he treated my mother as if she was a saint or someone who was very special.

Jack said he'd been in Carricklea because his mother and father were dead. This was a state school for kids who had problems. Innocent children ended up in places like this, brought there, left there, abandoned to the place, some of them just because they were 'illegitimate'. We didn't push him for any stories about his childhood. Carricklea couldn't have been much fun. I remembered Jack hanging around the Buildings on and off for a good while before he came to us, usually chatting up this girl Sheila, who had spectacular breasts, and he told me he knew my brother Joe for a while before he went to England.

For a few weeks after Jack came into our lives, I kept an eye on him and Ma. I knew this was just stupidity on my part but the situation was like a picture I'd seen where the young brother from nowhere turns up and ends up having the woman of the house who's his sister-in-law. In fairness to Jack, you could see he adored Ma, but it was respect and reverence he showed to her, as if she was his own mother.

Jack was with us about a month and I'd say he was paying his way, even though he hadn't got a regular job. Then Ma got a visit from one of our local curates called Father O'Keeffe. She was more than surprised: 'Of all the priests in Rathmines parish, he'd be the last one I'd expect to see come into the flats. He might get his shoes dirty or some young fella might lean against his Hillman Minx.'

Enough said. When Ma didn't care for someone, even one of the local clergy, she wasn't behind the door about letting you know it. The priest was there to give Ma a message. She was to be at the Archbishop's Palace in Drumcondra on a matter of some urgency the following day.

When Ma got back from Drumcondra she had been given money by Father Mangan, private secretary to the Archbishop of Dublin, Dr John Charles

McQuaid. Father Mangan had no chance with Ma. 'He never once looked me in the eye, nor so much as offered me a cup of tea.' She unleashed a wicked smile. 'So I got a taxi home to Mount Pleasant Avenue with some of the money he gave me.'

The Archbishop had a special interest in Jack Johnson, so this Father Mangan told Ma. It had been observed that our family had taken him in off the street and that he was sleeping on a mattress on the floor of our flat. Ma was to be commended for the charity of her gesture in view of her own circumstances and the Archbishop wished to improve Jack's situation without delay. Would she rent a room for him? Father Mangan produced money for several months' rent, and more money for a bed, bedclothes, and all that would be needed to turn a room into a self-contained bed-sitting room. He would remain in touch from time to time to see in what way the Archbishop could help further. The question of Jack's need of regular employment was already in hand and would be resolved in a matter of days.

Ma took the money from Father Mangan to do the necessary for Jack, or if you like, for the Archbishop. When I asked her did she put the bite on the priest for a job for Da, she was more than surprised. 'I wouldn't ask that man for a drink of water if I was dying!'

Jack was delighted to have a room of his own and I envied him the double bed he had all to himself. So from then on, if anybody came home from England we had the extra space, which Jack shared willingly. I don't know what was said between him and Ma about this sudden interest from John Charles McQuaid, but I hoped that some day Ma would tell me the whole story. One thing sticks in my mind. Jack never referred to the Archbishop as anything other than 'John Charles'.

Within a couple of weeks Jack was working for the Archbishop in the palace gardens in Drumcondra, or he was cycling out to Killiney to attend to things at McQuaid's summer residence on Military Road, and at other times he laboured on the College Farm in Stillorgan. Later I wrote a few words about what it was like out of town, not all that long ago:

In them days Stillorgan was country,
Old Goatstown was farmland and hicks,
I used to pick blackberries out there,
Boiling tea on a fire made from sticks . . .

We were all very impressed by whatever pull Jack had with the Archbishop, but we asked no questions of him. I tried but Ma quickly told me to shut up and leave him alone. Jack was now weighing in with money every Friday and soon he began to bring in a chair that could stand without crutches, or a can of paint, or other things that were useful. He helped Da wallpaper our kitchen and between the two of them they made a nice job of it. The big roses all over the walls and the fresh paint gave the place a lift and within a few months Ma was sleeping on something called a divan bed, with a good second-hand sofa under the other window for us to sit on.

Though Ma was delighted with the rise in our fortunes, she never accepted the right of the church to snoop around and find out about our living circumstances without our family even knowing we were being investigated. But she let it go like so many other things that didn't seem right.

Having Jack around was like having a big brother for the first time. I mean Michael was older but he didn't have any time for me. And though I might have been bigger than Brendan he was a shagging nuisance most of the time; if I did anything for him I was only following Ma's orders. There was no generosity in it, as Jack showed to everyone, particularly to Brendan and me.

He used to take us to the pictures and he'd give me the odd kiss on the cheek sometimes in the dark. He had big soft lips and his face was very blue where he shaved. He put brilliantine in his hair and I saw him get the eye from a woman now and again. I didn't mind the odd kiss on the face. There was a Brownie Boy around the Buildings for years called Harry who'd give you a tanner if you'd let him kiss your cheek, which I did any time he was in the mood, provided he gave me the sixpence first. Then off to the Prinner for the fourpenny rush and tuppence worth of broken biscuits!

And there was another quare fella who lived on the Avenue. Willie Something we called him, and he gave each kid sixpence for dropping his pants and hunching down as though he was going to do a Number Two. This happened in a narrow lane behind the house Willie lived in with his well-off mammy and daddy. Willie never put a hand on you and he'd give you an extra threepence, imagine, an extra three dee, which was money for jam if you could work up a good fart.

So Jack kissing me in the picture house never cost me a thought. The odd time Jack's hand would touch my leg but I didn't think much about it.

Once when his hand landed on my flies I said, 'Cut that out, don't do it!' and it never happened again, in the pictures.

4

Aunty Kay never warmed to Jack but then she didn't like many people and she more or less lived up to Ma's claim that 'She hasn't a good word to say about anybody. Her oul' mother was just the same. And she broke my mother's heart so she did, may God forgive the oul' bitch.'

The story went that Ma's mother, Molly Geraghty, wasn't good enough for Paddy Rogers because she had nothing and the Rogers family had land and a dairy and the devil knows what all in and around the village of Ranelagh. Aunty Kay often reminded us that she herself had been going to marry the captain of a Cunard ship 'but he was lost at sea and there was no other man for me'.

Ma sneered at this version of the tale. In her account, your man had run off with a floozie, but she admitted that himself and Kay were the handsomest couple ever seen in Ranelagh.

Granny Rogers — the Ma's mother — and Aunty Kay were sworn enemies because they both loved a man, the same man, who was too busy drinking himself to death to love either of them: the Grandfather Rogers, 'Six feet two in his stocking feet, sing the birds off the bushes, but God love him, he was a martyr, a slave to the demon drink.' He must have been because it's recorded fact that Granda died at the age of forty-two from alcoholic poisoning. This didn't bother me all that much since I never even knew the man. What did bother me, though, was a picture Ma had of her father, because it was me there in the photograph looking out; such a likeness you never saw, I swear. It was enough to make you stop sneering at the idea of reincarnation. I was very concerned that if the rest of me was his double as well, I could end up as big a boozer as he was, and I didn't fancy that.

Aunty Kay and Ma griped at each other a lot, so that you'd wonder why they chose to be in each other's company so much of the time. Kay could have been cleaning houses five or six days a week which would have given her a fair bit of money. And with her older sister Biddy dead a few years from the drink, she'd have nobody hanging out of her, and she could have had a very comfortable life for herself. 'She's a lonely woman,' Ma said in answer to my question, 'and she's an old maid, that's why she's so bitter. And she drives me to distraction. But we're all she has. Though I dread to think of my mother coming home for a visit. The pair of them together doesn't bear thinking about.'

I liked Aunty Kay a lot and not just because she was generous whenever she had any money. She was an oul' bitch really, a full-time backbiter, but she was brave in her own quiet way, even if she was snooty about some of the neighbours: 'Common as dishwater,' she would say, so human, good and bad all mixed up into a person who was a really decent skin.

Ma had given me a good answer to my question about Aunty Kay. But typical her, she avoided telling me why she tolerated her father's sister day in day out, with the sniping and the snotty remarks and all that. I'd worked it out that Ma put up with Kay because it meant she herself could be out all day if she liked and she did like because she was hardly ever in the flat except at mealtimes. And nobody, not even me, ever thought to ask her where she went when she wasn't at home.

I'd been noticing for a while that Aunty Kay was drinking an awful lot of water, and that when she had money she'd send Michael or me running down to Coffee's shop for a bottle of red lemonade. She always gave you a penny for yourself for going, but there was no chance of getting as much as a sip of the lemonade. The top came off the bottle the minute you got in the door, and then it was down the hatch with it in no time flat, like a woman dying of the thirst.

I didn't say anything to Ma for a while because they all thought I was dramatic enough already. But I'd read in the *Evening Herald* a while back about a fella who was in court for being drunk in charge of a pony and cart. The Head's defence was that he only drank as much as he did that day because he suffered from drinking diabetes. I'd never even heard of drinking diabetes but it stuck in my mind because your man got off without a fine or anything. I laughed when I read that the District Justice told him: 'If it ever happens again you should get between the shafts of the cart and let the pony drive you home.'

Finally, I told Ma there was something wrong with Aunty Kay. Ma seemed to be about to say something like 'Yeh, insanity,' but she heard the concern in my voice and she didn't resist when I urged her to take Kay up to see Dr Lemass at the dispensary in Rathmines. Need I tell you that the lemonade killer went into a spin, unleashing some very serious resistance. Ma let her say her piece and then she said quietly, 'Lee has been keeping an eye on you. He's worried about you. The least you can do is go and see Lemass. It'll put his mind at rest, anyway.' That was the first time I ever heard Ma call me by my new name to another person and I was delighted with her. Then to make me feel even better, Kay threw in the towel and agreed to go with Ma to see the doctor.

In the heel of the hunt it turns out that she has diabetes and suddenly nobody's laughing, especially when this huge nurse from Kerry comes to the flat to show us how to give the insulin injection Kay has to have twice a day. I stand there and pay some attention to what the nurse is saying and I watch as she administers the insulin. I feel a bit queasy for a second or two, but it passes. When I turn around to make sure the others are taking it all in as well as me, what do I find? I find I'm the only one left in the room, meaning there's just the nurse and the patient and me.

So what choice do I have? None. I am the one who will give Kay her insulin twice a day and that's that. Except to say that Aunty Kay was so brave as I pushed the hypodermic into her arm morning and evening, so brave, I began to feel humble around her. A year or so later, she was steadily losing weight and her arms were getting thinner; sometimes I had to try two or three times before I'd manage to get the needle in. I wanted to run out of there many a day, my insides scrunching up.

'Don't worry, Leo, just get it in anywhere you can.' Aunty Kay was very ladylike in how she carried herself except when she lost her temper. 'It doesn't hurt, honest,' she would say sometimes, lying to try and reassure me, so very aware of how I felt, while I had to get away from her fast to make sure she didn't see the tears I couldn't hold back.

Once the diabetes was under control, everybody in the family just forgot about it except me and Aunty Kay. So twice a day we had this little bit of time that concerned just the two of us, and sometimes, after I had injected the insulin into her arm, I'd make her a cup of tea. She talked to me sometimes about her life, of how she'd been left to look after her mother, who did sound like the oul' bitch Ma claimed she had always been. 'Forcing Kay to sleep in the bed with her and she roarin' from the pain of the cancer. No Christian woman'd do a thing like that to her own daughter.'

I asked Aunty Kay how her mother had died. Not that I doubted Ma but she could dress a story up sometimes when it suited her or when she was just being thoughtless and gave her very active imagination a long lead. 'The last ten months were very hard on her,' Kay said, nodding her head in confirmation. 'It was cancer of the bowel and she suffered grievously. People said they could hear her roaring in Milltown. Exaggeration. But I had to be there day and night for the ten months.' She sighed: 'My mother. Release is the only word I could apply to her dying. And I was released by God the day he took my mother to his bosom.'

'Was that when your sea captain got drowned?' The question surprised me as much as it shook Aunty Kay. She darted a look my way and lowered her eyes. I got my breath back, wondering where the question had come from. 'He didn't drown, Leo,' Kay said, taking my hand. Her voice shook but there were no tears in her eyes when she said: 'He found someone else while I was looking after my mother. He didn't wait for me like he promised he would when romance was in the air.' She shrugged and I noticed how slight her once grand shoulders had become under the old wraparound apron she wore all day every day. 'There was no knowing how long my mother would last, you see. Who could tell? And then of course, there was Biddy.'

Biddy was another story, another old maid never had a man look at her, according to Ma. 'She'd a mouth on her like a rat trap all the years she didn't drink,' Ma said without any hint of the unkindness that could be there if she was in a bad mood answering you. 'That whole family was riddled with the curse; the doctors ought to call it a virus or something, this thing where certain families can't drink without destroying themselves and losing everything.'

'Biddy was a lovely girl,' Aunty Kay told me. 'She wanted a husband and a family and that's all she wanted but God decided otherwise.' Kay looked around to make sure nobody else would hear what everybody already knew anyway. 'Drove her to drink, her disappointment. And drink took her life in the end, just like poor Paddy — that's your granda Rogers I'm talking about now.'

Aunty Kay no longer went out to clean houses for people on Sandford Road. The truth is that she wouldn't have been able to do the work and before long, when she was leaving our place at night, one of us would walk her home, or part of the way, anyway, to Byrne's shop where she loved to stop and gossip with Mrs Byrne.

There didn't seem to be any shortage of time and people willing to get into a good backbite. Certainly not with Aunty Kay anyway and the people she chatted with. Mind you, there was very little in the way of entertainment available, so the behaviour of the neighbours got plenty of eyeball. And there was the bush telegraph passing the word along, and need I tell you that the stories grew mouth to mouth, every storyteller adding a hint of something extra, a bit more spice to the original script.

Thanks to Ma going to see Mr Gallagher at Tranquilla National School, I'm a pupil there and I'm starting to learn the kind of things that might come in handy if I ever get down to earth enough to decide I have to take a job. As opposed to being a writer like, or the latest, which is a film star.

It's okay to laugh. Ma certainly did when I told her my new idea. 'So what happened to being a writer then?' And she gives me one of her smart looks, the ones that tell you you've a lot to learn, without her saying a word.

'Ah Ma, I know I'm only twelve going on thirteen, but right now I'm taller than Edward G. and Cagney and George Raft. And Alan Ladd's only a tall midget. When I was seven I was bigger than him.'

Because you were only twelve years old you couldn't explain you knew things you hadn't been taught. Things that were just there. In you. Like how to breathe, how to scrunch up your eyes when the sun was deadly. Things like that, which sorta meant you were never a kid in one sense, if you see what I mean. Like somehow your mind, everybody's mind, was as old as old can be. But you couldn't say things like that or they'd send for the man with the net. You were only a kid, right.

The idea about being a film star starts in Nellie Rafter's milk shop on a real Kitty the Hare of a morning near the end of January 1946. It's cold enough to freeze the ball bearings off a roller skate and I'm very grateful for the duffle coat I got from the St Vincent de Paul via the Madonna House Boys' Club a few weeks before Christmas. It's a blanket with a hood really, wooden toggles through loops, and it's a gift as winter flexes her biceps. But you wouldn't buy it, unless you wanted to look like an unmade bed. And you can get tired of people saying as you pass by: 'Hey! It's your man! Snot of the Antarctic!'

I'm not in the door when Nellie asks me without so much as a good morning: 'Who's Constance Smith?' As usual, when she's after something, Nellie manages to sound fairly agreeable. If you didn't know her, you could mistake her for a nice woman. I don't know who Constance Smith is but even if I did, I probably wouldn't tell Nellie.

'You must know her,' she assures me, while Rosie gives me a sly smile and goes back to scrubbing the bejaysus out of a milk churn that never did her a bad turn. 'She's from the Buildings. She lives up in the flats.'

I know Nellie is serious. Her chest is sticking out because her head is back and however the light in the shop hits her wire-framed glasses she looks like a nosy oul' owl. 'The only Smith I know is Connie Smith.' Curiosity is getting the better of me now. 'Why? What's going on?'

'It's there in the *Independent*,' Nellie said, pointing at the paper lying on the counter. 'She won a contest last night and she's going to be a fillum star, so it says.' I stand there assuming she's lost her scapulars and she gets my drift even though I haven't said a word. 'Look for yourself, there's a photograph an' everything.' Nellie's tone is a storm warning; she's not used to having her sanity questioned.

A few moments later my heart is beating as though I've won a fortune in the Sweepstake or something. Really beating like, as though what has happened for Connie Smith has happened for me. Which of course it hasn't, but the miracle of the night before for Connie, it helped me relaunch in my own mind the right to go on dreaming, and the feeling this gave me warmed me up very nicely on that January morning.

The article in the *Indo* came with a terrific picture of Connie wearing a really expensive-looking evening dress. The story said she had won a beauty contest the previous night in the Metropole ballroom in O'Connell Street.

'That's Connie all right,' I heard myself say. 'I know her well.'

'I told you, Rosie,' Nellie said to my little friend with the Ronnie on her upper lip. 'I told you Leo'd know her!' Nellie sounded triumphant in some way and she smiled at me for the first time ever. It was as if I was famous or something because I knew somebody who had got their name in the paper. Somebody from the flats, who wasn't the defendant in a courtroom!

Connie Smith lived in the flats with her father Sil, who really was a gent, her mother, her brothers and her sister Brenda, who was my age, Connie being a few years older. According to the article in the paper, Connie had borrowed the gown she was wearing from a friend. As it turned out, she'd been loaned it by the Cafolla women she worked for who ran fish and chippers in the city, only they called them ice cream parlours.

Connie was slim, her beauty would startle you; jet-black hair, an exquisite oval face, deep blue-green eyes fringed with lashes like luxury. She had spent half a crown to get her picture taken and she had posted it to a magazine that was running a contest for Film Star Doubles, along with a photo of Hedy Lemarr who starred with Victor Mature in *Samson and Delilah*, and would you believe it, Connie had won the contest. For this she got the prize of one guinea but what really mattered was her picture going into *Screen* magazine alongside a shot of Hedy Lemarr.

Soon after this Connie went to London to get the treatment that would turn her into some kind of film actress. This terrific young one, a working girl, being turned into someone I'd see one day in the pictures. Unbelievable, when you think about how slim the chances were of that happening to someone like Connie. Where did she get the wit to send in her picture in the first place? And where did she find the guts? We'd been brainwashed to settle for next to nothing; above all don't rock the boat. Obviously Connie said shag it! She took the chance and something big was happening for her. I was going to go the same route: make something happen for myself. That way I mightn't have to star in a remake of the story of my Mother and Father.

Going to Tranquilla was tough for a week or so after Connie Smith got her big break because my mind almost drowned in the fantastic thoughts that came around again and again as if they were on some kind of conveyor belt in my head. To try and calm myself, I wrote down everything I felt in the Reading Room at the library and the way the stuff flowed out of me gave me great heart that I might one day be a writer. I mean it wasn't impossible to be a film star and a writer at the same time. Nothing was impossible if you wanted it badly enough. Look at Connie. A few weeks before, who wouldn't have laughed into her lovely face if she had said she was going to be a film star.

To encourage us to write better essays, Mr Gallagher, the headmaster at Tranquilla, created an in-class competition. We would write an essay a day and he would give them so many marks out of ten, adding the total up on a Friday. The boy with the most marks would get a prize worth two shillings. This would be presented in the form of copybooks, jotters, a ruler, a pen, all done with a view to creating a goal and a new level of interest.

Mr Gallagher, this gigantic Corkman, was a truly decent man, who cared for the kids in his school and who treated you fairly, even if that included a caning. He had no favourites and he never abused anyone in Tranquilla; which just proved that you didn't have to behave like a monster to get kids to work.

I won the prize for eighteen weeks, bartering whatever I didn't need for sweets, chocolate, and any glam magazine that had women in it. I was only interested in suggestive stuff, which had to come from England, of course; like most of my classmates I was clinging to the ultimate fantasy, to see a girl, any girl anywhere, anyhow, as long as she was in the Jeyes Fluid — the nude.

By now I was convinced I'd been born to be famous, never more so than when Eamonn Andrews read out a poem of mine in a lunchtime programme on our national radio station. He and a journalist called Terry O'Sullivan hosted a weekly radio show sponsored by Imco Cleaners. They played records, they made jokes, and they started a poetry competition. About this time the luxury in our flat knew no bounds. I mean, now we were renting a radio set at three bob a week and Michael had got himself a turntable you could play records on.

My poem for *The Imco Show* could only be a hatchet job. I genuinely thought it was a crap programme, even though I was an Eamonn Andrews fan. When I sent in my verse I never expected it to get a mention, but I made sure I was there by the radio at Friday lunchtime, just in case a miracle happened. Then, one Friday, Eamonn says my name loud and clear. Ma automatically slaps my face. 'Jesus Christ, what have you gone and done now?'

Eamonn is reading the poem, managing to sound as if he agrees with every critical word about himself, Terry O and *The Imco Show*. And we sit there, Ma, Michael, Brendan, Jack and I. I can hardly believe it. My words being read out by one of our most famous men, a guy who would go on to be Britain's biggest television star. I can't remember the whole poem but I know it ended with the lines:

> *Wet Friday, wet Sunday, so they say,*
> *We wish that Imco would change their day.*
> *If they did, they would have more friends*
> *For we would have more Fine Weekends!*

The opus earned me a voucher from Imco for a pound's worth of cleaning, which was all right and I enjoyed opening their letter and looking at the piece of paper that represented my first earnings from writing. That was all I could think about: I had got paid for writing something, and I wasn't even out of primary school yet.

Unfortunately this was at a time when the value of my entire wardrobe was about five or six shillings, so I sold the voucher to one of our neighbours, who was the smartest Catholic I had ever met at that time: she practised her religion but she had only two kids. She paid me fifteen shillings for the cleaning voucher, and I even got a compliment from Ma, who was delighted that I got my name on the radio, now that she knew I wasn't Public Enemy Number One.

I found myself putting the envelope from *The Imco Show* into this copybook I wrote notes and bits of verse into. I wanted to keep it as a souvenir of the day I first heard my name on the radio. I felt good hiding that envelope and for weeks I touched it and had a bit of a smile. Not that long before, Connie Smith had got a guinea for winning the beauty contest that would make her rich and famous. My prize was just a shilling less than that, my few moments of fame not in the same league, but hearing my poem over the air seemed just as memorable.

In another way my Confirmation day was a big event. Not because I became a Strong and Perfect Christian as the church said, but due to the fact of my meeting the great man himself, John Charles McQuaid, who was taking the Confirmation day in the church on Rathmines Road. I got to speak to the Archbishop because I was on the centre aisle end of a pew three or four rows from the front of the church: 'That's where they put the bright pupils, so the Archbishop'll get the right answers,' Ma said, hitting the nail on the head.

I remember John Charles asking me what the word fortitude meant and I said courage in adversity. He seemed pleased. I noticed the little shimmer in his eyes only because I was looking into his narrow face to see was there some family resemblance to Jack. Don't get me wrong. I didn't for one second think that the Archbishop of Dublin was Jack's Da, but it wasn't impossible that our adopted brother was related to him in some way.

'Jack's Da, he was maybe a Remittance Man in the Archbishop's family,' Ma said philosophically. She had never bought Jack's story that he was an orphan who had been put into Carricklea Industrial School to be reared. 'He's not common; not out of common people like.' Ma sounded certain about this. 'He's fine in many ways, though he's a bit strange sometimes.' 'You don't know the half of it,' I thought to myself, knowing that I'd never tell her what Jack was like at certain times. But I was dead sure I wouldn't be sharing a bed with him ever again, not if every relation we had came home from England at the same time, bringing their neighbours with them.

A Remittance Man was usually the black sheep, Ma said. He was given money to stay away from the family, supported as long as he didn't make trouble, embarrass his relations any more than he'd done already to become a Remittance Man in the first place.

'Usually it's about a child born the wrong side of the blanket.' Ma talked to me in a way she didn't talk to anybody else in the family. 'What they call a bastard, Ma? Is that right?' 'Oh trust you!' She smiled as though she was pleased by the fact that I knew what she was talking about. 'You've a dirty mind like a writer anyway, or are you a star this week!' she said, closing the subject on Jack and the McQuaid family for the time being.

5

I already saw myself as the star of every situation in which I appeared and unfortunately I let this idea slip out a few times, which didn't help me onto anybody's Christmas card list. I know that Rose barely said goodbye when she left to join the ATS in England, and to my knowledge, Michael hadn't moved me up a place on his popularity parade. But things were picking up generally, we had a few quid coming into the flat every week, and I was looking forward to the bright-lighted star-studded future I had going in my head. And in the meantime, I was crazy about Ma, I loved Da, I didn't mind Jack, and the rest, well, enough said.

So in the tale of our first turkey, the way the story unfolded, my brother Michael turned out to be the hero instead of me. He was the Chap and I was just like the kid who didn't want to play Sitting Bull! Michael was a very straight, clean-cut fella who took no messing from anybody. He'd gone the Nellie Rafter route with the early morning milk deliveries until I took over. Later on he used to help out on one of Kennedy's bread vans on a Saturday. This was a horse-drawn yoke driven by a decent skin named Joe O'Connor who played football for County Offaly.

Gaelic was a culchie's game but even so, to play for your county was a great honour, so I was very impressed by Joe. And that was even before I saw his picture in the sports section of the *Evening Herald*: 'Offaly veteran Joe O'Connor turns out for his county at Croke Park on Sunday next.' After that, I hated the fact that Michael had got to him first. He helped Joe deliver the bread, he got a few bob for that, fair enough. But much more important, he got a chance to take the reins; he actually drove the horse at times. I saw him doing it, driving the nag up on Palmerston Road, sitting up on the front seat of the box van perched on two iron-rimmed wheels. I know I turned green that day, even though I was getting well paid to mow a lawn for a woman who kept her garden in very good nick. The money didn't make up for the fact that it was Michael driving the bleedin' stage-coach and not me.

Joe lived in a boarding house run by Mrs Redmond in Mount Pleasant Square, so when he wins this turkey in a raffle in Guinan's pub, what does he do but arrive at our door on Christmas Eve and put this half-a-ton turkey on the table in the kitchen and tells Ma it's a Christmas present for the family.

Ma sniffed back a few tears after Joe left. She was always the same in the face of decency. Minutes later it's, 'We have to have stuffing for the turkey. You can't have a turkey and no stuffing,' her panic only taking a walk when the huge bird was stuffed to the Pope's Nose and back again, and was finally ready for the oven. Ma had already bought a shoulder of bacon for our Christmas dinner.

My thirteenth birthday was just four days gone by and no trumpets had blown this year either. But sitting down to the first turkey, it was like being in a movie. And, for a change in our house, there was a ton of meat. When Ma hit it with her gravy, the roast spuds, the sprouts, and stuffing like a meal in itself, I ate so much I nearly had to force myself to devour the Christmas pud buried in custard. You had to admit it was a great way to be ending the year of 1947. With me thinking about the lucky bastards who ate like this every day of the year!

Afterwards Da went for his afternoon nap and Ma went up to Gulistan Cottages to visit Mrs Masterson, a really nice woman even if she was as deaf as a doorpost. My brothers were out and about, Aunty Kay had gone for a walk and a gossip, and suddenly I found I had the kitchen cum living room all to myself. The last time this had happened was six years before; I was seven years old. That day I knew I was different. And whether that was a good thing or a bad thing didn't come into it. It just was, and there wasn't a thing I could do about the feeling except live with it. The change in me started like something that had been waiting to happen. It was as if I had nothing to do with it from the moment my seven-year-old mind realised I was king of the castle. From that moment, that first second of total freedom in the flat, to the actual presentation of my first concert, my God, it must have taken all of half an hour! And this included rapid advertising of the occasion to other kids which had to include the info that the price of admission was a ha'penny.

Just moments before, I had never had a thought of putting on a show, in our flat or anywhere else. But there it was, this idea to stage something, worse, the compulsion to put on an entertainment, regardless of the consequences. Up to now I had never been to a theatrical show but I'd seen films that had a showbiz theme, knew that all variety shows had a lot of singing and dancing and gags, and with this under my belt, I felt I was ready to produce, God bless the ignorant and the insane! I brought the Curtain Up or to be more accurate, before an audience of four kids, I stood on the sofa bed and I parted the two bits of blanket I'd hung over this length of string that I'd nailed into the wall either side of the room. And I didn't even think that Da might not like me doing such a thing.

I sang a song to open the proceedings. Then I told this joke which can still raise a laugh today.

Two Dublin kids walk along the street. One says to the other: 'Hey Shamey! I got sumtin' behind me back annit starts with N an' you can eat it. What is it?'

Shamey says: 'It starts with N an' you can eat it? Norange.'

'No.'

'Napple?'

'No.'

'Negg?'

'No.'

'Ah,' says Shamey, 'I give in. Whawrris it?'

'Nonion!'

Then I sang 'The Miller's Daughter', having learned the words from a penny song sheet this oul' fella was selling in the street a few weeks earlier. I went on with 'Scarlet Ribbons', which Ma taught me because I loved it so much. And then I got a young fella who was a good singer up on the stage and he chanted 'Red River Valley' better than Gene Autry ever did.

I sang one of Aunt Lily's songs, 'That Little Kid Sister of Mine', and then I told my audience the show was over. I got one of them to help me get the blanket off the string, then I pulled the nails out of the wall with Da's claw hammer. I was highly delighted with myself. Not every day in the week you can make two dee (tuppence) while you're having a good time. From that day on I was hooked on Showbusiness and I knew I'd do anything in theatre, films or music hall to get a start on the boards. The fact that I left out opera wasn't modesty; it just never occurred to me. I mean, anyone that counted in opera (certainly in the films I'd seen) seemed to be very fat and very Italian and I didn't qualify on either count!

As we got into the New Year of 1948, Aunt Molly was very sick again and once more I had to watch Ma go through hell at the thought of losing her only sister. I was still pumping the insulin into poor Kay, who seemed to get braver as she was getting smaller. She was very concerned about the effect that giving the injections was having on me. She offered to ask if a nurse could come in twice a day to inject her. We both knew she was spitting into the wind.

'It's all right, Kay, I'm just worried all the time about hurting you.' I felt sad that she looked so old, so beaten. I finally got the needle into her skinny little arm again, glad really that I could cope, and I found myself picturing the photo of her and her sea captain, wondering why he had run off on her. She was an oul' bitch sometimes yeh, but nobody was perfect. And it's a dead cert she would have made some special kind of mother.

Aunt Molly was the same: no kids, but a heart big as a suitcase and the soft nature of a mother'd cuddle you to death if you were her child. And now it looked as if she was going to kiss the world goodbye, leaving my poor mother behind, in a million bits.

No matter how brave people are, and I always felt my mother had courage beyond the call of duty, you see something happen to them one day and later on you're able to define it as a moment when a part of that person began to die. A bit fanciful perhaps, but there was a Friday night when Katy came in the door off the 47 bus from Molly's cottage above Rathfarnham, and I knew she had been wounded from a blow so grievous that she might never get over it.

Molly was dead. She had died just after Ma got there about half six that evening. What disturbed me, even more than Molly's going, was hearing Ma sound so beaten, so battle-weary I feared she might weep, and I was afraid that if she started she might never stop until there was nothing left but her clothes in a pile on the floor.

For years every one of us knew that Aunt Molly was dying — Molly with the sexy smile, the cigarette stuck to her bottom lip like Lily and Mrs Doyle. She'd been under the sentence of death since I was a little fella. And here I was thirteen years old feeling like an oul' fella in the shadow of my mother's terrible suffering.

That Molly survived as long as she did surprised everyone. You had people dying all over the place, taken in a matter of a few weeks by the curse of Galloping Consumption, sometimes dead and buried in as little as ten days or a fortnight. In recent times I'd seen so many coffins, walked behind so many funerals, it was heading to commonplace. What I didn't see until the night Molly died was that Ma had all this time been hoping that Molly would survive, wanting this so fiercely that she couldn't see anything else, desperately holding on to the impractical belief that her sister would come through the cursed tuberculosis.

It was a terrible time as the funeral confirmed and, yes, guaranteed that Molly was dead. Somehow the pain gets stronger as the ritual unfolds, as though you're believing the fact of death more than earlier on, and you see your mother and the friends from Jacob's biscuit factory mourning in their tears and in their hearts the loss of long, tall, gentle Molly, who died as she lived, coughing on the cigarette between her lips.

Molly's passing and Rose taking the mailboat to Holyhead were the two major happenings that left Ma rent asunder. I felt worse about Molly knowing that Rose could always come home to see Ma and my sister had never touched me the way Ma's kid sister did. Not liking Rose was easy. She was a very cold girl and I thought she was a real cow a lot of the time while Ma was in St Anne's. Easy now to see that this young girl was just afraid that Ma wasn't going to live. That hardly left her much juice to be our mother, when she was only a big kid herself.

As Molly was buried I managed to get a picture going, a memory I cherished. Seeing Da, his narrow face bearing the look of a man who felt he'd been robbed by life, fixing a light by Molly's bed in the cottage, because her husband Dick — a good skin for a County Dublin culchie, Da called him — was ham-handed when it came to anything to do with electricity. In my mind I see Molly trying to slip Da a ten-bob note, Da backing away from her in his pride, the same pride that had kept him jobless and us pauper poor for over a decade. The same pride that allowed him to walk tall, even in want. That very morning we had walked the five miles from our place up to Molly's cottage because Da had had no money for the bus fare.

Granny Rogers came to mind, during the war. She came home because Molly was going through a particularly bad time. It was probably 1942. The crazy old bitch was taking the mailboat — Holyhead to Dún Laoghaire — just to be with her youngest child, letting us know in her pride-sodden voice: 'Jerry's torpedos don't scare me, Dirty Huns!' I've wondered since was this the reason herself and Da hated each other so much, because they were so alike, both of them too proud for their own good?

Granny Rogers acted very strong as Molly was buried and, even if you hated her, which I certainly didn't, you had to admire the way she held her end up in the situation. She reminded me of Molly herself, well remembered as she told Ma in my company: 'When I do kick the bucket, Katy, don't have the kids at the funeral. They'll know enough misery without seein' me in the wooden topcoat.'

Granny stayed for a week after Molly's funeral. I used to watch her sitting by the fire in our flat, mulling the porter by putting the hot poker into a glass of stout, the only time I ever saw drink in our flat. Da wouldn't touch it with a bargepole and he wouldn't have it near the place. Not that we ever needed it. We never had anybody come to visit except Aunt Lily and she brought the drink with her.

The Granny had this thick woollen sock she brought with her and it was half-filled with English threepenny bits, which were eight-sided. She allowed us kids to put a hand into the sock and take out a coin. I'm not saying this wasn't decent, but the way she went on about it, you'd think she was giving you a quid instead of a threepenny bit. As I dipped into the sock, I tried to think of some way I could nick another couple of coins on the way out, but she was like a hawk, so that even as you thought about it, you felt the old buzzard was reading your mind and you let the idea go.

One night just before she went back to Enfield in Middlesex where she lived, Granny, out of the blue really, mentioned the Silver Strand in County Wicklow. I saw Ma start.

'You could be forgiven if you'd forgotten that years ago,' Ma said, really looking at the old doll.

'How old were you that year, Katy?' Chuckling, the Granny sipped at the mulled Guinness.

Ma recollected she was just over thirteen, Molly had gone ten. They rented a caravan. In moments they were sniffing the tears away, the memory of Molly's eyes saucerlike, as they had called her in to see the birthday cake they had bought for her that day in Arklow. It was after her birthday, an even bigger surprise. 'Better late than never!' Molly had said, grinning in delight. My mother and my grandmother sat together by the fire, talking a lot, with the odd bout of whispering to make sure I didn't hear any of the juicy bits, now and then shedding a few tears over Molly, recalling the past, mostly with sadness, the old woman angry still with Da, regretful that Ma had never been able to talk him into going to live in England.

The Granny mulled her stout all the time, reheating the poker again and again, pouring more of the brew into herself, no bother. Ma didn't have any, but she was as easy as could be expected in the circumstances, relieved that Da was staying away while her mother was home. Ma never drank but she had a few fags that night. The Granny Rogers blamed the cigarettes and the fact that Molly had married a farm labourer as the twin causes of her early death. 'City people shouldn't marry bogmen,' she said, end of story, leaving me wondering if she was the first woman in Ireland to ignore the power of tuberculosis.

They ate a sandwich of batch bread and butter, only the best now that Granny was home, with a Hafners sausage sliced into the middle, and Ma drank strong sweet tea with the food, before they turned their attention to Uncle Jim and the time he went AWOL during World War II and everyone thought he was dead. Up to the day Jimbo went missing, 'the Emergency' hadn't affected us all that much. Ireland was neutral in the affair engulfing Europe. It was such an important fight, a battle for the freedom of the world so some people said, that even America had to come into it, yet Ireland stayed neutral. As soon as I got the hang of what this meant, I felt our country was shamed by sitting on the sidelines.

I kept up with what was going on in the war because Jack used to buy *The People* every Sunday. So I had read about the Battle for Stalingrad and it made me love the Russian people. I was also aware of what Hitler's bombers had done to London and Coventry and Liverpool, and I loved the English people for saying Never Say Die. I was a big fan of the English King and Queen too (the stuttery king Da called him) for staying in Buckingham Palace right through the worst of the bombing raids on London.

A lot of Irish people hated the English, many of them claiming that the Black and Tans were a true representation of the English as a nation. My Uncle Paddy, who was a straight talker, said he'd always had a fair shake in England, in and out of the army, and Uncle Jim-Jimbo said the same thing. And of course the Granny Rogers had become more English than Winston Churchill: her accent was so law-di-da you could have photographed it with a decent camera. If my Granny, the granddaughter of a Prod clergyman from Manchester, was going to adopt an English accent, it was never going to be working-class!

Da slagged the Granny and England and the English all the time, even though his two eldest sons were working and living in Enfield. They survived, like the Granny Rogers, who sent a few quid when she could, though Ma didn't see much from the lads. I didn't blame them. Their life in Mount Pleasant hadn't been much cop. They went away and they forgot about the Buildings as soon as possible. Ma could have done with a bit of financial help but she never mentioned it, except two or three hundred times a month.

When the Germans bombed the North Strand in Dublin, in 1941, there was blue murder going on for weeks. Screams at every level of society, letters to the papers, and God knows what else. Germany claimed it was accidental, they apologised, and that was that! At this time there was a German living up in Templeogue, which was above Terenure on the city's south side as you headed for the high rolling hills of west Wicklow. This gentleman, Herr Held, was an engineer with a business premises in Francis Street in the Liberties. Soon after the bombing of the North Strand, Herr Held was taken into custody and he was well and truly held by the authorities. The story has been written into Irish folklore, of a huge glass swastika fitted into the flat roof of Herr Held's wonderful white house in Templeogue. Apparently there was also a great glass arrow, a finger in glass pointing in the general direction of Belfast.

The swastika and this arrow were both powerfully lit from inside the house, to guide German fliers to Northern Ireland where Belfast, the capital of 'The Six Counties', lay, a hundred miles north of Dublin, in the United Kingdom. When Held was interned, a lot of people in the Liberties who liked the man said it was criminal to lock him up. One old boiling hen, nursing a glass of stout, was heard to say with some feeling: 'I t'ink it's diabolical lockin' that man up. Sure wasn't he on'y makin' sure the bombs didn't fuckin' drop on us.'

Thank God for the humour that snorts its way out of whatever is going on. If it wasn't there, the pain might be too much to handle. And whatever the situation, the opportunity for a laugh is never buried too deep, even when Molly dies and we're all broken-hearted. Granny Rogers is home and herself and Ma, sitting in front of the range, go over old times and relive some of the memories. Mixed through their tears and the overall sadness, there is still, here and there, a moment, a pinpoint of relief from the overall pain of losing Molly. One of these turns out to be Jimbo going AWOL during the war, though when the news first broke with the telegram from the Granny, the world quit turning for Ma. The telegram said: 'My poor boy has been murdered by Hitler stop pray for his soul stop letter follows stop Mother.' Nobody fainted better than Ma. If she was a film star, producers would have had three faints in every movie she did. We revived her. Ma wept before she had words with God, certainly yelling loud enough for him to hear it. She warned him and us that this was the last straw. Twenty years! How much did a body have to endure. And if Jim was dead, then 'Dear God, you might as well come and take me as well.'

My problem was this. While we waited for further word as to whether Jimbo was dead or alive, Ma forced me to go to Mass and even Confession, which I didn't do at all because I was not the least bit sorry for the sins I had committed. Ma gave me my orders 'and make sure you ask the priest to pray for Jim' and she herself said a decade of the Rosary — for the first time in a decade.

I lied to Ma, said I'd gone to Confession. I said I'd given her message to the priest who was already praying for Jimbo. Within a day or two Ma told me she was sleeping a bit easier in the knowledge that a man who actively worked for God around the clock was on his knees making a big pitch for Jimbo's safe return. And people say you should never tell a lie.

The real reason for not going to Confession was this priest in Rathmines church who got very short of breath when I told him about this girl who let me look at her breasts. She actually lifted her jumper and let me see them in the flesh after I had begged her for a whole week. I swear the priest's breathing changed so seriously, a deaf man would have heard it through the mesh screen between us. He wanted me to tell him her name. In a second I'm dripping sweat, but he pushes me for the name. Finally, I just lie to him through the grille, swearing that I don't know her name. I can't believe it. I'm here to confess that I lie, cheat, jerk off, all of it, and I have to lie to this man who is supposed to be my confessor. I come out of the box, weak at the knees, soaked in sweat and already an ex-Catholic, sickened by the priest with the dodgy breathing. So, no more 'Bless me father for I have sinned!' I have just made my last confession, lies an' all.

I'd love to get Jimbo unmurdered, but I have to lie to Ma. The lie helps her sleep better, while the lie to the priest about the girl who showed me her lovely breasts set me free from any further fear of having to go and say I was sorry. I wasn't in the least bit sorry for doing things with girls. I was thrilled to be lucky enough that girls wanted to do things with me. And anyway, of course Hitler hadn't murdered Jimbo. He was too busy trying to wipe out a whole lump of the human race.

Within weeks I am asking myself am I being punished for giving up religion, until I see the whole family's afflicted, the whole city practically, even people who hadn't given up Mass and Confession. We were all in the same boat, and overnight the bed became known as the Scratcher. Our affliction? The scabies epidemic that hit Dublin like a tornado. Someone said it was God taking our mind off the ration books, but it was more to do with the lack of hot water in the life of the ordinary people, so Ma said, and she was usually right about these things.

Bird-bathing was okay in August, but standing at the cold water sink in our scullery in November was no picnic. So we went to Tara Street baths every week once we could afford the bus fare and the tanner admission fee. The Corporation should have let poor people bathe themselves for nothing in places like Tara Street and the Iveagh in the Liberties, since there were no baths in the flats for the poor. If there had been anybody bright enough, powerful enough, working in local government to help the poor be cleaner than our living situation encouraged, we might have been spared this epidemic that knocked the country sideways, probably causing more annoyance and creating a bigger reaction than World War II. That's if you leave out the bombs in the North Strand.

I know now that the word scabies is a noun, that it comes from the verb to scratch, but when I was trying to reef the skin off my body to get some relief from those cursed scabs I don't remember about words or meanings or grammar of any kind. To describe the kind of itch we're talking about: I suppose if a herd of ants was scurrying about as busy as ants can get under your skin with a few chasing each other up and down inside your veins and arteries, you might want to tear some skin, rip out an artery, to get relief. Standing in the Iveagh Baths with a Corporation guy in a white coat slapping this whitewash stuff all over your naked body with the sort of brush you use to paste wallpaper cannot be anybody's idea of a good time. To deepen the gloom further, you are so close to the most awful itching in living memory that you don't care, you can't mind that you're naked, that you're being slapped by a brush as though you're just a number that has to be moved along as quickly as possible, which was exactly what was happening. You don't mind, you can't, because the moment the whitewash hits you, you know it's just got to work. It's got to work because it burns as if you've been set alight, since you're just out of a hot bath to open your pores. We all had to be whitewashed, including Ma and Aunty Kay. And even the Granny Dunne, who for the first time in her life admitted, 'Bloody Molly Rogers made a smart move gointa England in thirty-seven!'

A great compliment to Granny Rogers from Da's Ma pushing eighty, standing in her pelt, while a woman in a white coat slapped antiseptic paste all over her. I thought Granny Dunne was really great, the style she showed by letting this happen. Not forgetting Ma. And poor Aunty Kay with not a word out of her and one of her legs looking very sore. And all the other Dublin women who stood naked in the fight to beat the scabies, women who might not have been seen totally in the flesh even by their husbands. They did what they had to do, just got on with it, the way they did every day of the week, every week!

Rose got the wobbly brush like the rest of us and she didn't have to have her beautiful golden tresses cut off, though the prospect had reared its head, sending her demented. My guess is that it was in the Iveagh Baths that my sister finally decided she was leaving home for good, just as soon as she was old enough to go. But you'd never know, Rose would tell you nothing.

I didn't know what was so magical about the number eighteen, but Ma wouldn't let Rose go until she got there. Then just days later it's okay for her to take off to join the ATS with no guarantee she'll ever come back. I felt relief but Ma was shattered by the door closing on Rose's back and I wondered would she ever get over it. For weeks afterwards, Ma was impossible and Da got the rough edge of the tongue he'd taken for better or for worse, somehow copping most of the blame for my sister kissing the unhappy home bye-bye. Nobody could deny Rose had to get out if only to have a room of her own, some little chamber of privacy, and other things that an emerging woman would need to herself. Ma dumped on Da because we all knew that his only daughter couldn't stand him.

6

It was because of the scabies epidemic that we began getting visits from the members of the St Camillus' Brigade. These volunteer workers came to our flats with medical care and advice to people living on the floor, have-nots who needed help without having to trek to a hospital during times when the bus fare was as scarce as optimism. I remember one time I was going nuts with pain. I'd had a thumbnail pulled and a nurse just jammed cotton wool into the flesh, bandaged it, sent me home. A few hours later I'm in serious pain, and I wasn't a kid to make a drama of suffering, I already had an image to look after. But the thumb had me praying in a way that the nuns hadn't got around to yet: 'Sweet corrugated Christ. Jesus. Where the fuck is the Seventh Cavalry?' A minute later a girl from St Camillus arrived, a gentle blonde girl, she soaked the cotton wool off my flesh and started getting rid of the agony. She gave me two pills that made me feel grateful very quickly and she left me a few more to take to keep the pain at bay. Within a few days I was as right as ninepence.

So when the St Camillus' flag day came along, I was more than happy to put in the time needed to get my flag box full to help the cause. When I felt the weight of the box in my hand as I shoved it under the bed, I got to thinking about a cake. A big cream cake, all to myself. There had never been enough cake in my life. If one appeared you got a thin slice because it had to go round. Your tongue could hang out for more but you couldn't have what wasn't there, and that was that. So a cake of my own had always been a special kind of dream to me. And I used to spend a few minutes at a time looking at all the different cakes they'd have in the window of the Monument Creamery on Rathmines Road.

When I got the box of flags to sell I had no intention of keeping any of the money as the other kids were doing. Even when I saw some of them jiggling with a knife in the slit on top of the box, I didn't think it was right. And I didn't do it because it seemed like a lousy thing to do. Until one day in Rathmines as I passed the shop, I knew that if I didn't have a whole cake to myself just once, I'd go mad for thinking about it. I ran all the way home, so obsessed with what I wanted I'd no trouble pushing the guilty feeling out of my mind. I got the box, climbed out the window into the drying yards — the area the flats backed onto where people hung their washing — and smashed it to pieces with a brick that was handy. As fast as I could, I picked up the coins and put them in my pocket, then I gathered up the bits of wood. On the way to the bus stop, I pushed some of them down a shore, into the drains where they wouldn't be found, and I scattered the other bits around the streets as I hurried on. Twenty-seven shillings. I counted it again and again on the way into O'Connell Street on the top deck of the 12 bus. It was a lot of dough, and I was so excited because I knew I was going to the Carlton cinema, having first of all made a stop at a shop just up the street. I suppose I was so crazy with delight for what was happening that I didn't have the room inside to be frightened at what I'd just done.

Near the Carlton was a big cake shop, and when I looked into the window I saw a beauty of a cake that made me go weak just looking at it. I went in and the oul' one behind the counter gave me the once-over, twice. Not that you could blame her. In my badly beaten shirt and trousers, dirty runners on my feet, I didn't look like any of the other customers waiting to be served.

She put the cake into a box and took my five and threepence. When I walked out of the shop it felt like a ton weight in my hand. I paid for a one and eightpenny seat and went up to the balcony in the Carlton and sat there in the dark and ate every single crumb. I sat back then to enjoy the picture. It was called *Step Lively* and Frank Sinatra, George Murphy and Gloria De Haven were in it.

When I came out of the cinema I knew I'd never be the same again. Then for a few seconds I got an attack of the collywobbles. What was going to happen when the St Camillus crowd came looking for their flag box? Right there and then I knew I'd have to own up, tell them what I'd done. This didn't fill me with delight, I can tell you. Shag it, I did what I did; I'd face them and the lawmen if they reported me. To my surprise and, need I add, to my relief, the flag box was never mentioned again, nobody from St Camillus came to collect it. I need hardly tell you I didn't go out of my way to remind anybody about it. I couldn't see any fun in that.

Fun? It was about as plentiful as money on the home front, very little gas in our house, unless it came from the new cooker, little or no joy living with Ma and Da, even at the best of times. And you sort of knew there never would be because Ma was just too strong for Da. Every so often you could practically see this truth land between the eyes yet again, and the fury in him then could scare you. And when the gloves came off and they were really at it, they were blind to everything else. Their fights were so passionate, you could only imagine what it would have been like if they'd liked each other, got along instead of going into battle every day, each of them trying to beat down the other for once and for all. Then there were their silent skirmishes within the continuing battle to live together, and you could tell at those times that Ma couldn't bear the sight of Da. I was very aware of the tension between them and he captured all my respect because he was man enough to let the hare sit till she remembered his name again, and that they were together for better or for worse and probably till the day the heels would go first. It was like that between them for weeks sometimes. You'd be piggy in the middle. Ma asking you to ask your Da if he'd eat a rasher for his dinner, Da saying, 'Tell your Ma I'm so hungry I'd eat a slice off an oul' man's arse!' You trying not to laugh as you said yes to Ma, who might have been stone deaf to any sound falling from your father's lips.

Great stuff in a story, terrific in a picture house, but hard to live with. And Katy would not be worn down, not by Da or by poverty. Somehow, for all that had been dumped on her, she was her own woman. I would have loved the story from her own lips, the tale she kept imprisoned in her heart, a word about her hopes and dreams for herself before 'I got tied up with your Da'. But Katy wasn't likely ever to cough up the truth. She was burdened by pride of her own, she just wasn't free to show you her postcards from the past. But she did let you see the odd flash of her greatness in some of the things she did without giving them a second thought.

Even when we were really on the breadline it didn't stop her adopting Jack. Did she put an advert in the paper for a maid? Of course not. But Aunty Kay arrives and more or less moves in. So there's Ma, pauperish but not very papist, proud as Da that she slagged for carrying the same deadly sin, with at least one of the family, me, profane, while our all-day maid sometimes works cleaning houses to subsidise the little bit of living we are allowed by our circumstances. To my mind it was all due to Ma, who was like a fly-paper to which everything stuck.

Next thing you know, the newspapers are saying the world would never be the same again now the war was over. This was just fine by me. If it was true, it could mean some change in the lives of people on the bottom rung. Things needed to change so that everybody got a fairer crack of the whip. I was as mad as hell with politicians turning up at the flats. Anything you needed to hear by way of promises, these conmen would make it to get a vote. Strangers in decent suits and white shirts hustling strangers, shaking hands, talking to people as though they mattered, ensuring by the very promises they were never going to keep that they would remain strangers.

The only politician I could bear in those days was Alfie Byrne, who was Lord Mayor of Dublin for a good while. Alfie used to ride around on an auto cycle, which was a pedal bike with a tiny engine, and he used this mount to get about in the war years when there was little or no petrol available. Like Roy Rogers with a waxed moustache, he spent a lot of time in the saddle. Alfie was a people's politician. I can't honestly recall if he ever did anything that was beneficial to anybody, but he took the trouble to be decent and ordinary Dubs swore they loved him. Which you could take with a grain of salt.

Then we got some really good news, the headlines we'd been looking for in the papers. Hitler was dead! Died in his bunker so we were told and what could we do but believe what it said in the papers and on the radio. Churchill was like the uncrowned King of England for his courage and his never-say-die attitude right through the war. Word had it that he had more brandy than blood in his veins. Maybe so, but so had a lot of other people and they didn't win the war for the Allies.

From what I had read about Churchill, I thought he was a great man. To *out-think* Hitler surely meant he had a genuine criminal mind, by all accounts a very handy thing in a politician. So you can imagine my amazement when he got the elbow from the British people in 1945 as Clement Attlee led Labour into power and the great man found himself on the Opposition benches at Westminster.

I know I was only eleven years old at this time but I was reading better than many of the adults I knew, and if my memory was not quite in the total recall bracket, it was close to it. Most of what I read I would remember without trying. Every film I saw seemed to be there on a roller in my head, and because I was a fund of facts, I spouted out a lot of opinions which of course annoyed the hell out of people who felt — as my sister Rose did — that little pigs should be seen and not heard.

Long after the war ended we still had ration books but we were eating better than ever before. It was nothing to get excited about but things were definitely looking up since Da had finally got a permanent job. This gave a lift to all of us, especially Da himself, proud of the fact that he was now working for the Electricity Supply Board.

It wasn't long before we began to see some material benefits in the flat: chairs you could sit on without doing a balancing act, a new second-hand table with pull-out leaves. Soon came a sideboard with a flat top, which became home to Michael's record turntable: this did a balancing act on an old shoe polish tin because my brother couldn't afford to buy a wooden base for it to lodge in. Michael was working too by now. He was a storeman in a wholesale motor supply outfit in Pearse Street and, though Ma found it hard to get him out on time many's the morning, when he did go he was clean and pressed and well capable of doing the job. He had always been like that and I well remember him coming up Coffee's Lane one Sunday after Mass in his scout's uniform. One of the kids I was standing with said something about him being a boaster on account of the way he walked and someone else wondered where the money for the uniform had come from. I told the first guy to close his gob or I'd close it for him, and I told the second kid 'He collected waste paper for a year to get that uniform, that's where he got the money!' It was true enough but what surprised me was the sense of pride I felt at Michael's achievement. Not that I'd have told him that.

I was no longer delivering milk for Nellie Rafter. She turned me down for a raise so I walked out one morning. She fumed at me but I didn't care. I said goodbye to Rosie, who smiled and went back to scrubbing a churn. Before long she was dead, bowel cancer so another shopkeeper on the avenue told me. But the hare-baiter herself, Nellie, wouldn't kick the bucket for a long time.

When we got the electricity into the flat, we spent a few minutes turning the light on and off, making a joke as we acted surprised to find that the walls were green. Like kids we were, delighted with our place now that there was lino and more food about. What a difference a couple of years could make. Even Ma, who never seemed happy, was taken with the electric light. That first evening in our brightly lit kitchen, I found her reading *The Great Gatsby*, devouring it as I had in the library; I had bought it second-hand so that I could have my very own copy. F. Scott Fitzgerald's characters were interesting and very complicated, though he presented them in simple terms. Gatsby and Daisy were both deluded. Daisy's husband Tom slags Gatsby as a phoney while he cheats on the wife he is fighting to hold onto. Jay Gatsby wasn't Gatsby's real name, so he was phoney too, but he'd made a pile of money and that impressed me.

'Things are going to be great when I get rich and famous,' I told Ma.

'Don't forget your poor Ma when you do,' she chuckled. In her eyes you were going to be nothing but a labourer if you didn't get the right kind of education. 'Don't build your hopes up,' she'd warn me, 'then you won't be too disappointed.' I couldn't hear this kind of talk. It sounded too practical to the wayward ear and I just wouldn't let it land on my hopes and my dreams. There was some little guy inside who knew you could *make it* if you wanted it badly enough and you were willing to do whatever it took to get there.

'I'm going to be rich and famous, women falling over themselves to get at me, Ma. You wait and see.'

Her eyes rolling upwards as though she could see God while she asked him: 'Where did I get him from?' Turning away from me to hide the smile battling with the concern that always marked her face when I talked like that. It was one of the saddest things about Ma: the need to have you think within the narrow little passage that she believed life allowed to people like us. To accept and not get ideas beyond your station and stuff like this, which I couldn't give lodging to, and I wouldn't.

'You're like my father and I can't help worrying about you,' Ma would say, looking right at me. 'He destroyed part of us all while he was destroying himself. I don't want that for you.'

When Ma talked to me like that I liked it, even though sometimes her remarks were critical. I loved the secrets shared just between the two of us. Finding the two quid on a Saturday night to get Da's suit out of the pawn office, begging it sometimes, borrowing it always, and somehow saving Da from having to admit that his one and only suit had to go into Gibson's every Monday to get the week off the ground. And pray that things might be different by Saturday when the suit had to be redeemed. And I do mean had to.

I enjoyed Ma relying on me to come back home in the mornings bearing an egg stolen daily from Walker's farm in Clonskeagh. I used to borrow a fella's bike without him knowing it, and cycle out there in the middle of doing Nuala Madigan's huge paper round, which earned me twelve bob a week. Your man who owned the bike never woke up before nine, which was a great help. Ma lit up when I came in the door with the hen's pearl, nobody daring to moan about more French toast even though we ate enough of it to put you off it for life.

You could have taken a bite out of Ma's relief when I got an extra job, a full day on Saturday with a butcher in Rathmines, who gave me five shillings for the day. Plus the Wrap-Up, bits of meat, cut-offs, that would make a great stew on Sunday. As you might imagine, the five shillings was hard-earned, a twelve-hour day, eight to eight, but after Nellie Rafter I wasn't complaining.

Ma was there one evening when I came out of Dewhurst's and she was in bits. She hadn't got the money to redeem Da's suit from the pawn office and she was pretty desperate. This man came to mind in an instant and I took the pawn ticket from Ma. She went to buy the bits and pieces for the next day while I went to see the man I'd christened Mighty Joe-Joe because I heard he was very well endowed, especially for a little jockey of a bloke like him.

He had a thriving little business of his own in Ranelagh and we knew each other as casual neighbours, but people didn't give much time or thought to kids back then. So you can imagine Mighty Joe-Joe's surprise when I turned up on his Saturday evening doorstep, asking could he loan my mother two pound to get my father's suit out of the pawn office or my father would strangle her in the morning. He was more than surprised, but I could see he was sort of impressed by my cheek. I stood there practically holding my breath while he looked straight at me for about a fortnight, with me hoping above all else that he wasn't remembering the last time we had seen each other. If he did get a rerun he might think I was trying to blackmail him.

I knew Mighty Joe-Joe was riding a woman in the flats without permission from his wife, or the husband of the lady. I knew about him and her because I'd seen him come out her back window into the drying yards between the flat blocks one lunchtime. I was there looking for an old tennis ball I'd lost. He must have seen me while he was stuffing his shirt into his pants, buttoning his flies, attempting to look as if he was just out for a walk in the fresh air, all at the same time. Neither of us said anything and that was that.

On his own doorstep he makes no bones about handing me the two quid, accepting my word, my promise that he'd have it back by ten o'clock on the Monday morning. And he got the two pounds back but I had to hit him again the next Saturday night, and every Saturday night after that until we just didn't need the loan any more. When this time came, he laughed as he told me: 'After the first year, I didn't know whether it was you or me owned the two quid.'

In time came the day the Da's one and only suit wasn't going into Gibson's on a Monday morning. Just as well. One sad black Tuesday — I remember we'd just bought our own wireless — Gibson's pawn office went on fire. People said it was like an act of God; it was such a perfect leave-nothing-but-ashes kind of fire that it had the hand of God all over it. Just about every Mass suit in our flats and Holyfields must have been in there when the heavenly lightning struck, because a lot of women in both flats were wearing shiners they didn't get from walking into any door.

7

S o by 1948 we had music to go with the electric light, which really brightened the place up. No more of the gas mantle spitting out a tubercular light that made the oil lamp seem like a great idea. Except that going electric wasn't just about having more light; it meant that things were looking up, it meant we were getting off the floor at last.

As I headed for my fourteenth birthday I knew I was through with school. I had sat for the Primary Examination in June and I wasn't going back in September. Needing 40 per cent to scrape by, I got 41 in Irish, a bit more in Arithmetic and 80 per cent for the essay in English. So I scraped a Pass but as the man said 'Every front has a back.' Like, thank God I wasn't 15 per cent smarter; that would have made me one of the smartest kids in the class. Our brightest lad flew through the Primary, then passed the exam to be a telegraph boy, someone who rode around on a bicycle delivering telegrams, a role that had no place in the plans I had for myself.

I did manage to get out of going back to Tranquilla and I said goodbye to Mr Gallagher with some feeling. This man could listen to you when you talked to him, a teacher apart from all the others I had. 'The only decent Corkman I ever met,' Ma said charitably.

He had caught me writing one day when I should have been doing long division. I was so taken by this story in my head I got lost in it, forgetting I was in any kind of class. Mr Gallagher took me up to the top of the room and gave me twelve of the best, six on each hand, for not paying attention. He asked me what I had been writing. I said it was a story. He asked if he might read it and I gave it to him. He sat and he read and I saw him smile a couple of times before he said it was a good short story. Then he complimented me on the research needed to produce the twist in the tail of the tale. I had found the information in an old *Irish Times* in the library in Rathmines.

Mr Gallagher has to be praised. He encouraged me to study, made discipline seem like a good idea because he was always fair. These words come from the heart once fearful and closed tightly against the threat of violence and malicious behaviour from men and women who should have known better. He was the tallest teacher I had ever known, but it had nothing to do with height. He was just bigger in his heart, where it counts.

Now out of school, I wanted a job even if I had to do a paper round to pay for the bicycle I had my heart set on. Not only did I want a bike; I needed one. I was growing up and I was prepared to look after myself. I had secrets, like Eileen for example.

In July I'd had my first girl, or she'd had me, depending on how you look at it. Let's say I'd gone through the motion of sexual intercourse for the first time, with a very generous sixteen-year-old girl with large breasts. Her name was Eileen and I thought she was terrific, gorgeous, lovely even. You couldn't have convinced her of that, though, so after telling her forty or fifty times, I gave up. She said that all her friends thought I looked like John Derek and Farley Granger. I was made up to hear this, trying to be patient about getting my lips to her beautiful breasts. Eileen took the initiative, kissing me gently at first, working up to a more active spit-swapping operation, and she educated me into the art of French kissing. The first time I felt her lovely tongue in my mouth, I thought some part of me would just explode. Sensation shot through me and I wrapped my arms and my lips around her, giving her my own tongue with a heart and a half.

In 1948 French kissing was very definitely regarded as a 'Mortaller' in the Irish Free State. A Mortaller was a mortal sin, one of which on your soul at the time of your death was enough to keep you in hell for all eternity. Which, as the man said, is a long time to be waiting for a bus.

Imagine, you get lucky, the gods go laughing for you, a lovely girl shares saliva with you, trusts you enough to put her velvet tongue in your mouth, allows you to do the same to her, and if, by ill fortune, you were to die in the moment, you would go to hell. From heaven to hell in a heartbeat!

I have never forgotten that first time with Eileen in Palmerston Park, half-naked, buried in the bushes. I felt so excited, it might have been over for me before I even got started. But I got there. And when I did, I had to lie still, I had to be a corpse, one breath and I would surely explode before I even got to the first bend. God, it was wonderful, just wonderful in the waiting, still as light, until it was safe to move, on a tightrope, overcome by the sheer amazement of what was happening, then a breath, and one more, and still no explosion. Moving then, very carefully moving, wanting to know everything in the world, wanting to be good at doing this, wanting to laugh a little laugh that's caught my throat in a gentle grip that says thank you to some god gone laughing somewhere at the folly of men who threaten you with hellfire for tasting life's joy. I had no fear of hellfire there with Eileen. I was so joyously free for a few minutes that there was nowhere about me for fear to land and spoil the magic.

Immediately afterwards I felt sort of down, but I couldn't have expressed it right there and then. It worked out all right, but if Eileen hadn't been as warm and as kind as she was, I might have had a bad time. She kissed me gently and then we were laughing because I was ready to go again in a matter of minutes. Eileen smoked and I had my first cigarette with her in Palmerston Park while we lay in the grass with our clothes all straightened out. She told me she was surprised that I didn't want to get up and take off as soon as I'd 'come off'. She said all the boys she'd done it with so far, they wanted to go as 'as soon as they came'. And some of them hadn't spoken to her since, which was a pity she said, because she had liked one or two, apart altogether from doing it with them.

Even though we were dressed and she had hooked up the clips of her brassiere, I was fascinated by the lovely mounds under her blouse and I kept kissing them through the cotton material. She didn't mind. She said every boy she had ever met had been tit-mad and she hoped that sometime she would come across a guy who thought tits were okay but nothing more. I couldn't believe that having breasts like she had could ever be a nuisance. They were so beautiful, covered or naked. The shape of them made you want to put your mouth to them even if you didn't know the girl standing behind them. It was hard to look right when you had big tits, Eileen said. If you wore tight things you wondered if you looked like a tart and if you had a loose top you looked like a tent. I don't know if it helped her when I assured her that breasts like hers were enough to make a heathen believe in God. As I left Eileen, I realised how much I was looking forward to seeing her again. There was something about her, a softness like all girls should have. Her body made my mouth water, but it wasn't just that, and for some reason that made me feel good.

I sang on my way down to Belgrave Square and the Avenue going back to the flats. I sang all the time. All the popular songs that I heard on the radio, I had them off by heart in no time. I had become a big Vera Lynn fan towards the end of the war when I first heard her singing 'The White Cliffs of Dover' and 'I'll Be Seeing You' and fell in love with her voice.

We were listening most of the time to Radio Luxembourg, which came in on '208 metres of the Medium Wave'. This became *our station* because we listened to nothing else. We loved the easygoing, chatty style of Pete Murray and Geoffrey Everett. They soon had us singing new songs, even seasonal songs: 'Spring is Here', 'Summertime', 'Autumn Leaves', 'Stormy Weather'. The first song to really knock me out was 'Don't Fence Me In!' It was sung by Roy Rogers in the film of the same name, with everybody's favourite Pal, Gabby Hayes, playing 'Wild Cat Kelly', the outlaw that Cole Porter wrote the song about. Right away I nicked it as my own, wondering if you could get a cowboy song played at your funeral.

In 1948 Irish radio was still part-time and with so many people out of work I used to say to myself, 'This whole country is part-time.' Dublin was like a graveyard with lights which reinforced my resolve to *pick up my gur cake and milk and get out of town!* To me the Irish were too submissive. It drove me nuts the way they just accepted the gloom and repression hanging over the country like a fog that had rolled in from the sea with no intention of leaving again. The country was full of people who didn't mind books and films being censored, others who thought the Archbishop of Dublin was right to have spies all over the place making sure that Communists weren't about to undermine all the years of Catholic indoctrination and dogmatic effort. For me it was so stifling my anger threatened to choke me.

I know I got this from my mother. Da just seemed to mosey along. If he'd had a job for the first fifteen years of my life, a ride once a week with Ma, a few shillings to go and watch Drumcondra play soccer at Tolka Park, he'd never have had a bad minute. Ma had ideas, wishes that would never be fulfilled but she never got up and said this is what I want and this is what I'm going to get. In some ways she was like the country itself. And since Ireland stuck in my craw because she was tailoring her young to leave, I wondered with some feeling of guilt if, in a way, Ma wasn't doing the same thing. Either way, it didn't feel right.

Of course I was keen on heroes and often thought I was one myself. I know that by the end of August 1948, I felt like one. I'd done everything I could do to get Ma to see my situation the way I did. I pulled all my strokes, all my faces and expressions, did enough good deeds to be knighted if I was an Englishman! I might as well have been trying to get a coat of paint on a breeze.

'Ma, Bolton Street Tech's for fellas want to be plumbers, plasterers!' There was nothing wrong with tradesmen but to get this exam idea out of Ma's head, I'd have got circumcised and become a Jew.

'Something'll give you a living for life, that's what you need and never mind the famous.' Ma stood there with her feet planted wide, a sure sign that this was another argument she was going to win.

'Ma! The minute you finish any kind of apprenticeship here, soon as you've served your time, it's the boat to England to look for a job.'

None of this washed with her. When she made up her mind Ma got what she wanted. I was mad as hell, still I go to Bolton Street Tech and I fill in a paper saying that I'd like to be a carpenter, a voice in my head pleading, 'Jaysus, have you forgotten what happened to St Joseph!' I burst out laughing at the joke. When I glance at the paper for the Irish exam I stop laughing rapidly. With the best will in the world I have no chance of answering the questions on the pages in front of me, it may as well be Chinese. So, in the neatest handwriting I am capable of, I tell the powers that be I am sorry but I can't even read the exam questions, never mind come up with answers. I go on to tell them I could get to like being a carpenter because 'I love the feel of wood and I'm a big St Joseph fan. And my mother thinks I should have a trade, even though I'm going to be a famous writer.'

That autumn of 1948 Rose came home for a week from playing soldiers in England. She was stationed in Devizes and she'd worked her way into a good English accent. I thought it was funny but nobody said anything and Ma was thrilled to see her so well. She wore regular clothes while she was home but we had pictures of her in her army uniform and she looked great. Her hair was still lovely, very fair, even though it had been cut some to conform with army regulations.

Rose and I didn't have much to say to each other while she was home. She was only really interested in Ma. When she went back, Ma was unbelievably sad for a few weeks and then she adjusted and it was back to the old routine. So Rose was free to go back to Britain as I was sentenced to Bolton Street Tech, provided I'd passed the exam. The only escape I had was the lovemaking, as Eileen called it. Despite all that I had on my plate, I was still seeing her once or twice a week. The great thing was we liked each other, and we had a lot of fun together. And because I was curious enough, as usual wanting to know about everything, she showed me how to touch a girl, and she helped me take longer before I let the vinegar strokes grab me and fling me into an orgasm. She suggested I take deep breaths, think of something for a few seconds, a line in a poem, words of a song, something from a film, anything at all to help keep from what she called *early ejaculation*. I didn't say anything to that, but it was a while before I found out what Eileen meant. She laughed with me when I finally admitted I hadn't known what premature orgasm was. We could laugh together, we were pals more than a couple going together. This was due to Eileen, who was quite a girl. But then she was two years older than me. And that never came between us, especially where sex was concerned. We still got worked up very rapidly whenever our circumstances made it possible.

By the end of the week after Rose returned to barracks, Ma brought me down to earth with one of her lemon drop smiles. I'd been offered a place in a small technical school in Lower Mount Street and the law according to Ma went as follows: 'You're going to this tech and you'll pay attention to what you're taught. And I don't want to hear any more I'm going to be rich and famous for a few years, all right?'

Two days later, a Friday morning: 'Oh sweet holy Jesus, spare us all!' This fervent prayer, practically dripping blood it came from so deep in her heart, was Ma's reaction as she read the acceptance note from the *Times Pictorial*. As true as God they were going to publish an article of mine in their next issue. I stood there smiling, my hair shiny with some of the brilliantine Jack bought in little skinny bottles for about threepence a go. It was as if I was suddenly just a huge grin of a thing that loved itself so much it didn't even need to look in the mirror to feel good.

'You think you're great, don't you!' Ma was thrilled skinny though she was playing Annie Oakley, pretending hard-boiled for a second before we were hugging each other and laughing. By the time I let her go, the worry lines were back like tram-tracks across her forehead.

'Everyone who ever wrote anything was a raving lunatic, Lee. And that's the truth. And I'm afraid of you being near people like that.'

'What about the people wrote the Gospels? And the Handbook of Religious Knowledge?'

'Don't make me mad with your smart questions. You know very well what I mean,' Ma warned me. 'It's like writing and being happy or halfway decent just don't go together.' She was genuinely ruffled, as though she believed I could be successful enough to be in the kind of company who sent shivers up her spine.

'Ma, I'll work to earn a living. But you have to admit I must have some ability. Mr Gallagher said it, and I've had the poem on the radio and now this article. So nothing's going to stop me.' I left it at that, knew for sure I couldn't stop the voice with the stories; I couldn't stop the words and ideas. On top of which, I didn't want to. I loved the wild distant dream of somehow making a crust from scribbling.

The *Times Pictorial* was a fortnightly magazine paper published by *The Irish Times*. My article was about money. Not the money I didn't have, for a change. In this pub on the corner of South King Street, the Four Provinces Lounge Bar, the manager was a collector of souvenir money. He asked foreign visitors to leave a currency note from home and he stuck the dough up on this huge mirror behind the bar. So I wrote a piece about the many-coloured currencies and speculated about the people who left it.

When I dropped the article into the *Times* office I didn't speak to anyone there. If they knew the writer was only fourteen years old, they'd just assume that the piece was no good. I showed it to Brigid Kelly, my first friend, who I'd taken to school on her first day at the age of five, and she thought it was a clever thing to write. Brigid lived near the flats and we were great pals. She had read a few pages of what I thought could be a book that I was writing. About her father really, driving his tram down Rathmines Road early in the morning while I was delivering the milk. Now the last tram had run to Dartry and Terenure, Mr Kelly and other men were out to grass. Things were changing all over as they always did. I remember how Brigid said to me one day at her front door: 'Some day you'll be a famous writer.' It came out of the blue but she sounded definite, so I wasn't going to argue with her. Apart from being far brighter than I was, she was a redhead.

I dreamed about what Brigid said, seeing my name on dust jackets in bookshop windows. I'd been visualising screenplay credits in my name, though I couldn't have articulated it in this way, right back to the age of ten in the Prinner. And I often wondered had Connie Smith seen her name on the screen as an actress in the movies, before it had happened. At times I felt confused at the way doubts could just step all over the dreams inside your head, even when I was determined to be positive. Mind you, I had to fight a lot of the time to beat off feelings like they're right when they say you're nothing but a nutcase, a dreamer fulla wind and piss. I hated this kind of thinking. I couldn't be like this. Then I discovered that feeling could be like acting. If you acted happy you got to feel happy. So I practised acting inside if only to keep the misery out of my head. And though I couldn't have explained it, I never had to ask myself was it the right thing to be doing.

In September 1949, I start going to the technical school in Lower Mount Street but my heart isn't in it. I become captain of the soccer team which means I get to play every week, and I also stroke time off class to organise a team for every game, and anything else I can use to keep me away from sitting behind a desk. I mean, what possible interest could I have in metalwork and mechanical drawing? There's a physics class I like because going in I don't even know what physics means, so I can learn something. By the time we're into December I've had enough school to last me a lifetime. I want out for once and for all. but Ma refuses to give the idea houseroom, she won't even listen to me.

Meanwhile something happened with Jack that shut us all up for a day or two. I liked Jack more than ever now that he had finally quit groping me. After the last time when I caught him at me on his knees by my bed, I was so angry I punched him in the face, and actually made him believe that if he ever laid a hand or a lip on me again, I would tell Ma. He begged me not to, fell on his knees again, and began to pray like a man demented, pleading with God to relieve him of his burden. Being honest, I thought he was nuts. Anybody getting into prayer like that, they'd frighten you on a dark night. But he kept his word, and he never backed off being decent with the few bob even though he knew that he had to keep his hands to himself.

Going back for a minute to that early time after Ma had gone to see Fr Mangan at the Archbishop's Palace, it surprised all of us how quickly the White-Collar Mafia, my nickname for the clerics, had Jack working when there were at least 200,000 men out on the streets protesting about the lack of jobs. But that was just the start. Before long Jack had to report to the bus company. In no time at all after that he had a job cleaning buses at night. Not a very salubrious way to earn a crust, but my father and thousands of other men would have jumped at it. Jack was a good guy and later I came to believe he'd been abused sexually as a child. He'd been in Carricklea, where those in charge did what they liked with the boys and nobody did a thing about it. In my gut I knew that the Archbishop — who knew even that Jack was sleeping on our floor — had to know that children were being abused in the most vile way. But he did nothing and Jack never moaned about any of what had happened to him. He had a good heart, and when it called for it, he wasn't without courage, even out on the street where he never walked away from a fight. Now the bus company needs his birth certificate, since Jack's *getting permanent*.

He is due back from the Custom House, hopefully with the cert in his pocket and no problems. As we sit down that Friday lunchtime with a one and one from the chipper, Jack comes in the door. The minute I see him I know something has gone badly. Ma gets it instantly, glancing at me as though she's remembering that our adopted brother may have been born on the wrong side of the blanket. Jack, this big strong fella, is sitting at the table facing me, and he's blubbering like a kid with his heart broken, tears suddenly streaming down his face, his whole body rocking as he tries to free himself of the pain that's beating him up.

Ma leaves him a minute to see if he'll snap out of it. Then she pushes a cup of cold water into his hand, makes him drink it even though he chokes a bit as he forces it down. He wipes his eyes then on the sleeve of his shirt, and very quietly he says: 'Take a good look at the bastard from Carricklea.'

I remember Ma comforting Jack and I've never forgotten the soreness wrapped around my heart like a glove that lunchtime. On his worst day Jack was a good guy, there was no badness in him, but enough sadness to float a boat in. Suddenly he was beyond us, beyond any help we could give him, though we weighed in the best we could. None of it mattered. From that day Jack wasn't the same any more and soon after he went away to work in England.

By December 1948 I've saved the pound deposit I need to buy a bike on the hire purchase. We call hire purchase 'the Kathleen Mavourneen' system, like it may be for years and it may be for ever! But whatever name we put on it, it's a godsend to me, except I'm stuck for someone to act as guarantor, someone who is what's called 'solvent'. I rack my brains, figuring out if I know any-body in this position. The only person who fits the bill is Mighty Joe-Joe, who saved Ma and me for the couple of years with the two quid Saturdays for Gibson's pawn office. He signs the paper, no problem, and he grins when he talks to me about my poem on the radio. He had a laugh with me that I had to sell the cleaning voucher because I had nothing worth getting cleaned. 'You will have,' he told me in this matter-of-fact way he had about him. 'You'll do well, young Dunne, it's stamped all over you.'

Ten days later I threw my leg over the crossbar of my own bike for the first time and if it had been Trigger himself I couldn't have been more excited. I felt like a king as I rode down Castlewood Avenue heading home. The bike was a gift to ride, especially after the yoke I had delivered the meat on. Very handy for doing the paper round before going to tech. And even though I'd be a year paying for it, it was like an early present, Christmas, birthday, all rolled into one, from me to Lee.

As we approach the school holidays, I'm still at Ma to let me look for a job. 'Less than three weeks I'll be fourteen, legally entitled to work full-time.' Ma didn't want to know but I felt a twinge of change in her attitude so I knew I'd keep working on her till I got what I wanted. I wasn't her son for nothing. And anyway, we weren't battling all the time, we had some fun too.

'You'll wash your face away so you will!' she'd yell at me when she heard the scullery tap, me singing while I washed. 'Then you'll have nothing left to look at.'

'I can't help being vain, Ma, girls never stop telling me how good-looking I am. Not my fault having such a beautiful-looking Ma! The apple doesn't fall far from the tree, you told me that yourself.'

'That doesn't apply to *looks*,' Ma could chide with the best when the mood was on her. 'Only to madness and we all know you got your share of that.' Getting serious then: 'But y'are getting too vain, joking aside. Watch out, pride comes before the fall. Don't say I didn't warn you.'

Within about three weeks I had good cause to remember Ma's words. There I was one morning delivering the papers, my inbuilt appreciation of my good looks in place, when I come off the bike thanks to early morning ice I didn't see in the dark.

Checking the damage later in our scullery I feel like crying. One of my centre top teeth is broken in half, and I'm halfway to being demented. After waiting three hours in the Dental Hospital I'm handed over to a big country guy who has been a dentist for about three weeks. For the next two or three hours I am at the mercy of this mountain man who should have been scything a meadow or something, the hands he had on him. The guy is so nervous he wrecks my front tooth totally and then they break the news to me that it has to come out. Now I cry, but keep it inside, not letting these gobshites see, so upset I'm not sure I remember the pain of my broken tooth being pulled. I certainly don't have any memory of leaving the hospital or how I got home. I was inconsolable, knowing again the awful vomit-making taste of us once more not having the money to get the job done properly. On my own I cried for the loss, but from somewhere inside me came the question, suggesting maybe I wasn't the agnostic I was now claiming to be: 'Why? What are you trying to tell me?' A little plate sticking to the roof of my mouth supports the false tooth replacing the one nature gave me. I hate it but I have to get used to it. It's a life sentence.

Before we break up for Christmas, the head teacher at the tech mentions the chance of a job in an insurance office. I tell him I'd love it. I'll go for anything if it means no more school. I dress the story up for Ma: the teacher thinks I'm too sensitive for metalwork, stuff like that; an office job seems like a better bet for someone of my temperament. I go easy, you have to tread carefully around Ma, something of an actress in her own right with a lot more experience than me. God bless her always, but that Christmas in particular. For my fourteenth birthday, I get a pair of gabardine trousers and a sports jacket, a pair of shoes and a shirt and tie, and I'm as happy as a dog with two pricks. Michael gets the same outfit only larger, but I don't ask him how he feels about it any more than he asks me.

In January 1949 I go for the job interview. I'm a bit worried about my chances of getting the job, the Primary Cert isn't worth framing. In a few moments, Harry starts up in my mind. 'So what! So tell a real big story, lie. Tell the truth you deffo won't get the job, nothin' to lose by spoofin'. You do it right, you can't lose.' So far Harry had never lied to me. Why would he? He is some secret part of me nobody knows about. I talk so much but who can you really talk to? So Harry Redmond arrived; maybe I brought him to the table in my head. I never really thought about it. One day I needed him, needed someone to talk to privately, and there he was. So if he says lie, all right, I'll lie. It's just a question of getting the stuff in your head in the right order. The way Da and me did that Sunday morning when we were late for Mass and needed a good story to give to Ma.

On the bench on Leinster Road I sit quietly with Harry right up front in my mind. All I can think about is the interview. I need the job, but I'm never going to get it, I'm too young.

'So don't tell them your right age,' Harry says. 'The guy asks your age, you say "Seventeen, sir." And remember, you can't say "sir" too often when you're telling lies.'

'They're bound to ask about school before the tech?'

'Say "I couldn't go to one, sir." He asks you why not? You say, "I had to work, sir, my father's an invalid." Give him a real story. Tell it right, the job is yours.'

I can feel myself getting hooked on the idea. How I love to tell the tale, pull off a good spoof. Times that was all that was between me and death at my mother's hands. 'Suppose he hasn't thrown me out of the office by now. How do I get around the age thing? That's the big one, isn't it?'

'Yeh. It's a dot on the card he'll want your birth certificate. So you take your time and you speak with controlled emotion, holding it back, a touch of John Wayne is what you need.'

'Fine, Harry, but what do I tell the man?'

'You say, "I went to collect it on my way here, sir, I nearly didn't come for the interview at all." He asks you, "And why was that, Mister Dunne?" "Well sir," you take your time now, you say, "when I went for the certificate, well, I just found out, sir, that when I was born, my mother and father, they weren't married, sir!"'

'Jesus, I can't say that. Ma'll kill me if she finds out.' I'm serious about this, then I'm thinking of poor Jack and how finding out had demolished him.

'You have to go over the top,' Harry urges. 'When you spoof you have to give them a story nobody in his right mind would make up. That's the trick.'

My doubts don't just disappear but what can I do. I need the job; I'll go crazy in the tech. I'll take the Foreign Legion ahead of more school. I want wine, women and song, and lots and lots of money!

Two days later I go for the real thing. In his private office with Mr Cowman, who has a classy accent for a Corkman. I can see he's not a bad man. Basically decent, in line for some surprises as I answer his questions. Basically the man has no chance. Like, one Corkman against two Dubs, no contest.

I get a month's trial. Mr Cowman shakes my hand. 'I'll be writing to you about all this.' He looks at his notes: 'At number seven Rugby Villas, Ranelagh.' I'd given him Brigid Kelly's address.

When I tell Ma the news her look belongs to someone past being surprised. 'So somehow a suit has to be found,' she says in a matter-of-fact way. 'With the help of God, we'll find the money we need.' And guess what? We did.

The suit was tweed the colour of the heather up at Glencree. It didn't have much of a cut to it but I thought I looked deadly in it, a real ladykiller.

8

I was part of the Picture Generation, people who came under the spell of the movies, and for an emerging nutcase like myself, well, it was total immersion. Even after I quit directing cowboy pictures in the street, I still acted most of the time. Except I didn't advertise that I was doing it.

I know that my ability to act older than my age came from watching Mickey Rooney and the Dead End Kids. Maybe that's why my age never came up at work. I had the gift of the gab, my handwriting was considered excellent, I wasn't afraid to work, my timekeeping was good and I was naturally polite, plus I was willing to feel good. This was the key. Acting as if you felt good. It helped you get along with people and most of the time it improved your own mood as well.

Looking back I can see why I was considered a colourful young fella. I was basically happy or I acted as if I was, I was always willing to make a joke, I seemed to have a facility to give people a laugh and I looked after my appearance even though my wardrobe was still in the bare necessities category.

I also had a photographic memory. When I read something it was there behind my eyes waiting to be shared, delivered if you like. People seemed to enjoy the fact that I had a story for just about every occasion. Most people like to laugh and people who can make people laugh are popular. And I was well liked once you weren't overexposed to me. As the man said I tended to come on strong and that can be wearing.

I got along very well with the young women in the insurance office; one of them had a double-barrelled name and she also sported a double-barrelled sweater, so beautifully stacked it made me want to weep because I knew I was never going to get near those amazing breasts. Like the rest, she was a nice girl, and all I could do was wonder how she could tear herself away from the mirror and gaping at the shape she so naturally wore, as though it didn't mean a thing. There were two good guys there I really got to like but, sadly, an office manager came with the job. He must have read the *You Have to be a*

Shit to be a Manager handbook, lived by it, was detested for it, and went straight to number one on my list of people to avoid as much as possible.

Patrick Cowman, the working head of the firm, was a gent and he treated me fairly all the way down the line. He admitted to me one day that he'd never be a good driver and I thought that was really something in a place like Dublin where every guy behind a car wheel thought he was Dan Dare!

I realise now what a busy life I led, at the time it never occurred to me how much ground I covered in any one day. I was lucky that I enjoyed working in the insurance office. It wasn't what I wanted for my life but while I was marking time it was more than bearable and they got their money's worth out of me every day. I opened and sorted the post each morning, I hand-delivered letters to other companies within a reasonable walking distance, I did all the filing, copied proposal forms by hand, saw that the dictaphone cylinders were shaved on time, and attended to the outgoing evening mail, keeping a record of the names and addresses in a special book kept for that purpose, before dropping all the letters at the College Green post office as I headed home. Nothing exciting but a lot of work, yet I was never tired coming away in the evening, even though I'd been out early with the papers before I got to the office at a quarter past nine five days a week.

Saturday was the toughest day but still the best day of the week because once I got through with the meat deliveries and made sure Ma didn't need me for any emergency, I could go and wallow in a nice hot bath with my great friend, Claire Kearney. Claire was this terrific woman on my meat round, the first adult friend I had ever had. She was the first person to remark on how well groomed I was when I delivered the meat, though she must have noticed I always wore the same clothes. Jimmy, the butcher, had given me a brown shop coat but I didn't fancy myself in it, so I usually turned up at Claire's house in Terenure in my office suit, which just happened to be my only one. *Oh Mrs Kearney!* This is what Jimmy and the apprentice, Slattery, called Claire. They made it sound exciting, giving it some kind of sexual quality, laughing at something between themselves as Slattery made some kind of joke. 'She likes good meat, that Oh Mrs Kearney,' the red-headed bogman would say with a cackle and Jimmy would join in. 'That's how she got them big headlamps and them lovely childbearing hips,' he'd go, laughing as though somebody was tickling him.

The first time she opened her hall door to me I knew what Jimmy had in mind when he said headlamps. Claire's breasts were so stunning I nearly dropped the meat on the doorstep. Apart from her amazing chest she was a fairly good-looking woman even if she did wear glasses. I swear I was shaking visibly as I handed her the parcel of meat. She asked me my name, I told her. Then she shook my hand, saying, 'I'm Claire Kearney.'

I knew Claire for the guts of a year before anything happened between us. Thinking back on it, I'm sure I used to look at her, well, at her breasts, like a Labrador dying for his dinner. And when she finally invited me into the house, asking me if I'd like a cup of tea, I said yes thanks and then we were in the kitchen. Even as I talked to her, I was doing mental novenas that something would happen between us and I didn't care a damn that she was probably old enough to be my mother. With breasts like that she could have been sixty-five and I couldn't have cared less.

It may sound crazy or even stupid, being so affected by the nearness of a middle-aged woman, but I was fascinated by breasts. So much so that I'd willingly have put my lips to the breasts of most of the women I knew by sight. Just about every guy I knew was the same as I was, dreaming about bed with a woman who had headlamps like a Ford Prefect. I knew one guy who carried around with him ladies' lingerie ads cut out of a newspaper. A far cry from *Playboy* and the rest but this guy put Sellotape over an advert for a front-lacing corset so it wouldn't fall apart. When he showed it to me, I had to choke back the need to laugh. Your man was so turned on by the thing he didn't seem to notice the price tag, which was forty-seven and sixpence.

'Excuse me, ma'am,' I remember saying to Claire. 'Could I use your toilet, please?'

'Of course, Lee. It's upstairs. I'll show you.'

I walked behind her up the stairs. Just watching her move in front of me was a fifty-fifty mix of pure joy and sheer agony, and I know I was actually sweating by the time I stood over the toilet bowl, knowing there was no way on earth I wanted to take a leak, and even if I did it wouldn't have been possible, the state I was in. She never made a move to go out. She bent over the bath and began to put some clothes that were lying in it into a bundle. I didn't move. Talk about fear and excitement, I could hardly breathe. I just knew something was going to happen. A sane young guy would have been out of there because he was embarrassed, but when she turned to me from the bath, I was actually waiting for her to do with me whatever she wanted.

She smiled at me. I was like a fella hypnotised as she put her arms around me and kissed me on the mouth, her friendly breath so lovely on my waiting tongue which surprised the hell out of her, so she told me weeks later. This horny young fella waiting with his mouth wide open to her kiss. Her lips felt lovely and soft and her breasts were molten, so hot, or so it seemed, boring holes in my shirt and my chest and I came right then and there, my shoulders heaving from the thrill of it all.

In moments she was cuddling me. She pressed my face gently to her breasts and it's impossible to describe the feeling. I thought for a second I was going to cry. Then I knew it was time for me to go. She understood and anyway she knew that before very long I'd be back.

The following Wednesday Claire Kearney rang me at the office. When I gave her the number I was showing off, never expecting her to actually phone me. Hearing her voice I felt a little bit threatened, excited. She wanted to talk about some jobs that needed doing around the house; she was offering me the chance to work for her of an evening. I jumped at her offer, which was to be the start of my friendship with this terrific woman who was never less than decent to me in or out of bed.

I was reading a lot, scribbling for some part of every week, and I was very busy with the girls, developing a great street patter for picking up strangers in minutes. I still loved the films and I'd been to my first play, having already acted in one, *The Bishop's Candlesticks*, with Madonna House Boys' Club.

The first play I saw was *The Monkey's Paw*, staged in the Bernadette Hall of my Penny Dinner Days. It was produced by a man called Pat O'Rourke and it was only brilliant. Afterwards, feeling stunned by the impact the play had made on me, I crept away on my own to take a quiet walk, knowing I didn't want to talk to anyone until I'd had time to savour what the play had said to me as a young lad dreaming of being a writer. From that night, the wish inside me grew even deeper to write, act, do anything to satisfy the urge in me to be a bit special in some way.

Ma had no time for the theatre, blaming some guy who took her to the Abbey a lot before she met Da. Her West Brit heart couldn't stomach the heavily Irish plays the national theatre was producing at that time. *The Playboy of the Western World* was 'like havin' pneumonia', so she assured me. 'Must be the best-fed actors on earth,' she'd say, half-joking, whole in earnest. 'Every five minutes someone on the stage says, "Yerra! Would yever put down a panna rashers for the dacent man,"' which is never said in *The Playboy*, but that didn't stop Ma going with her own brand of dramatic licence.

When I went on about acting and writing, she tolerated me as best she could, but she was deadly scared I just might get a break on the very last road she would have chosen for my journey in life. I would, occasionally, play it down then, lying that it was all just a dream. I'd remind her I was doing well in the office, my first raise under the belt, but her anxiety about me was increasing by the month. She seemed to know that no matter what she did to clip my wings it wouldn't be long before I'd fly the nest. And she didn't know the half of it!

I'd quit going to the Prinner by now, the cinema of my first dreaming no longer giving me what I needed. My interest in sex had come between me and my interest in Roy Rogers kissing Trigger. So I began going to the Stella on a regular basis. Here the best seat in the house cost about one and eightpence, as opposed to one and threepence in the Princess. They got a different type of picture to the Prinner; there was no shortage of laughs and thrills, but above all I was hungry to see the guy kissing the girl, and of course the Stella was also a great pick-up joint on Sunday afternoon. You picked up a girl as easy as sitting down beside her, and the more it became known as a great place for heavy petting, the more girls seemed to show up. I was just one of a group of guys who never failed to end up snogging some girl. But that was it. You didn't make dates, no guy I knew wanted to go steady with a girl, not when there were lots of lassies curious enough about the magic of boy meets girl to experiment in picture houses.

There was one Sunday afternoon when I didn't go for a pick-up. I was only interested in the film they were showing that day. It was called *The Mudlark* with Andrew Ray in the title role. And guess who was playing the maid in Buckingham Palace, the one who finds the Mudlark hiding under a dining room table? It was Connie, Constance Smith, our very own Hedy Lemarr. There was Connie before me on the screen and I swear she was unbelievably believable as that gentle Irish maid. I gaped as this girl, who truly was one of us, more than held her own with all kinds of top actors. Connie went on to make several Hollywood movies. Before long I saw her starring with Dan Dailey, the legendary song-and-dance man, in *Taxi*. She played opposite Larry Parks, who starred in *The Jolson Story*, in *Tiger by the Tail*. And Connie looked every inch the film star and I believed that if it had happened for Connie, it could happen for me.

As I headed towards the magical seventeenth birthday, I was still giving Aunty Kay her insulin, immune to worry about hurting her as I found some spot in her tiny arms to accommodate the hypodermic. She was like an old woman but still the spit and vinegar flowed. The fire in her belly burned and she could fly into a rage over the least thing.

I loved the old bird and I admired her. Life hadn't given her much to write home about, one after another her dreams had been dashed on the rocks of other people's insensibility, but she never complained, never beat her breast about what she had missed out on or what might have been. She just gossiped more than most, her only sin. That and keeping her mouth shut about a serious leg wound she'd picked up in our flat, something she hid for so long that by the time we got her to the doctor, Aunty Kay had gangrene.

What can you say about a woman who at her age stands on the broken wooden seat of a lavatory to hang some old floorcloth on a string line inside the narrow window. The seat moves, she slips and somehow cuts her shin against the rim of the toilet bowl. I can hear her even now saying, 'Well the cursa Christ on it, in anyways,' as she hauls herself out of the tiny lavatory to go and find a bit of petroleum jelly or something to put on the bleeding wound, tying a bit of a bandage around the damaged leg before she forgets all about it. Until she ends up in hospital, finally needing to tell me all about it, unaware that I need to run out of there, to yell and yell and yell till the taste of my own helplessness stops fouling up my mouth.

'When it started paining me and my foot got sore, Lee, I took a few aspirins. At my age you come to expect aches and pains, and sure what was one more on top of all the others.'

When we got word that her leg had to be amputated I almost fell over in shock. There was no option, the doctors assured us, and I have to admit I steered clear of the hospital the day before the surgery was due to happen. Kay knew about her leg coming off but I couldn't bear the idea. It was a sort of a bridge too far for me. I felt such sadness and probably pity. I just didn't know if the pity was for Aunty Kay or for me.

Meanwhile Ma had a new problem. 'Your Da wants a hot lunch taken down to him Sundays at the Pigeon House. What am I going to do?' We both know Ma's informing me that she needs my help. Just as we're both aware that Da isn't as well as he's letting on, and we can't deny that hot food would be better for him than sandwiches. I can practically hear the sigh I let out of me. I didn't need the job of pushing the bike through Ringsend and down along the East Wall to the power station every Sunday. But the need was so real, you could taste it. So I didn't hem and haw, not even for a second. I took on the job, glad there was no law saying you had to enjoy everything you were asked to do in life. And grateful that Michael agreed to make the run every now and then.

Da was a watchman now, still doing shift work but no longer shovelling coal, which might have killed him in the first year at the power station, He never missed a shift, working eight hours shovelling coal, a lightweight with the heart of a lion. And if someone didn't show up to relieve him, Da would take the extra shift and be glad to get it. It was as if he was trying to say, 'See, I would have worked if there had been any work to go to.' Sometimes I'd be home when he'd come in as grey as November, the coal washed off his face, the chest pains showing up in his eyes after the bike ride from the Pigeon House to Mount Pleasant. It didn't seem fair but I couldn't say anything about it, so I just had to stew in my own misery.

But you couldn't take your sadness to work with you. Like, you could feel down, but you were dealing with other people all day, anxious customers in need of the right premium quotation, the name of a good solicitor to help them cope with an upcoming court appearance after a car accident or whatever. Each day brought its own busy problems for you to tackle head-on, with no room for moping about what was wrong with your private life. So I kept quiet about the things that hurt and about what mattered to me a lot of the time, which I suppose most people do. Even with Peggy Keavey, who was a divine girl, she never heard from me about Aunty Kay losing her leg, just as she never had any inkling I had friends like Claire and Eileen. Or that I had serious dreams to be famous.

Peggy worked in Burton's tailoring factory in the Liberties, where she helped produce men's suits for the mass market, and like me she rode a bicycle to and from work. She earned little money, gave much of it to her mother, put a few bob into a 'Club' each week for Christmas and holidays, and dreamed of a life with a good husband and a bunch of children.

Before me she'd been 'going with' a pal of mine, Mick Cunningham, one of my early heroes. Some months later Peggy and I ran into each other at a dance, we made a date and we fell fairly desperately in love. Is there any other way to fall in love? Peggy wanted the same things my mother wanted: a husband with a steady job being top of the list, along with being happy and in love with your partner. I knew in my heart that this wouldn't be enough for me, but Peggy and I became quickly involved, and I give credit to both of us for keeping the temperature down for most of a year. Money was still scarce but we went to the pictures once or twice a week and when the weather was halfway decent we'd walk and talk and make each other laugh a lot.

The Keavey family lived in Ballyfermot. They rented a house from Dublin Corporation which had some kind of garden back and front, and above all, their own front door to shut out the world. I used to cycle up the South Circular Road to Inchicore and then on to Ballyfermot. When we had the money, Peggy and I took the bus into town to go to the flicks. When we got her home again, we'd have some time together in the tiny hallway of her house before I rode the four or five miles home at about midnight.

Heading home on the bike thinking about Peggy, remembering her smile, the touch of her hand, her lips on mine, I'd shut out the doubts and the fears for another day, another week. Something inside me knew that we were going nowhere — how could we when we wanted different things, Peggy hoping for love, stability in her own family, while I was dreaming of sex and success. But for all my dreaming and the ache inside me that spelled the strength of my wanting, I was crazy about this lovely girl who thought I was so very special. I got sad at times when a fantasy grabbed my mind — I'd see life a few months ahead, see Peggy and me after we'd broken up. Peggy would be sad and lonely, but not left alone for long. Guys would be all over her, and though her heart belonged to me, what could she do but try and repair her life. And my own heart would feel shredded till I snapped out of the misery back into the present. Peggy knew nothing of the turmoil I had to endure because I wanted her and, impossibly, all my own madcap dreams as well. How could you tell anybody you were so mixed up!

I can see now that I was spreading myself around too much but, in the eye of the hurricane day to day, my only problems were never having enough money and the time I had to waste sleeping. To me sleep was some kind of sin; something was going on when you were snoring in the scratcher and you were missing the action. But Jack the Lad as I thought I was, how could I admit that anything could get the better of me. I liked to drink, I loved sex, and all I could think was that I'd like more than I was getting, even though I knew for a fact I was getting more than most guys of my age.

Often on a Monday or a Tuesday night I'm going to what we call Singing Pubs with a fella called Jack Savage I got to know around Rathmines. I want to practise singing in front of an audience and Jack just likes to sing, so we team up, because it's always easier to sell a song if there's even one person you know in the audience.

Jack sang love songs in a big voice and he did a terrific job on 'You Are My Heart's Delight', made so famous by Richard Tauber, the great Austrian tenor. Tauber had this thick accent and sounded like a fella singing with a bit of hot spud stuck to the roof of his mouth. So naturally I christened him 'Hot Potato'! He was another guy who loved the birds and the brandy and all the other luxuries life had to offer. I often wondered what he would have thought if he'd heard me at home yelling to Michael: 'Mickey, come in quick. Hot Potato's on the wireless singing Franz Lehar.'

I used to croon trying to sound like Sinatra or Perry Como, my singing heroes, aiming to sell the song as they did, which was just about impossible. But I kept hitting those pubs and the smaller hotels with a resident piano player. Since I'd always had to sing a cappella it was very important to get used to doing it with musical accompaniment, which is a lot harder than it sounds. Not that I was looking for a living as a singer. I saw singing as another string to my bow, like acting, or compèring, anything that would help me earn while I was trying to find my feet as a writer.

So Savage and I, we sang our way around the city on the nights I didn't see Claire or Peggy or, more occasionally now, Eileen. Jack used to chuckle when I picked up some female in a pub or hotel: 'You're some bleedin' teenager you are. As true as Jaysus, you'll die in the saddle!'

Myles Breslin, grandfather to the Nolan Sisters, entered my life when he auditioned me for one of his charity concerts in Harold's Cross. So there I am on a Tuesday night, waiting to go on, one of a bunch of dreamers. I was lucky because I was the only crooner auditioning that night, and as luck would have it, I won the contest. Myles Breslin was delighted with me, shaking my hand with the kind of enthusiasm could leave you in need of a plaster cast and he tells me to be at Marymount Hall, on Sunday, looking good. 'And be sure and bring that voice along with you!'

At home I didn't say anything about the concert. Ma would just worry and I needed encouragement, not aggravation. At work I wanted to tell everybody in the office. But I couldn't risk any of them turning up on Sunday night in case I was diabolical, so just for once, I kept my mouth shut. On the Sunday two things happened that scared me in the worst way. First the piano player didn't show up. Then just to really get my adrenalin pumping I'm told as I go on stage that the microphone is not working. Myles Breslin can't understand what's happened to it. Does it bother him? Are you kidding! 'Y'know Al Jolson never used a microphone, don't you? You just go out there and deliver the song from the ticker, and they won't even notice there's no mike. All you need is a big heart!'

As I walk on I can't see anything beyond row three, probably because my heart is hammering at a rate I'd consider life-threatening today. And my right arm feels quite numb. But somehow, I begin to sing. The song is called 'Heartbreaker'. It has a beat to it but there's a poignant spine running through the lyric which reminds me how sad I sometimes get over Peggy and me going nowhere. I use this for all it's worth to help me sell the number. In a matter of seconds I'm getting all the help anybody could possibly wish for from a guy in the front row who hates me on sight. He's a big guy with a big voice, and the minute I start to croon he joins me as though he's getting time and a half. And not only does he sing so loudly you wouldn't hear me behind a tram ticket, he's smiling, as if he knows he's a good singer, much better than me. All I know is I'd like to launch myself feet first right into his big smug mush.

From row two back people thought his voice was mine, and I got a huge ovation. I got doubly lucky then because when I said I'd sing 'Chattanooga Choo-choo' I could see your man knew the number. 'We' went so well Myles Breslin came on stage to ask me back the next Sunday. I said yes knowing I wouldn't be back. Not even if I could guarantee that my singing partner would be there again for me in the front row!

After the concert I took a taxi up to Claire's house, and fell into a hot bath while she ironed my wet shirt. I was full of hurt, seeing what had happened as a disaster. Claire gave me a glass of brandy, said I was just great to get up and do it, and that, given half a chance, I could be a real success. This cheered me up, another couple of brandies helped some more and I began to enjoy myself until the face of Peggy Keavey got in between me and the great time I thought I was having.

Right through the early part of the week following the show in the Marymount Hall, I was half in and half out of my head. At times, I felt low as a snake's belly as I seriously wondered had I any talent at all. Maybe all the people who dismissed me as a nutcase weren't wrong. I thought I might be ill, which wasn't like me. I seemed to have springs inside, always bouncing back no matter what happened. On the Wednesday morning as I cycled down to Ranelagh Road, I found myself mouthing the oath I'd been swearing for the last couple of years, as morning after morning I rode the bike down the hill on the way to work: 'Some day I'm going to say goodbye to this fucking place.' I heard the words out loud as opposed to just running through my mind. This was a first and it left me asking myself if the time had come to just get up and go. Crazy if you think in terms of the marvellous females in my life. I mean, what young guy in his right mind would even think of leaving Claire, not forgetting Eileen, who was still there for me any time we could organise it. But for all the loving and the excitement of the sex with my two friends, I was troubled over cheating Peggy, using the fact that she was still a virgin as an alibi for my behaviour.

At times the idea of being married to Peggy engendered some touch of bliss, there's no denying it. Then I'd get this sort of scraping noise in my head, as though I was trying to rip out the very notion before it got any kind of a hold. For as sure as God made little apples, I knew that if Peggy and I went over the top and she was to end up pregnant, I would marry her. I would marry her because she was so decent and so loving. But I couldn't ignore the fear-filled thought that if I had to get married like that, I would kill myself before I was twenty-two. Seems dramatic, but I just knew I couldn't be happy doing the kind of job I was doing at present for the rest of my life. And if you were not going to be happy, how could you go on living?

During the following few weeks I could have earned a Ph.D. in self-pity. I spent a lot of evenings with Claire, who not only loved me but poured me brandies which helped keep the cursed devils at bay. I saw Peggy only once. Lying, I said on the phone that I had flu and just had to hit the sack early night after night until I got rid of it. As for my big dreams, well, it felt like good-night and goodbye to them. I was drowning in my own misery. Then, as though the bloody devils were rubbing it in, who walks into the office as I'm at the counter only Jack Doyle. I hadn't seen him in five or six years, not since the night he bought me a one and one in the chipper in Ranelagh when he was living with Angela Brady. He was a giant from County Cork who had left home to conquer the world with blarney and a certain degree of bellicose behaviour in the boxing ring. As he looked down at me across the office counter he chuckled when I reminded him how we'd known each other those years before.

Jack was six feet five in height and he was reputed to have laid some of the richest and most beautiful women in the world. He was a singer first. Correction. He was a lover and a drinker first. Then he was a tenor with a melodious voice. He was also a sometime boxer who could have gone all the way had he trained on something other than pints of porter, had he not been addicted to going all the way with every female who gave him the eye! We discussed Pluvius insurance for his wrestling match in Tolka Park. A smart move to get insurance cover against the weather for any outdoor event in Ireland, which was what Jack was interested in. I'd seen a photo of his opponent in the papers having some suits made by Burton's in Dame Street. There was one wonderful shot of a tailor standing on a chair to run a tape measure across your man's shoulders, which were about as wide as your average barn door. Need I tell you that his name was Gargantua!

While I was getting premium quotations for Jack, fantasising that some day I'd be as famous as he was, the man himself was downstairs in the Bodega bar having drinks and talking to reporters. His story from the high stool was a warning, so the papers told us later. Jack told the people in charge of the event in Tolka Park they shouldn't have anybody sitting in the first three rows around the ring. When he was asked why not, he said: 'I'll be throwing this guy out of the ring, I just can't be certain in which direction. I don't want any member of the public getting killed when he lands. He's a big fella!' This was a master stroke, guaranteeing front-page coverage for the wrestling match. The following day there was another picture of Gargantua in the papers. This time he was standing on the deck of the mailboat to Holyhead, heading for the hills you might say, having taken the threat from the Gorgeous Gael very seriously indeed. And if he looked better dressed going than he did coming, wasn't it a credit to Burton's tailoring at the time?

Jack Doyle became an unbelievable mess at times. Then he would bounce back, recreate himself, yet, in the finish, booze and more booze and the profligacy of his existence would tear him down, leaving him in relative poverty for the last years of his life.

I know now there was a warning for me in the Jack Doyle story. At the time I heard something but Harry in my head told me not to mind what happened to Doyler. 'You're not him, you're you, and anyway, you're smarter than he was.' What else was I going to do when Harry was telling me just what I wanted to hear?

The following week the office manager asked me if I had any famous people coming in this week. He wasn't being amusing, the bastard was just in another of his nasty moods so you had to tread softly — after Mr Phillips and Mr Cowman he was the boss.

'How d'you mean, Mister Murphy?' I looked right at him aware of a streak of belligerence lurking just under the surface of my Mass card expression. That evening when I meet Peggy to go for a walk out at Bluebell I'm still smouldering, knowing it's not just Murphy and the snide way he can be when he's having a rough day. It's all kinds of things, including Aunty Kay in hospital long-term, now the word is her other leg will probably have to be amputated, and Ma and me fighting about the hours I'm keeping and my few shirts ruined with lipstick and face powder and anything else that Katy can find to throw at me because she knows she is losing the battle to have me knuckle down and be a happy little insurance clerk for the rest of my life.

Peggy and I walked a lot because we couldn't go anywhere that cost money. We never had a meal in any kind of decent restaurant, we never went to the theatre together. Something like a weekend away was unheard of then, and not just because money was scarce. This had to be very hard on guys who were totally committed to one girl. I'd have been climbing the walls.

Peggy took me home to meet her family. This gesture, and the fact that I was willing to go, was like an unspoken sign that we were serious about one another. And this developed into card playing evenings which were more fun than I would have admitted. Part of me could be happy enough playing cards, having tea later with a slice of this very good custard tart that Mrs K made, but before long I would become uneasy, feeling I was getting roped in, while all Peggy was really doing was enjoying my company, maybe hoping things would work out for us, she in love with me as I most certainly was with her.

On Sundays in the summer the Keaveys would head off en masse for Portmarnock and since Peggy's father had a taxi, they got a lift out there. The old man would come and pick them up again at the end of the day. So Ma K, Peggy, her three sisters, two brothers, all crammed into the cab, happy as sandboys the lot of them. When they asked me would I like to join them one Sunday, I said sure. I liked the Keavey kids, and I wouldn't refuse in case it made Peggy look bad; anyway, it would be a new experience, going to the seaside with a family.

Portmarnock has a wonderful beach and the sea is kind there on a sunny day. We swam and played football and Relievio and I embraced Peggy in the water in her one-piece swimsuit and I thought she was one of the most beautiful girls I had ever met. At some time during the afternoon somebody gave me a boiled sweet, some kind of barley sugar. I never ate things like that any more but I was having such a good time I wasn't thinking straight, so I popped the sweet in my mouth and started chomping on it. Suddenly, something terrible happens. In one second, one poxy second, I am in the middle of a fucking nightmare. I realise that though the barley sugar is still in one piece in my mouth, my denture plate is falling in bits onto the fucking beach, the entire Keavey family looking at me in some kind of amused horror, their faces frozen as if they are in aspic. They can't take their eyes off me but they don't want to be seen looking, having to appear serious when they need to break their sides laughing.

Peggy is wonderful, picking up the pieces from the sand, holding them in her hand as though it's the most natural thing in the world. I just want to die right there on the sand of Portmarnock beach. I want a tidal wave to come in and sweep me away to oblivion. But I'm left standing seeing nothing but the hole in my face I'd like to disappear into.

Of course I can't even get the dental plate repaired until Monday so everybody in the office suddenly knows I have a false tooth, which really helps the week get off to a brilliant start! I'm smiling at nobody till I get my tooth back, that's if I ever manage to smile again. Whether I do or not, I know for sure I'm never going to forget how I felt on that Sunday afternoon at Portmarnock.

The start of a new week, a Monday morning, a gap where my beautiful front tooth used to be. And oh yeh! I had a shilling in my pocket. One shilling! Apart from which I hadn't a clue where the money for the denture repair was coming from. Apart from which everything was just perfect!

No need to tell you I was feeling seriously sorry for myself, delivering the hand post locally. In and out of insurance offices like a flash, no chat, no gossip, no jokes this morning, pal! I felt lousy, genuinely sick. Which I was over my gone-forever tooth and the hole it had left in my life. But I felt ill as well, as if I was coming down with flu or something.

By the time I got as far as the Olympia Theatre at the other end of Dame Street, the way I felt I hadn't a word to throw to a dog. I saw something then to renew my heart, like a sign to me, this huge billboard over the façade of the theatre, telling the world Barry Keegan was starring in *Seagulls Over Sorrento*!

I stood there with my pathetic Wicklow Gap mouth hanging open. Jesus! Barry Keegan was from Herbert Park just up the road from the Gut. Like Connie Smith, my inspiration as a milk delivery boy, Barry Keegan was a Dub, one of our own, and here he was back home as a star!

As I gazed up at the billboard, I suddenly felt really nauseous. At the same moment I got a nudge from someone and there was Granny Dunne on her way home from her weekly visit to the Jewman's office.

'You're not looking well, Leo,' she said, sticking to her favourite name.

'I don't feel great, Granny,' I said, passing out right there on the street. When I woke up I was in St Kevin's hospital, sick and sore enough that they'd keep me there for the next four weeks, with no time out to go and see Barry Keegan in his three-week run at the Olympia!

9

The first person I saw when I came around in the hospital was the Granny. She was sitting by the bed like the Dublin version of the Rock of Gibraltar. The minute I stirred her face came very close, I got the smell of lavender and for some reason I almost burst into tears. She gave me a hug, not really her style, and she sat back on her chair.

'I wasn't leaving till you woke up.' She smiled to hide her relief. 'Wanted to make sure you hadn't gone for your tea before I get down to tell Katy you're in here.'

In fairness to Granny Dunne she never put Ma down in my company and she never moaned about things, not even her husband, who sort of earned a Ph.D. in not measuring up as a man. When I brought my article torn from the *Times Pictorial* down to her room in the Gut, Granny read it through a couple of times and told me I was great. She said this in a way that made you believe her. I think it was this memory that had me nearly in tears when I woke up in St Kevin's and found her sitting there waiting for me to show her I wasn't dead.

Once I was awake the hospital machinery went to work and in a couple of days they told me, in Ma's company, that I had an abscess between the kidney and the spine. They decided not to perform surgery, the abscess being in a tricky spot, difficult to get at. So I would be on a course of injections, four jabs a day until things improved.

I'd already had painkillers so I wasn't suffering all that much. But it would be at least two weeks before the doctors would know if the jabs were breaking up the abscess. Until the first results came through I was bound to the bed.

I had many visitors, including Vincent Phillips himself, the MD of the small company I worked for. He told me not to worry myself about anything, just get well and come back to work when I was good and ready. Very decent really, but the company had always been like that, excluding the manager who had to show you his snotty side just to keep you in check. Thinking back, in my case, he was probably right, but at the time I found him hard to take.

Granny Dunne came up to the hospital every other day, a trip involving two buses each way but no bother to her, she was as odd as two left feet by times. So her husband claimed anyway after she gave him the bum's rush when he lost it completely to the booze. She poured me the first bottle of stout I ever drank straight the Christmas morning of my fifteenth birthday. She gave it to me with a slice of her home-made Christmas pudding, which was black like chewing tobacco and certainly had a cure in it. As a matter of fact you felt that if you could handle two good slices of it you'd be pissed as a pudding! She told me that morning that it was time I learned how to take a drink, so I'd learn not to abuse it the way some men did.

In my case she was talking about two grandfathers out of two but I didn't say anything about percentages. And I didn't bring up the fact that every picture I saw of my mother's father left me feeling that I had just looked into the mirror.

The Granny chuckled as I pulled a face at the bitter Guinness stout on that Christmas morning. She believed it was my first drink but she was wrong. Cackling at my innocence she told me to eat a bit of the pudding and keep it in my mouth till I got used to the taste of the drink.

I'd already learned to deal with the bitter taste of Guinness the day I bought stout and cider in Humphries' in Ranelagh, heading on down to Herbert Park to drink it, see what it'd be like to be really pissed.

I passed out that day, all on my own. The park was shut tight for the day by the time I came around, the summer light just going to bed. It was a long story involving getting my bike out over the high railings, trying to let it down on the road outside without damaging it. Nearly breaking my fucking neck when I finally managed to haul myself up over the spiky railings.

I fell in love with a nurse in St Kevin's Hospital, a woman with slow eyes and a smile that'd warm your feet on a cold day. The nurses there, they were all great, looked after me and the other guys very well. One fella had fallen off a lorry, damaged his spine, he was lying on the flat of his back on a bed of boards, as he said himself, with a permanent hard-on. He was sexually obsessed this guy, so we got along great, sharing our ideas and our fantasies, the pair of us addicted to some wild notions that would get you excommunicated if you hadn't left already. The other lad, a decent skin from the inner city, born a long way from Easy Street, was just over an operation for a hernia, having done a month in Mountjoy for punching a bus conductor one night while he was drunk. He'd had a fight with his mot, the conductor gave him a hard time over no change, late night, whatever, and he gave him a knuckle sandwich.

The three of us talked about booze, we'd all been drinking by the age of fourteen. They had started young too with the girls, mad for sex from the time they hit puberty. Paddy, the puncher, got a surprise visitor who brought him whiskey. He offered me a shot of Jameson Ten from the half-bottle, I passed, scared enough to be practical. I didn't want to mess up the stuff in the injections, maybe do myself harm. The chat we'd had got me thinking about booze in a way I hadn't done before. Maybe I was just trying to escape the ward, making an escape back to the yesterdays where the boozing started.

Booze had made a wonderful difference in my life. Apart from the warm feeling you got, it was like having a pal on the inside to back you up when you were feeling down or nervous or whatever. I felt I could do anything when I had enough of it inside me. If only I'd had the money for more than the one miserable jar when I went for the quiz show in the Royal, I might have won it. But things just didn't work out for me on the stage of Dublin's largest theatre. It wouldn't have been so bad if I hadn't planned the operation with such a lot of care, in the hope I might get noticed, get some kind of showbiz job out of it.

I'd given the butcher a good story about my aunt dying, I wouldn't be back from the funeral till late because she lived in the country. Once I provided a stand-in to deliver the meat, Jimmy didn't scream. So I had the afternoon off with a view to giving my life a lift. And hopefully I'd earn at least a quid and maybe two at the same time.

The Capitol and the Royal were the only two spots in Dublin that ran cine/variety shows at this time. Which meant you got a film and a stage production, like two shows for the price of one. I went to both when I had the money and I always enjoyed Jack Kirwan and Frankie Blowers, the brilliant Noel Purcell with Jack Cruise and Mickser Reid, and maybe the best comic of them all, Harry Bailey.

The Royal also included a very popular English musician, Tommy Dando. He played a Hammond organ, coming up out of the orchestra pit. He conducted a singalong, with the words of popular songs showing on the cinema screen, a little white ball bouncing on top of the lyric to help the punters get the rhythm. It was great fun and opened the variety show, which included singers and dancers, comics and all the usual acts to make up a good bill. Besides all this the Royal included an item called 'Double or Nothing!' — a simple quiz handled by an actor called Eddie Byrne. The contestants came out of the audience, you could win a pound note if you got things right. If you were lucky you earned the chance to win *another pound* in some kind of grand finale! I was now earning two pounds a week in the office job so you can understand why the prize money seemed like a tidy sum.

The compère came out on stage after he'd been given a build-up by a voice (probably his own) off stage. He'd ask for people to come up and take part in the quiz. Within weeks of this item being introduced, the battle was not just to win the prize money, you deserved a medal just for getting up on the stage still wearing your coat and your shirt and whatever else you came in with, such was the frenzy to make it as a contestant. I mean it, like, if someone heard you'd actually made it onto the stage in the Royal, their respect for you went up several notches.

So, as Eddie Byrne comes on stage I am up there! I am up there with the man! Using elbows and whatever else it took, I am now clinging to him so hard he'll need surgery to get me off him. There were three other people behind me and about another hundred that didn't make the cut!

The contest begins, I tell him my name and I answer two questions for five shillings each, with no problem. I am now ten shillings ahead.

'Will Lee take the *ten-bob note* or will he sing a song to take it to fifteen shillings? Will he take the ten-shilling note I have here in my hand, or will Lee from Rathmines risk it all on his way to the top prize!' Fair play to Eddie Byrne as he makes himself sound like a man giving away a small fortune.

Will I sing a song? Will I dance a jig? Will I break out in a sweat? Will I ride a bike? For a pound in my hand there isn't a whole lot I won't do! Besides, I want to sing, I am desperate to sing, I may even be dying to sing! Hoping as I warble that Jimmy Campbell, the Royal's musical director with the Brylcreem look, dentures with a life of their own, will like my style, sign me up to croon to the people of Dublin for a lot of money every week while I'm waiting to get really rich and famous!

I sing 'Too Young', a big hit for Nat King Cole, and even though I say so myself, which of course I do, I sing it very well and I get a really terrific sitting ovation! So now I'm worth fifteen shillings. Will I take this princely sum and walk? Or? Eddie holds a pause with real style. I want to walk believe me, I want to walk, I want to run with the fifteen. But I need the extra five shillings for God.

That's right. I promised God 25 per cent if he'd let me win. And if he could interest Jimmy Campbell in my talent, I'd give up swearing and quit telling dirty jokes. So I couldn't run, much as I wanted to. But if I stayed I could lose what I already had. I had to risk losing the fifteen shillings to have a chance of winning the pound, so that I could make good the deal I'd made with the Creator of the Universe. If I stayed I would end up with a pound or nothing!

'Ladies and gentlemen, Lee is going to risk it all, he's going to risk losing everything so that he can go for the top prize!' Eddie Byrne makes it sound as if I'm coming down Mount Everest on a roller skate, the audience applauds as if it's being paid double time. And Eddie says triumphantly, 'He Goes For The Pound Note, Folks! Lee Is Going For The Top Prize!'

The orchestra strikes up a tune. Eddie Byrne asks me to name the melody for one pound. 'And! You remain in the contest with the chance to win the Grand Finale and walk away with Two Pounds!'

I know the tune. I can sing the words of the song any time. I'm standing fairly close to Eddie Byrne, I become very aware of the make-up plastered all over his face, and the smell of whiskey on his breath. And right up there on the stage of Dublin's Theatre Royal I am drawing blanks from a mind that is capable of total recall at any time of the day or night.

Fair play to Eddie Byrne he looks right at me and he says, 'You're UNDECIDED, aren't you!'

Whether it's the fascination with Eddie's make-up or the aftershock of singing solo in front of over two thousand people, I don't know. But what happens? My mind stays blank. And not only that, I am so lost I don't even hear Eddie Byrne telling me the title of the song each of the three times he said the word 'undecided'. The guy was hitting me over the head with the 'undecided' hammer, but my mind was out of town!

> First you say you will and then you won't
> First you say you do and then you don't
> You're undecided now so what're you gonna do!

I'll admit to tears as I stumbled out of the Royal. I choked on my own frustration. To have been so close and to have lost it all. I stuttered up Hawkins Street, the inside of my chest feeling raw as though it had been standing too close to a blowlamp without actually burning. I stopped around the entrance to Trinity College on the long walk home and when I looked up I said with all my heart, 'Fuck you! It wasn't too much to ask!' And that was when I really turned my back on God and the whole idea of God, for the first time.

Back in the present I get my third injection of the day and a cup of tea with a few biscuits. I could smile then, looking back on that carry-on in the Royal. Besides, it wasn't too long before some good did come out of that experience.

As a result of singing on stage there I got an audition for a folk group that was starting up but I didn't get the gig. I didn't care, so I told myself. The truth was I had to audition cold, without any jar in me because I was broke that week. So I'd been a bit nervous, not as good as I might have been with a few scoops inside me. Anyway, I didn't want to sing Irish ballads and stuff like that. I wanted to sing love songs, Cole Porter, Rodgers and Hart; romantic lyrics suited the way I sang and the way I felt about singing. And I wasn't sure I wanted to be part of a group anyway. I had a good outside routine going, at the same time I was facing up to the fact that, inside, I was a loner.

Peggy was relieved I blew out on the folk group possibility, she felt there were enough distractions keeping us from seeing more of each other, and she wasn't talking about my financial state. I could see that even though she loved me, she wasn't happy about us, and a lot of the time, even though I was crazy about her, I felt the same way. In August when her holiday club came up she went off to Blackpool with a couple of girls from her job. I felt sad the night we said goodbye, then ten minutes later cycling home through Rialto, I was in some way relieved.

She'd been complaining that I never took her dancing. I said sorry but I didn't do anything about it. For me dance halls were pick-up joints. Taking your own mot to a dance was too square for comfort. Like a trial run at marriage, as if you go everywhere, do everything together. Just the thought of it scared the hell out of me. You just didn't do it!

I took to dancing as though I was born to it. I got the steps of the quickstep, tango, slow waltz, foxtrot and rhumba by studying this *Victor Sylvester's Dance Book*, bought second-hand. But no book could teach you how to get really close to a girl in a slow waltz with the lights low. That had to come naturally, the nose to sniff out a fast girl for a slow waltz, in minutes dancing so tight you were nearly behind her, with French kissing to send your head into orbit. For a half a dollar — where would you get it!

Having rhythm built in is a gift, but it's handy to know how not to walk all over your partner's feet. One Dublin bird said to a learner as they struggled around a dance floor together: 'Do you like the floor?' 'Oh I do,' says your man, 'I like it a lot!' 'Well,' says the lady who was no lady, 'why don't you try dancing on it!' I once asked a gorgeous tarty-looking creature up for a dance. 'Ask me sister,' says she, 'I'm sweatin'!'

For all my jazz about knowing the steps and being able to throw a few shapes, I needed booze to make a go of dancing, I knew that the first time I went stone cold sober to the Four Provinces. This really was the place where girls French kissed you with a will and the music was perfect.

I'm in the Four Ps with Mick Cunningham, the coolest guy I ever met. He's tall, a good-looking guy, big with the birds, doesn't give a shit about anyone, secure in himself and in his talent as a lithographic artist, financially ahead of the game compared to the rest of us. Above all, this fella can stop in front of a shop window, take out his comb, do a real number on his hairstyle. To me that was all kinds of freedom, something I hoped to experience some day. Cunnyer was also a good guy, a truly decent skin.

I watch my mate dancing his legs off, his only problem being which girl he might give a break to later on. Meanwhile, I'm having real problems, because big-headed or not, despite knowing I can really dance, I'm glued to the floor of the ballroom. It's so bad my legs hurt from trying to tear them free so I can walk over and ask a girl, any girl, if she'll dance with me.

I can't believe it. I mean, I'd never allowed any kind of shyness to stop me from doing things. I just couldn't understand what was going on. I loved being there in the Four Ps. I loved the mouth-watering variety of girls, just to be that close, to be able to look at them, study them, enjoy the sight of them, that alone was worth the price of admission.

That night, finally, in desperation, I get a Pass Out from Tucker on the door. I hurry around to Sinnott's pub, drink a pint of sweet cider with a whiskey poured into it. I repeat the dose, enjoying it because the cider kills the whiskey taste I don't like. The drink bounces my inhibitions out the door in a few minutes flat. Walking back to the Four Ps I'm on top of the world, wondering why I put myself through all that agony before I got the good sense to walk around to the boozer.

Back in the dance hall, I walked over and took this lovely dark-haired girl up to dance, no bother at all. As it happened we spent a lot of that evening dancing together and when it came to dancing closely she gave as good as she got. Like it wasn't just that her breasts were against my chest in the slow waltzes, she jammed her pelvis against mine as if that was the only way to travel.

That night in the Four Ps I found a new friend in booze. Up to then I'd been hiding from it, taking it, drinking it, but never admitting to myself I needed it. I could admit for the first time I *used alcohol*, which an awful lot of people seemed to be doing, in real life as well as in the pictures. And why not! Weren't stout and whiskey and brandy advertised all over the place? And didn't people expect a man to take a drink? Even women like the Granny who'd lost her husband to booze, she thought every man should be able to have a jar once he learned how to hold it. I ignored that bit!

The two guys in the ward were sipping away at the half-bottle of Jameson Ten, getting merry by the sound of them. Nowhere was sacred when it came to the gargle. Drink was everywhere, like the hub of whatever was going on that was any kind of fun. In every other film you saw, people were either ordering drinks, drinking drinks, or pouring drinks for themselves and others. Many of the gangster pictures in the forties showed guys riddling each other to death with machine guns because of the money that could be made from bootleg booze while America was officially on the wagon.

As far as I could work it out, people everywhere were lashing all the booze they could afford into themselves, I wasn't the only person who used drink to get through some situation. The only booze problem I had was getting enough of it. I mean, in all honesty, if the money was there, what fella in his right mind wouldn't want to wrap himself around a right few jars every chance he got, whether he was going dancing or not.

Dancing was something Claire never mentioned to me so I let the hare sit. She had to know I went dancing. Everybody under thirty-five went to dances in the fifties. And I was such a natural-born shaper I just had to be a jiver. Claire and I sometimes mooched around her lounge to music from the radiogram, a slow waltz that always ended up in lovemaking.

Claire would be jarred before we'd get to dancing in her front room, and I wouldn't be feeling any pain. I was happy in her company, there were no demands made on me and I responded by giving her whatever I had to give. I liked Claire and she liked me. She never looked beyond the day, a great idea, I believed, though my eyes were so firmly focused on the future, it's a wonder I could see where I was going at all.

When Peggy came back from her holiday in the Isle of Man she told me she'd met a guy who was a wonderful person. She was thinking of going to England, she said, what did I think about that? Part of me wanted to tell her not to go. But what could I offer her? I was eighteen years old with a head full of dreams that might yet prove dangerous. Ma was still striding around in my head — *dreams beyond your station!* All that stuff had made its mark even if I denied it at the time.

Within a few weeks Peggy and I were over and it hurt me more than I can say. I could scarcely believe how painful it was when I was asked how she was, how we were getting along. Trying to explain it was over without showing any pain was far from easy. I missed her like hell and I had to believe she was missing me. We'd been too close to walk away feeling nothing. Yet something stopped me giving her the *let's try again* routine. Peggy and me married wasn't part of the dream I had for my life. The hurt was like a demand my dreams were making on me, a demand being paid in advance.

Then like a signal Peggy and I had done the right thing, I get a gig singing with a small pro band. Their crooner is in John of Gods, an expensive hide-away for people avoiding the sheriff and the bailiffs and all the other people who haunt the coat-tails of serious drinkers.

The band is heading for the late night Irish hillsides to play dance music to country people, with a crooner thrown in as a touch of class! We're all jammed in comfortable as sardines in this big old American car. If I can survive the propinquity of this journey, doing the gig should be a breeze. Mind you I have a half-bottle of Hennessy in my pocket, insurance!

The band leader is a lady violinist with genuine blonde hair and blue eyes that'd melt concrete, but she's warm enough when she tells me she heard about my singing in the Royal. An ill wind, I thought to myself as I meet the keyboard player, a drummer, and a saxophonist doubling on clarinet. The percussion stuff is jammed into the open boot tied down with heavy-duty string, and the other gear is on a roof-rack covered with a rainproof sheet.

I don't know where we played that night, but it took three and a half hours of fairly hard driving by the drummer to get us there. We're greeted by a priest who really welcomes us, he provides a good fry-up, giving us an hour before we go on. Fair play to him we get a bottle of Jameson Ten to give the weak tea the kiss of life; the whiskey helps me to recover from the journey. In the toilet I take a couple of belts from the brandy and I'm ready to give my first professional gig a go!

We're close to going on stage so I ask Maureen, the blonde violinist who runs the show, 'What's the story about what I sing?'

'No problem,' she assures me. 'Anything we play in your key you give me the nod and pick it up on the second chorus.' And that was it. My total rehearsal for my first singing gig.

In a way I was relieved because had she asked me what key I sang in I wouldn't have been able to give her an honest answer. Though knowing me I'd probably have said, 'You name it, I can sing in it!'

So they play a long quickstep medley to get the evening going and the dancers dancing and after about four numbers I get up and take 'Bye Bye

Blackbird' along from the second chorus. They're a decent outfit musically and I have no problem. I'm wearing a dress suit that Maureen supplies along with my five quid wages for the night. Five pounds was two and a half times my wages from the office, so I was very glad to get it, apart from the experience of the gig itself, maybe my first break.

In the first hour and a half I sing maybe fifteen songs and I'm getting very encouraging signs from Maureen and the guys. But it's a lot of singing so I'm spreading it a bit more the second hour, taking care of the pipes as the man said. Maureen prods me in the back with her violin bow. I turn to see what's going on and she's telling me, 'Give them another one,' so I get up and sing some more. And some more. And some more until something like half two in the morning.

We have one twenty-minute break in the four and a half hour gig and I cannot even begin to suggest how many songs I sang. I had to keep going because if I let two or three numbers go by without getting up on my feet, I got the bow in the back again, and the later it got the harder old Maureen prodded. Earlier on I'd been getting the eye from one or two of the girls from the dance floor and I was interested in whatever might come my way, country-style, but by the time the dance ended, I was so tired, so weary, that I couldn't have made my lips work well enough to kiss a girl. When I got home Ma was up getting Brendan out to work. She said plenty about the kind of life that kept me out all night, I didn't even answer her back. I couldn't because I had a first division case of laryngitis!

Maureen did come back to me with the offer of more work but I turned it down. If it interfered with the day job I'd have to leave home, Ma just wouldn't stand for that, and anyway, it seemed to me a very hard way to make a living.

Claire came back from seeing her sister in England, bringing me some badly needed clothes. My trousers were worn away so that I was afraid of taking a long step, walking around with my ass as tight as a duck's in case the women'd see the bare flesh at the top of my leg, like the top of the leg over the stocking which I so loved to see when a girl rode by on her bicycle.

You could hardly blame the trousers for falling apart through sheer friction. The poor suit had been on twenty-four-hour call, getting more action than most clobber would in five years.

Claire didn't think about how I was going to explain the suit and the other gear to my mother. I might get away with some spoof about getting a shirt, maybe even a pair of trousers, but to walk in with what you could call a complete wardrobe, there was no way on earth I could kid Ma that such a stroke of good fortune had just fallen into my lap. Ma may well have believed in the Virgin Birth, and the Loaves and the Fishes, but a miracle in Terenure'd be stretching things!

I leave the clothes with Claire, ask her to put them into a dry-cleaner's next day. When they've been cleaned I take them home. I give Ma a story about this woman in Terenure I'm hanging wallpaper for. 'I landed on my feet with her, Ma, a real lady. Her son, my size, God, he joined the American army.' Ma runs her eye over the clobber, dry-cleaning dockets still fixed to the garments. I lied like a judge, giving Ma my best *amazement*. Since even Katy couldn't have dreamed up Claire and me as a couple, she bought the story.

Feeling very tasty in the new clobber, I'm spending a bit of time on my bench in the shadow of the Town Hall clock. Sitting on the bottle-green seat I called my own, tinkering with the current story in my head, letting it get where it had to go before it'd let you write it down.

The seat on Leinster Road, it's my own private place even if someone else is sitting on there at the same time as me. This is where Harry Redmond first lit up my head with his foul mind and a mouth that wouldn't quit. Here he cackled as an old neighbour, Noggler Green, went by on his bike: 'Look at him, he's a lip on him'd hold a fortnight's snots!', making me laugh out loud even if it was totally disgusting.

I go with the flow of reverie, from the boredom on the hospital bed, to the wooden seat, remembering Harry first talking to me as I sit there. A disturbing vision crosses my gaze, a priest in full uniform assisting an old woman on dodgy legs along the street. Just the sight of him sets my anger on fire. If he hadn't been in company, clearly helping the woman on her way, I swear to Jesus, I'd have given him such a root up the arse, his hole would have landed between his shoulder blades. The fucking bastard! Even after four years his skinny face was burned indelibly into the place where my rage lurked, waiting to get even. To pay him back for Blackrock.

I was maybe fourteen years old, having cycled out to Blackrock baths by the sea with a couple of guys, Kelly and O'Connell, to have a swim. They were still in the water but it was too cold for me and I was in this tiny cubicle rubbing myself down to get some life back into my body.

Then this priest steps into the cubicle with a cheery hello. He shakes my hand, tells me I made a couple of good dives from the three-metre springboard. Not true. The one-metre springboard yeh, but twice I almost bellyflopped from the higher one. I say, 'Thanks, Father,' because quite honestly I'm so surprised with him being there so close to me in the box I don't know what else to do.

I had an uneasy feeling I'd experienced before with a guy in Herbert Park, a Brownie Boy, a guy who wanted sex of some kind with kids.

The priest in the cubicle landed on me so fast I'd no time to think, in seconds he's got my man in his hand. Looking down at it like a doctor.

'I see you're not circumcised. And I suppose you know you're a very good-looking boy.'

His narrow face is no more than six inches from mine, he pulls my foreskin back, which is sore because I'm blue with the cold.

'You're hurting me, Father,' I tell him. 'So please let me go, I have to get dressed,' I say, totally lost about what to do next. It's so painfully shameful to feel completely inadequate that he must get some sense of how awful it is.

I'm frozen with fear. I can't move, I can't seem to say anything else. And I wasn't a kid who'd been protected from life on the streets. I knew about Queers, Brownie Boys, I'd had my face kissed by Harry Knowles at a tanner a go, I'd been messed with by Jack God knows how many times, but this was different to any of that. This priest has me terrified, I'm out of my depth, ashamed it's happening, double-ashamed I don't know what to do about it. Finally I manage to squeak out again, *Please let me go, Father!*

Whether he lost interest now that he had me numb, I don't know. He just turned and left the cubicle, going around the half-door with no fuss at all and a throwaway goodbye.

I'm no longer bored in the hospital bed. I'm in a sweat as I remember sitting on the bench, your man going by, that taking me back to his handling me, and me like a helpless eejit not even kicking him up the fly buttons.

How could he get away with doing something like that? A fully dressed man in his black suit and shoes and hat, his white collar standing out like a wedding ring, not a praying clergyman, more like a praying mantis, and getting away with it because nobody had the balls to speak up against a priest. Not even me with my big mouth and all my big ideas.

Who'd believe you for God's sake! Imagine me telling Ma? Even if she wanted to believe me, how could you expect her to? Love me or hate me, she thought I was a head case and she certainly didn't trust me as she used to. So I buried those cubicle minutes, it seemed like the only thing I could do at the time. But it hurt. A priest stroking me as though I was a piece of meat for him to do what he liked with — I wanted to vomit at my own powerlessness.

My favourite nurse, Jennifer, brought me back to the present, with the offer of more tea. I gave her my John Derek/Nick Romano smile though my well-being remained girdled by the vivid recall of what that guy in the white collar had done to me. It shows you the power of memory, in seconds sweating over something years before, one step into memory's mirror taking you back, that leap taking you back even deeper, leading me to suppose that if you were in hospital long enough you could go all the way, like looking into an infinity of mirrors.

Finally, my abscess left town and I was told I could go in a few days provided nothing untoward happened in the meantime. So three and a half weeks after I threw the wobbly in the Granny's company near the Olympia, I was about ready to Exit Stage Left.

Next morning there is a yellow-head pimple on the side of my pipe and I go into a double panic in four seconds flat. Why is it there? And how in the name of Jesus do I tell the nurse, especially Jennifer? I mean, I have a hard neck, but I can't see myself saying to her, 'Listen, I have a yellow-head pimple on my prick.' On my dick? On my mickey? Not even on my penis! I can't say any of these things to Jennifer.

I ask to see a doctor and I tell Jennifer, trying to make a joke of it, 'You wrecking my heart is what's wrong with me.'

She is a cow in her heart of course, assuming that the lady doctor she finds to come and see me is her idea of a bit of fun. A lady doctor! With me too conscious of my image to freeze now, the Doc is standing there wanting to know what my problem is.

I hem and haw so much that the doctor understands. 'Is your concern connected with your penis, your genitalia?' she asks as though enquiring if I have a headache. I manage a phoney offhand nod that puts years on me and I feel as if my teeth are sweating.

'Let's have a look, shall we!'

She makes a move to touch my man, move him around so she can see what the problem is. I move a tiny bit, a signal I can't handle her handling me like, something, I don't know. She nods in silent understanding.

'Can you show me what's bothering you?'

I move John Thomas to show her the pimple on the side. Just that one touch and up he comes. You have to remember I'd been in the hospital for three and a half weeks at this stage, no sex of any kind, not even on my own, for fear of causing my abscess to erupt like Stromboli or some fucking thing.

Now I have a hard-on, my face is beetroot, but at least the Doc can see the pimple, which looks as big as an egg yolk to me.

The doctor touches JT, moves him around to get a good overall look. Then she says casually, 'We don't need this.' She flicks the index finger of her right hand against his fireman's helmet and the hard-on rapidly becomes a soft-on. And all I want is for the bed to open up and swallow me!

The doctor squeezes the pimple in a deft movement you'd hardly notice, if it hurts I don't even feel it. She wipes the pus away with the cotton, adds a hint of antiseptic to a fresh swab and brushes it against JT. 'It shouldn't bother you again.'

I thank her and I really mean it. I do not have cancer of the cock-a-doodle-dandy. And I was grateful for how she dealt with it. I knew that she was doing her job, nothing more, but when it's your crown jewels exposed to the eye of a lady doctor, it's not so easy to hold your royal cool, believe me.

I had an extra week off work after I got out of the hospital. I have to admit I hated our matchbox bedroom, the particular smells of the flat, the lav and the offal under the scullery sink, and I spent much of the time out walking very gently, and up in the library, writing in the Reading Room. I visited Claire too, but platonically, because I was still getting back to abnormal!

I didn't beat myself up for hating the flat; after the space of the ward and the great feeling of being between the sheets in the hospital, it was to be expected. But I had a nagging guilt because of how good my bosses had been to me the last four weeks, knowing I wouldn't be staying in the office job any longer than I could help it.

I had the same feeling about living at home. The overall doom and gloom of life in the flats, the growth of feeling alien to Ma, who had no problem with Mount Pleasant Buildings but all kinds of niggles with me. Why would I want to stay, why would she want me to? It was as though we lived in different places, and it wasn't going to change, not unless I had a brain operation to make me into the steady little guy Ma wanted me to be.

December dawns. My eighteenth birthday is beckoning to me like a rescue boat to a drowning man. I'm reading the *Irish Independent* and I see this advert in the 'Stage' column. As I read it I go into an immediate fantasy, calling it *My Ad,* as though it's been placed in the newspaper simply so that I, and I alone, will see it, answer it, fulfil the need of the advertiser, while I take the first real step on the road to the fame and fortune I was born to experience.

That very same day I make the first move to get the job that will take me out of the flats, away from the insurance job that isn't for me, away from yesterday and today, into the tomorrows where my dreams can come to life.

10

ctor/Singer/Musician wanted for touring company. Solvent management. Reply to Box. There it was. My Ad! As I'd always dreamed it would one day be.

Looking at it again and again I somehow *knew* that this was my passport away from all the things I didn't want in my life. Harry steps into my head and he annoys me with his 'Is a touring company even worth the bother? You'd get no guarantees from some Mickey Mouse touring company.' I had to shut him out. He was sounding practical, who wants *practical* when the dream's in full flight?

That same evening with my writing paper and envelopes and some really good pictures of myself, I walked up to the Reading Room. I sat down and set about writing a letter that would get me the job. This meant doing some serious lying but that was okay. Now just a few weeks short of eighteen, if there was anything at all on this earth I was really good at it was telling lies. So writing a letter to people I didn't know with a view to getting something I really wanted, I knew I could handle that.

Harry reappears reminding me, 'If you're going to lie, lie good. No small stuff, no Mickey Mouse makee-uppers!'

I have a few things going for me as I contemplate the letter. I know I can sing well enough, I know lots of popular songs, I can carry a tune even without music. I also believed I could be a good actor, given half a chance. And girls and women were always telling me I was good-looking or very handsome; lately my looks had been compared to Scotty Beckett, who played the young Al Jolson in *The Jolson Story*. So I was hoping hard that these facts might help me get the job, backed up by the pictures I was sending, with some high-grade storytelling as the icing on the cake.

I begin by writing I've been singing and acting in London, Enfield in particular. This was the town in Middlesex where Granny Rogers and Joe were living. I was going on the principle *Never tell a complete lie* — I had been in Enfield for a week, I had sung there every day while I was shaving my face, and my sister-in-law, Eva, said I was a terrific crooner.

In my letter I focus on the acting and the singing. I have enough front to lie about things I can possibly handle, but I can't play anything except the comb and the bacon bones, so forget musician. And do a novena that the pics will make them think 'leading man'.

My acting? I'd put on a show at seven, played the Maid in *The Bishop's Candlesticks*. In addition to this startling amount of on-stage experience, I've been in a couple of operettas, bit parts, that was it.

I describe singing in the pubs and hotel lounges, suggesting I get some money for these appearances, without ever actually saying I am paid. I write about winning the Marymount Hall Talent Show, my very successful Sunday night there, the invite to return any time. I make a big play out of singing with 'Maureen's band', making out it was an ongoing thing whenever I had time to fit it in.

I mention my poem on Radio Éireann, how pleased I was that *Eamonn Andrews* himself had read it, as if we know each other! I tell them I am a contributor to the *Irish Times Pictorial*.

I mail it off the next day just *knowing* the job would be mine. Meanwhile I brush up on 'The Shooting of Dan McGrew' and 'The Cremation of Sam McGee' by Robert W. Service and 'If —' by Rudyard Kipling, reckoning stuff like that will go down well in the Irish countryside.

A week later there was a letter returning my photos with thanks waiting for me when I got home from work. It was a very considerate kind of a letter. The writer, Mae Giles, who produced the show, sent me words of encouragement, promising to keep me in mind in the future. I might have been grateful the lady had gone to so much trouble. But I wasn't. The rejection went into my heart like an icicle and I was physically sick into the sink in our scullery.

I smacked my fists on the lavatory door and I bitterly reproached the God I had rejected that Saturday when I'd lost out in the Royal. Inside I was screaming defiance. Would it have been too fucking much to let me get that job, get out of here, get away from this? I was so mad I stormed out of the flat and when I snapped out of the insane anger in my head I was at Claire's front door.

I got drunk. What you might call stinking drunk. And when I woke the next day I didn't know if Claire and I had made love or not. It was scary having no memory at all after a given point in the proceedings, something I was never going to get used to. And now? Jesus Christ, it was morning! Time for work. And I hadn't been home at all — Ma would be off the wall.

I looked like a dog's dinner as I pulled myself together to get ready for the office, my heart, my hopes and my dreams all in the same sling, all of them broken or fractured along with my sense of humour. And I was so hungover I couldn't give houseroom to the idea of taking a cure, a couple of scoops of brandy to save the day. I knew I'd vomit again if I put a drink near my lips. It was as bad as I had ever been after a long night's drinking.

If I hadn't been so very sick when I got to the office I just might have held onto my job. Of course I should have had a couple of cures before I left Claire's place. I should have forced booze into myself till I got the hit that would help me overcome feeling so lousy. But I didn't do the smart thing and when Murphy tore into me in front of everyone, all I did was react with the phoney energy of the fella who knows he's in the wrong. I told Murphy to go and do something to himself, a trick that was both morally wrong and physically impossible. He didn't take up my suggestion but he did account for me leaving the office in a very short time. For the last time!

When I got home that evening Ma gave me the silent treatment for staying out all night. Afraid to speak, so Michael told me, in case I disappeared again for a few days. It didn't feel good, Ma being afraid of me in some way, that wasn't fair to her, but my immediate problem was how I was going to break my news to her. When she steered clear of me I was relieved. It was only temporary, sooner or later the shit was going to hit the fan so hard the whole neighbourhood would be painted brown.

The next morning Ma stormed out of the kitchen after I answered her angry tirade with some smart remark that contained a warning of my taking off again before long. It had to happen. A saint couldn't have gone on taking the very heavy verbal Ma was dishing out by the shovelful whenever she felt the urge. Suddenly she pushed out of there, another breakfast gone west, aggravation riding the range. What can you do!

Lunchtime Ma was out of the flat visiting a sick neighbour, so the first thing I had to do was tell Michael: 'I've lost the job.'

We were facing each other across the table over the remains of our fish and chips. I told him about the final row with Murphy, and gave him a note to pass on to Ma that evening.

'Have you any idea where you're going?' he asks, a look of concern in his face. Michael thinks I'm the mother and father of all gobshites!

And me, with my usual penchant for the subtle, the underplay, a cooked ham if ever there was one: 'Some day I'll send you a postcard from the other end of the world.'

Michael curbed his impatience long enough to let me know he wouldn't be holding his breath. Then he was off with a 'See you sometime.' For the first time in my life I wanted to hug him, hold him, make an impression in myself of him, the feel and the smell and the way of him, decent skin that he is. But he was going out the door so it was too late. Ma was passing him coming in before I'd made the sleeveen's escape.

She began clearing the table, I started for the door, trying to sound casual as I said the usual goodbye.

'What's the rush? Ma asked, her knowing tone stopping me dead in my tracks for the door.

'I've got to get back to work.'

'Have you now?' The words were like the crack of a whip and in a moment she'd lurched across the kitchen, smacking me so hard across the face I almost fell over.

Ma'd phoned the office and she was just plain desolate when she told me: 'I called to say sorry for the row this morning.' This didn't surprise me. Even when we hated each other, not talking was poison, the silent treatment never lasted very long. One of us would have to say sorry.

'The manager told me he had to sack you himself yesterday. That you swore at him in front of the entire office. You stupid young pup! God, I feel like taking a whip to you! Oh, what's the use.' She threw her hands up in despair. 'The job he had and he just threw it away.'

'I have to go Ma, I've got to get out.'

'Go? Go where? You've no job to go to.'

'I'm talking about leaving, Ma. I can't take any more of this.'

I could see her clamp down on the need to flatten me with a punch that would send me into the middle of next week. 'You? You can't take it any more. What about me? What I've had to put up with all these years?'

'That's not my fault, Ma. I did all I could to help you.'

She grabbed the back of a chair to help her keep her hands off me. 'Oh yes. You did. You were a great fella altogether. Always the few bob, even the few pound when you wanted to hide what you were really up to. I know about your lady friend in Terenure. Woman in Rathmines pointed her out to me. Your whore! May God forgive me. I'd sooner see you dead at my feet than watch you take that road.' Horror rode across her eyes. I've no idea how long it was before I lurched out the door without a word.

I lay beside Claire later, the story told of the job loss, the twenty pounds I needed in my pocket, thanks once more to her very generous nature. I hadn't told her I was leaving, any bit of sincerity I had ever shared with her tucked away in some limbo, safely out of the picture until I could get out of town.

I left her at half five that afternoon. I bought a ticket in the shipping office in D'Olier Street for the mailboat ride to Holyhead. A bus ride out to the pier at Dún Laoghaire, Claire's score in my trouser pocket. All my worldly possessions, even my notebooks, left behind in the flat. I realised I didn't have so much as a clean shirt under my arm. And I have to say I liked the image. I was sore, hurting all over, but I felt good about travelling light!

The sadness didn't hit me until the harbour lights became a distant necklace about the throat of the bumpy wintry evening. Then I remembered it was December, my birthday and Christmas only weeks away. Jesus Christ! Where was I going to be for Christmas?

I rushed into the bar and threw down two bottles of cider, sipping the odd shot of brandy from what was left of the half-bottle I'd bought in town. I was getting rapidly jarred but then, like a giant leprechaun, Frank Keating put a large brandy in my hand.

'The drink in here is very fucking strong,' I said, certain it was Keating himself standing there beside me, wondering what the hell my workmate was doing on the boat. Along with two other guys, Gerry Shortall and Liam Derham, Keating's friendship and irrepressible good humour had helped me through many a tough day in the office with Murphy on my back.

Frank gave me the shit-eater's grin he used on occasion, touching his glass to mine: 'To temperance, in the hope it won't raise its head too often in the days to come!'

We drank more brandy before I thought of asking him what the hell he was doing heading for Holyhead. In no pain at all Keating got a cigarette going, exhaled in his Noël Coward impression: 'You were one of the very few reasons I could stand working in that office. When you got the bullet yesterday I thought to myself, Francesco me bhoy, this is goodnight and goodbye to the insurance biz. So here I am!'

He inhaled a good shot of the cognac into himself: 'Lily Gaffney told me you called today to say goodbye. That you were taking the mailboat out this evening. I thought I'd join you, see how the cookie crumbles.' He chuckled. 'I nearly applauded when you told Murphy to go and fuck himself. I wonder if he'll give it a try!'

'You're baling out because I am?' I didn't give a damn but you have to admit, it was a situation to make anybody curious.

'I'd had enough of the place. Lily Gaffney, Maura Murphy and you, you kept me there, the three of you. So when Lily said you were crossing the water, why not! says I to myself. Time to go! See if the big bad world is *really bad*. Y'know, bad enough to be terrific!'

I don't remember much of the boat ride. Brandy and cider can do that to a person. Memory loss after a piss-up was just part of the script now. It happened to a lot of people, so I heard. In a way, it was like scoring with a girl, another notch on the gun butt, something to tell to a bunch of hardchaws like myself from the high stool on a wet day.

At Crewe station, a long way from Holyhead, a long way from anywhere, I become conscious again. The train I'd ridden on from Holyhead is missing. I'm alive enough to know I'm dying, vomit on my clothes, no memory of the train ride, and above all no fucking choo-choo!

Frank Keating appears out of the station lavatory, heading for rigor mortis as fast as I am. It's essential we find a *medicinal* boozer. If this is all there is, life isn't worth the living.

A couple of hours later the pain is gone, we drink till lunchtime, and I'm well jarred. When I tell Frank I'm not going any further he looks as though he's been smacked very hard. For him the trip is a breeze, for me it's already a disastrous mistake. He is out of Dublin to take on the world, all I can think about is getting back home. I try to explain to him how I feel. He is not with me but that's his problem. I may have shed a few tears, I can't say.

Keating tries to talk me into going to London with him. He has mates there, a flop's no problem. What was I going to go back to anyway? The job was blown, the unemployed marching the streets in their thousands. He was right, I knew that, but I couldn't listen to him.

In the fifties the Liffey began stinking like a neglected person in very bad health.

> *I remember the sweet-smelling Liffey*
> *I swam in it many a time*
> *Before some stupid whore turned it into a sewer*
> *What happened to reason and rhyme!*

After the Crewe debacle I was trying to like myself. Not easy as the boat from Liverpool dropped me at the North Wall the morning after the morning after I had left from Dún Laoghaire. There's only one thing worse than thinking *I blew it*. And that's *I blew it again!*

The Liffey stank but like a small light bulb going on in my hopes I felt some kind of gentle lift in the embrace of her body odour. I would willingly have kissed her deeply and not complained about halitosis of breath or spirit. Sick as I felt, lost as I knew myself to be, somewhere in me Redmond was humming a tune that meant he was glad to be home. But for all the relief I felt beside my shame, I just wasn't that sure.

I found a café and ate a bacon sandwich and drank really awful coffee. I didn't care. People would say I'd made a mistake throwing my job away. So what! I'd get another job, maybe a better one than the one I'd lost. I'd be all right. I knew I would because I was me!

The idea of facing Ma was awesome as I walked up the hill past McGrath's pub. I got to Byrne's shop on the corner and my stomach turned at the sight of the flats, the grey stucco like a giant scab to my eyes, the iron bars. By the ball alley in the middle of the flat complex, a dustbin was on fire. A woman threw a pot of water over it, moments later the smoke signals started. 'Listen! Yis all can't be cowboys. Summa yis has to be fuckin' Indians!'

I stood there like a hard sweet in a set jelly, frozen by the irrefutable knowledge that I couldn't remain here, not any more. Just as I knew I'd had to come back to taste this. When next I left I wouldn't be wearing the pink specs hooked over the deaf ears I'd shown to Frank Keating's good counsel in a pub in Crewe.

I had no problem about being out of work, sick about not getting the stage job sure, but I knew I'd find something. Just as I knew I didn't have to feel bad about disliking Mount Pleasant Buildings as much as I did.

So, I'd go indoors, try and make peace with my mother. And I'd be good to her for whatever time I had to spend in the flats. And I would embrace her, kiss her goodbye when next I went away, because next time it would be for keeps.

Ma opened the door and I saw a light come on in her oil-brown eyes. She was happy to see me. Then we were in each other's arms apologising, sobs and tears, so much to say, when no words were needed. When she let me go she gave me a long searching look.

'Your Grandfather Rogers'll never be dead while you're alive. If we shaved the moustache off his photograph I'd be looking at you.'

The tears arrived, I didn't fight the weeping, what was the point? Love for Ma was pouring out of me through my eyes. We couldn't let go of each other, there was no getting away from the feelings.

While Ma went on into the kitchen I washed my face at the cold water tap in the scullery. As I reached for the towel hanging on the outside of the lavatory door, the combined smell of the bog and the pig feeding turned my stomach, another nail in the coffin of what time I'd remain at home.

Da, not long home from his shift as nightwatchman for the ESB, came out of his bed to greet me. I didn't know what to expect. He amazed me by embracing me, hugging me for the first time ever.

He sniffed, turned quickly to go back to bed. Before he closed the door he mumbled: 'I've a few quid for you, Leo.' I believe I said, 'Thanks, Da,' but I'm not sure. What I was sure of was the feeling of joy inside me, how warm I felt in the unexpected welcome home. With, just once, Ma and Da being on the same side.

The following weekend, I'm in the Four Ps on Saturday night when this gorgeous, Spanish-looking girl with a terrific figure and a hundred-watt smile tells me she works on the touring show.

'Oh yeh,' I try to sound offhand. 'The job I didn't get!'

The girl, Yvonne Casey, tells me she saw my pictures on tour, so she just wanted to say hello. 'And I hope it won't be long before we're working together! The guy they wanted, he's not available.' I gave her a look. 'Honest,' she promised. 'Expect them to contact you soon, maybe even this weekend. We're in town for the Christmas break.'

The next dance is a Ladies' Choice and I'm knocked out when Jenny Evers comes and asks me for a slow waltz. We're old pals and I can say I love her in a very special way. She was with me in Charlemont Street the day I first heard Johnnie Ray singing 'Cry' like the Eighth Wonder of the World! His amazing sound pumping out of the radio in Larry Farrell's bike shop while Jenny and I just gasped at the impact of the man with the hearing aid.

I was supposed to be on my way back to the office, another lunchtime with no lunch money, so I was fed up till I met Jenny. She had a room in the street that she worked out of though she didn't live there. She was a childhood girl of mine, two or three years older, developed in every way, a darling. And she'd always had a real grá for me. One winter evening when I was about fourteen, we were snogging together. When I wanted to do more, Jenny said she had to go and get her father's tea. 'Come round about half six,' she said, skipping up the steps, 'and I'll pull y'off!' Two years after that, one night, meeting casually, we ended up in a heavy petting session. But she tried to stop me going up under her jumper. 'Ah, leave me tits alone tonight.' We kissed some more and

I went back again, until she gave in and I raised her jumper. Before I could touch her I saw the reason she was keeping herself covered. Her lovely breasts were held up with bits of rag and twine tied together to make a crude uplift. I was angered by this, saying I was sorry. We were friends, she knew what I was feeling.

'I'm going to be a brasser,' she told me that night. 'I don't want to live in poverty. I hate it.'

That day in Charlemont Street she was getting ready to go to England. She smiled, as pretty as Connie Smith in a different way. 'I got the ticket yesterday, going to stay with a palla mine's on the game in Manchester. No choice.' I knew the story, part-time factory work, her father unemployed. 'Working for buttons in Burton's Buttons, no thanks very much.' Then she was gone and I didn't see her again until that night in the Four Ps. 'Home for the hollyers,' she laughed, a bit tipsy. 'Doin' great beyond. Plenty of business, and I'm savin'. And if you're free tonight, you can have one on the house!' She was wonderful, but I didn't see her again that night after we ended our slow waltz under the revolving mirrored ball to the music of Al Cole.

The next day, Sunday, at lunchtime I am just about to sit down to a dinner of bacon and cabbage when a local kid knocks on our front door. Michael answers it, comes back into the kitchen telling me: 'It's for you!'

When I stepped out of our flat block I could see a big man standing up close to the next hall and he had showman written all over him. A tan crombie overcoat wasn't something you saw around the flats every day of the week. The broad-brimmed hat and the brothel-creeper crêpe-soled shoes just yelled showbiz to me, and during the next week a neighbour said she thought George was a film star.

As I reached him he flashed a grin at me that was worth money and he told me his name was George Quinn. 'And you've got the job if you're still available.' He was shaking my hand with a good grip, saying he'd like me on-stage on the opening night of the January tour.

'You haven't heard me sing or anything,' I said. By *anything* I meant *acting* but I couldn't bring myself to use the word. 'You'll be great, Lee,' he said reassuringly. 'I have a nose for these things. And you look the part, which is all-important.'

I didn't argue with that but I insisted I wasn't happy going anywhere until he heard me sing a few songs. There was nothing noble about this, believe me. I knew I could sing a bit, that I could really carry a tune. But suppose I joined the show and George couldn't stand my style, where would I be then! Up crap creek without a paddle!

Next thing I knew Ma was on the footpath outside our hallway, just forty yards from George and me.

'Come in for your dinner,' she yelled, like a fishwife doing an audition of her own.

'I'll be right there, Ma,' I yelled back. Jesus! If she got near George, guessed he had anything to do with show business, he could get a smack that could stop him acting for a week. Thank God Ma went back inside and George agreed to meet me that evening to hear me sing.

A minute later as I came into the kitchen Ma hit me with a right-hander that slammed me back against the door. 'Jesus Christ, look at what you're after making me do!'

I was shaking my head to clear it. 'Ma, *I was out there* so how could I make you do something *in here*!'

To make a long story interminable, Ma was placing my dinner plate on top of a pot of warm cabbage water, to keep the grub alive while I'm talking to George. She failed to register the fact that the pot was larger in circumference than the plate, so bang! Bye-bye dinner, I hope you can swim!

Ma was weeping in frustration, her fury had just got the better of her. Reminding me of the times Da wilted in the face of this same carry-on, a fearless guy who just couldn't handle her, except when she'd give him a verbal opening as he was going out the door. The times I heard her yell at him in despair: 'Jesus, Mary and Holy Saint Joseph, you'll drive me to the madhouse!' Da then going, in his own laconic way, over his shoulder: 'Oh no I won't. If you want to go to the madhouse you can walk!'

Ma was trying to rescue the food, moaning at me like a broken record. I said, like a fella treading on eggshells: 'You needn't worry, you won't have to put up with me for much longer.'

When this hit her she dropped the rescued bacon and spuds back in for another length of the pot. 'What? What's that you said?'

Staying well clear of her hands I said: 'You won't have to put up with me annoying you for much longer.' I took a deep breath, hitting the ball on the hop in case my nerve deserted me: 'I'm going into show business.'

'Jesus, Mary and Holy Saint Joseph,' Ma cried from a heart that sounded battered and bruised: 'You'll drive me to the madhouse!'

I stood there biting my tongue not to come back with Da's immortal line.

Then Ma went out the door in her apron, blind in her unwillingness to accept that she could no longer expect to win every time she laid down the law.

That same Sunday evening George Quinn buys me a drink in Duignan's lounge, where I've just done my turn with Jimmy at the keyboard. As it happens, George likes my singing and he wants me in his company in three weeks in County Fermanagh. I get five pounds a week to start, pay my own digs, two quid a week.

I ask George for the fare to the North of Ireland and he gives me a tenner. We leave the pub after one more drink and while he goes home to his missus, I take a cab up to Claire Kearney in Terenure, knowing over the phone that she'll have a steak and onions waiting for me when I get there.

Claire was genuinely glad I was getting a chance to do what I wanted, even though we wouldn't see each other all that often. She'd come and visit me on the tour, great, but above all she gave me her backing even though she wouldn't have chosen for me to leave Dublin, her understanding reminding me that Ma was in the opposite camp.

I knew there was nothing I could do. Ma was Ma and Lee was Lee and on some issues, never the train shall meet! The joke came to my mind because as I got into bed with Claire I already had my rail ticket from Amiens Street booked in my mind. And no matter what Ma said in the meantime, I was going, going, gone!

11

As I boarded the train for Northern Ireland at Amiens Street station I was still chuckling over what Alfie Heffernan said as we pulled away from the flats in his taxi. Ma was standing there like a cripple at a cross, bitter tears flowing as she assured the neighbours I was going on tour with bloody tramps and gypsies. I urged Alfie to take me away before it got really dramatic. He was droll enough in his own way and he said, catching my eye in the rear-view mirror: 'You should do well with the acting all the same, with your mother like!'

I got off the train at Newtownbutler. I stepped onto the platform and found myself looking down a single stem of street. This was not a New Town, this was a village, there had to be some mistake!

The porter stood beside me where the platform met the street, with the demeanour of a man who had seen it all before. 'I'm supposed to join a theatrical company. Is this Newtownbutler?'

'Och! This is it all right, sir, the one and only!' He jerked his thumb to the left and I saw George Quinn hobbling up the street. He was wearing overalls now, looked like the father of the man who hired me. He seemed to have hurt his foot and this disability made him seem older, the illusion getting a shot in the arm as I realised George was losing his hair.

His handshake actually helped me to feel better. I don't know why, I just liked the feel of him as it reached me through his hand. Everything seemed all right just because George was there in front of me, reasonably happy even though he had all kinds of problems on his hands, without me arriving all arty-farty.

As I got to know George in the weeks that followed my arrival I realised he knew exactly what was going through my mind as he walked up to meet me off the train on that first, cold January Monday. He had smiled a lot, even though his arthritis was murdering him, he assured me my digs would be excellent, did all he could to make me feel welcome, carrying my basket as though it was a feather. Without comment he gave me what I needed, I would witness him doing this again and again with others in the months ahead. He was really a gifted psychologist except on those occasions when he got jarred, about twice a year and then, like the rest of us, he could lose the head.

'I just hope I won't let you down,' I said to George when he had me settled in the digs. George ignored this show of nervousness, he gave very little time to anything negative.

'The all-important thing, Lee, I need you to use your good looks on the ladies, young and old. They love a new face, you being here, it'll let some air into the shows we've been doing for years. And I just know you're going to be fine. So,' he gave me one of his nickel-plated grins, 'relax and keep the ladies happy for me.'

Without laying down any law he made it clear that if I was willing to listen to him, I could probably be sensational and go a very long way. He smiled as he said that and I felt a glow inside. He was talking my language.

My debut hall in Newtownbutler was a grey oblong building like many others I was to play in during the tour. The same bleak design, dashed concrete blocks, door centre front and back, six windows along each side, one emergency exit midway down the right-hand side. It had been painted grey a long time ago and I couldn't help thinking it needed a rub of the brush in the worst way. But so what! It was the show that mattered, not the hall. And I was ready to give whatever I had to offer, hoping it would fill the bill.

As I arrived first time with George, two guys were erecting the frame. Basically four legs and four arms of four by four batten, bolted together. The legs supported the arms, from this would hang the many sets of curtains used in the different productions through the week. A different-coloured curtain, a different location in ten seconds, George said. 'Say pink for a street, green for a field, and so on.'

Close by, a stack of chairs of the folding kind sat by the wall beside a number of tea chests and orange boxes crammed with all sorts of gear necessary to the mounting of the show.

Two women wearing overcoats and headscarves were taking costumes from a wicker basket. They turned out to be a character actress called Mona Lynch and her daughter Helen. The two guys were Noel Dalton, the main character actor on the tour, and a little guy, an all-round performer, Harry McCormick. I hid my surprise, shock more like — actors putting up the stage had no part in my picture of life as an actor.

Somebody began playing 'Come Back to Sorrento' with a light liquid touch. George introduced me to the pianist, Sally Devine, a very attractive dark-haired woman who had so far managed to keep her mileage hidden from the world. By that I mean that the knowing aura she manifested spoke of time and experience that wasn't yet showing up in her handsome face although her eyes tended to let you know she knew a lot more than she was ever going to say to you.

I liked her right away and I sorta fell in love with her because of the talent she displayed on the keyboards and the violin. She worked with me on some songs for that first night. The idea was that I would sing in the first half of the show, which was variety. I would also mind the door to make sure latecomers didn't bunk in for nothing.

By seven o'clock on Monday evening I'm back in the hall at Newtownbutler and I'm going through some kind of panic attack. Not just about having to sing a couple of numbers, more to do with me knowing very little about stage make-up.

I stand at the back of the hall trying to calm myself down by taking in the changes to the scene achieved in just a few hours. Where there had been quite a shambles, order is the order of the evening with straight lines of seats each side of the centre aisle, and two low-watt lamps softly lighting the pale blue curtains which mask the set, called the tabs. The sidestage masking material is black, draped double over rope lengths tied close to the top of the front upright of the stage frame, secured to the wall each side by a strong hook.

All the baskets and boxes, and the piano, are out of sight backstage; there is a small card table with admission tickets on it by the door, and it's all so warm and cosy that I feel it would be a shame to turn on the lights. I walk up the aisle to the stage, turning around to look back down the hall. The front seats are folding chairs, about four rows of them, the middle lot are bench seats covered in leatherette, the back rows timber benches.

I slip through the masking drape and go sidestage. Sally is already at the piano in full stage make-up and I notice her violin case sitting on top of the Jo. As she sits at the keyboard, the stage is to her right so that she can see whatever is going on there.

A heavy wooden box is the step up to the stage; beyond this is the door to the single small dressing room, which the women will use while the men dress sidestage. Property baskets are in a tight line against the wall, there are two big black trunks open like books, and a lot of suits and costumes are hanging up on freshly sunk nails.

The make-up I'd brought with me is lying on the table I'll share with the other actors. Standing there trying to figure out a way to get over this particular hurdle, I amn't feeling the best.

George comes sidestage at that moment and I make a small show of holding a stick of Nine up to the bulb, as though I'm trying to work out the best mix of make-up to go with the very ordinary lighting. This doesn't fool George for one second and he begins my rescue by having a look at what I have in my make-up box.

I tentatively suggest a little help wouldn't go astray until I get used to the lighting. George agrees and two minutes later I am Nined and Fived and I'm applying my own eyeliner. Then, carmined and powder-puffed, I sneak a wink at the good-looking guy in the mirror.

George hands me a soft white jacket and a red shirt with a red and white bow tie to match. A minute later, wearing the fabulous gear, I blink my eyes in gratitude to the Patron Saint of Chancers!

Now George takes me out front and tells me quietly: 'You step up to the door and every young bird that comes in, you smile at her like she's Betty Grable. And give the old dolls a smile. Make them wish you were their only son.'

As I arrive at the entrance door, Mae Giles, who is George's missus, nods her head with an appreciative glance at the jacket and my overall get-up and Yvonne's shiny dark eyes twinkle in approval. She looks stunning in her opening chorus costume, convincing me every fella in the audience will be fantasising about her wonderful breasts from now till July. The nipples pressed like diamonds against the skintight top she's wearing, you get the feeling that even without the support of a bra, they'd be looking right in your eye.

At ten minutes to eight Sally starts an overture that is a mix of popular songs and the better-known Irish tunes. By eight the place is about full and then I hear George's voice come over the sound system as he welcomes the punters to *Showtime Parade*!

My gut flips out! *This Is It!* Any minute the show is going to begin and I'm a part of it. Jesus, just minutes and I'll be up on that stage! I shiver with it, knowing there has to be more than a few beads of sweat sitting on my Nine and Five forehead.

The lights are out now. The curtains are opening. Sally is pounding out 'There's No Business Like Show Business' on the piano.

Mae, Yvonne and Helen wear lime-green skirts below orange tops and a slim white belt. Staggered behind them the three men wear costumes that add up to red, white and blue. George is clearly catering to Prods and RCs, real hands across the border stuff. A reminder that the volcano might be taking a kip but eruption was never that far away.

The three men on stage are George, looking very handsome in the gear and the make-up, Noel, looking totally out of place and barely managing to hide his boredom, and Harry McCormick, looking little and willing.

The buzz is wonderful, the music, the movement, the singing, the lighting. The audience are already approving, moving a bit to the rhythm of the song, and as the Opening Chorus ends there is a welcoming burst of applause and several yells of appreciation.

The nightly format of the show was the same with different music, songs and sketches in the variety half. During the interval George ran a raffle and this was followed by a play which ran for about an hour.

When the play ended, George came out front and made a pitch for the next night's show, telling the audience the name of the play with a brief outline of the story, and guaranteeing them a variety show with all new material. If he blushed when he said *new material* you couldn't tell on account of the make-up. He meant different gags, but then he knew that most people don't remember jokes, which is why the old ones usually work best.

The night's entertainment finished with 'A Long Laughable Sketch, to Send You Home with a Smile Instead of a Tear', as George said night after night, week after week, month after month, his tone laden with enough sincerity to suggest that the words were coming through him direct from God. No doubt about it, he was a master!

I carry two abiding memories of that first show in that village in County Fermanagh. First, the arrival on stage of Yvonne Casey for her solo singing spot. She'd already been on for the opening, one sketch and an acrobatic act that she delivered with the practised ease of a natural athlete. But nothing prepared me for her sheer talent as a singer. She was a lovely-looking girl, with the kind of Latin looks that show up even better on stage. Right away I felt that if she had the kind of ambition you needed to go anywhere, she could go all the way. She sang — you got goose bumps!

The second memory of that Monday night was Helen Lynch's singing act. Helen was everything that Yvonne Casey was not. But somehow the Man Above protected her from this realisation and she came on and wowed that audience out of their seats. You know what Miss World looks like. Helen wouldn't have made Miss Village, not even Miss Hamlet. Her dress? Rescued from the *Titanic*. She sang, my gut twisted like a wet towel being wrung out. Helen had no voice at all.

In Newtownbutler she presented 'The Hills Above Drumquin' and 'When Peggy O'Dea Came to Mullinalea' and when she finished with 'The Old Bog Road' I'm almost ashamed to admit that I had tears in my eyes.

This was a lesson in how to sell a song. The message was simple: you had to go with what you'd been given — if you could do that you had a chance to win. If you were easy in yourself while you performed, your audience would feel easy, feel good. Helen knew that and our audiences adored her. What a lesson that turned out to be.

On my first Thursday night with *Showtime Parade*, I played the juvenile lead in a play called *Noreen Bawn*.

'You're mad!' I told myself as I was going on stage, knowing there were times when those scars on the brain, the chevrons of the madman, came in very handy!

Noreen Bawn was a classic story of emigration — Paddy going to America vowing to send for his only love, Noreen, within the year, she vowing to wait even though her heart is in a sling. Events get in the way of the big dream. The postmistress is the unmarried virginal mother and father of all diabolical female characters, a woman who by definition would be safe on an over-crowded troopship stuck fast in the ice floes of Antarctica for a year and a half. But she tells everyone that Paddy is writing to her from America and that he wants to marry her, and everybody believes her. The truth is that the dreadful bitch is intercepting Paddy's letters to his one true love until he gives up writing while Noreen thinks he has forgotten her.

So she marries a guy who goes bad due to alcohol. Not that you could blame him. He's working as a slave-driver, an overseer on a plantation in Kentucky, which gives Yvonne Casey, her face blackened and a turban on her head, the chance to sing 'My Old Kentucky Home' or whatever. When Noreen starts to die from TB you know it's her broken heart, which is by now in a plaster cast.

Not that her husband, played very badly by George who simply could not act, gives a damn. He is preoccupied with running off-stage, whip in hand, to give the slaves more of a hard time. With Noel Dalton yelling sidestage, 'No more whip, masta!' or words to that effect as he shuffled around in his stocking feet to try and suggest there was more than one slave getting the whip from George.

I hadn't been given any character sketch with the lines I was handed on the Wednesday morning. Mae Giles gave me some pages with cue words and 'Paddy's' lines and she told me we'd be doing the play the next night. She ran me through my lines a couple of times but I didn't get any real direction. I didn't say a word about this because I didn't want her to think I needed help. I'd never been in a real play before but I learned my lines and now the play was on and I was going okay.

The final scene finds Paddy, upstage centre right, by a grave, a free-standing small white cross with the word Noreen printed on it in black paint. There is a coffin-length mound of grass downstage of the cross which I had gathered myself from a nearby field that afternoon. And there is a door frame covered in scrim that George had slipped into the centre of the set.

Paddy wears a belted raincoat I'd had for a while. He holds a hat in his hand. This was the hat George had worn when he came to see me at home and I had an idea that it might make me look as though I had just returned from America!

A piano chord is heard and I start to sing, the last verse of the song 'Noreen Bawn' on which the play is based:

> So fair youths and tender maidens
> Ponder well before you go
> From your humble homes in Ireland
> What's beyond you'll never know.
> What is gold and what is silver
> When your health and strength are gone
> When you speak of emigration,
> Won't you think of Noreen Bawn.

As I hit the first line of the song, George, sidestage, standing on a chair, hits the scrim-covered door frame with a large, very powerful flash lamp beam, the sort of light you'd be grateful for if your car broke down in the dark. Mae Giles, Noreen, is now revealed in a white wedding dress, a bouquet in her hand.

The audience gasp is audible even to me though I'm listening to my own sound to keep me on the melody line of the song. Noreen's Ma and Doctor Sean come on with flowers, stand with heads bowed, I hold the high note, Yvonne brings the general lighting down slowly, George cuts the torch, we get dark and the curtains close. Need I tell you there is not a dry eye in the hall.

On the Friday night of that first week with *Showtime Parade* I wore my tails for the first time. Evening wear bought the previous week in the Iveagh Market on Francis Street from a woman who could get more bullshit into a single sentence than some people could fit on a long-playing record. Especially when it came to discussing the price she wanted from me for the tailcoat, the dinner jacket, both fitting me perfectly, and the pants I was prepared to buy without a fit.

The tails were for my first entrance as Sir Francis Levison in *East Lynne*, the ever-popular melodrama by Mrs Henry Wood, often called 'The Little Willie Story!' We needed a small kid to play Little Willie every Friday night. George had gone to the local cleric, given him a few pounds for charity, finding out which family had a nice little boy who could be controlled without anybody having to step on him.

Mae is playing Isabel Carlisle, the boy's errant Ma, and she spends Friday's interval with the kid. She had a way with children and she always ensured the mother got front row seats for herself and her family. Which was okay if the family was Prod but could be dodgy when it was RC because you never knew how many kids they might have.

We reach the big moment. Little Willie's in a sort of crib, the upstage end raised so we can see his face. Isabel talks to her son, makes a speech of heartbreaking intensity; handkerchiefs are to be seen all over the hall.

Now Isabel turns profile to Little Willie. The audience know he is dying, that his train is pulling out for Pearly Gatesville. The child stirs. Isabel reacts startled. Is it possible? Will she get a moment or two to talk to her dying child? He tries to sit up.

Sidestage, George, standing on a chair, holds The Spot, the big flash lamp, on the child's face. Little Willie tries to speak. He's going to say something. The length of this moment is dependent on how gifted the kid is week to week. You have to go with what you've got. This kid was good.

Isabel uncovers her face, takes off the dark glasses, says to Willie, 'Look, it's me, your mother.' The audience hold their breath. The child, arms outstretched, face up to George's flash lamp, slumps back down. His eyes close. And your audience just know. The collective sigh tells you they know he's on the 10.45 just leaving the station, gone to a place somewhere close to the right hand of God, where the governess never wears shades in the house.

Isabel sobs, pours her pain all over the neighbourhood, and delivers the immortal line: 'Dead! and . . . never called me mother!' Mae Giles has to give the line muscle to be heard over the sniffs and the sobs, and Jesus! I've got a lump in my throat! But only until our kid wakes up again!

Oh yes! Lo and behold, he decides to sit up on his after-deathbed, to wave at his Ma and his Da right there in the front row. Applauding louder now, and continuing to clap long after the curtains have slowly closed. The feeling in the hall that night was fantastic, showing me it's not smart to look down your nose at other people's tastes. I was in good form as I crept away to meet Claire, who was waiting for me, having driven up from Dublin.

I was glad to see her, delighted we'd spend the night together. George was an attractive man, so Claire said. And that Mae was too old to play opposite me. Yvonne was stunning; she looked wistful for a moment when she said that. We made love in a hotel bed. Claire was warm to me, good to me as she'd always been from the day she answered my novenas by holding me close in her bathroom at the house in Terenure.

Claire needn't have worried about Yvonne and me. She was a lovely girl all right, very sexy in a kind of innocent way, what I called a *Who me?* female. She was also a nice girl, unattached which surprised me on account of her Latin good looks. She just wasn't the kind of girl a halfway decent guy would try and mess around with.

Saturday afternoon I was sweeping the hall when George came in and gave me my first five pounds wages. He commented on the way I cleaned the hall each day, the time and the effort, sprinkling cold water around to keep the dust down, doing it right. We chatted about audiences, the coming back to life in *East Lynne*, George grinning: 'Little Willie's a lucky little fucker he's still alive this morning!' My landlady had told him I hadn't got back the night before. I smiled, saying nothing. George grinned and gave me a nudge, his idea of a medal for the guy who struck oil in his first week on tour.

I sent Ma one pound ten, guilt money because it was more than I could afford, hoping to ease the tension she'd been feeling when I left. The money meant I was earning, I'd been paid, that might reassure her. If the company was solvent like, things couldn't be too bad.

The note to Ma was chatty and light, we needed time for the damage inflicted on each other to heal, so not much to say really. I felt relieved at being away from the flats and I wasn't suffering because Katy and I were separated for the first time. I didn't write any of this, just made small talk, a few words about the show, said I'd drop another line next week.

Now that I was playing parts I was a bit worried about my Dublin accent. It wasn't that bad but I knew I needed elocution lessons if I was seriously going into the acting game. I was a good mimic. I used an English accent to play Levison. It didn't make me sound English but I did get a West Brit effect which was good enough for touring the sticks of Ireland. Time would show me the way to go provided I was willing to listen — not something I was good at.

I got Claire's Dear John after she'd come north for the second time on the tour. We were in Lisnaskea, and after the show she asked why I kept her visits secret from the others. It never occurred to me to do anything else, it was my way of protecting her from gossip, the kind of stuff that could arise out of the young stud — older woman scenario. She seemed to accept this: 'Ah don't mind me, forget it!' We made great love that night, she left me saying she'd be in touch. Next thing I'm reading her letter: she'd met a man of her own age, he was quite serious about the prospect of marriage 'which I'd like to happen since I'm not getting any younger'.

I sent Claire a postcard wishing her well, thanking her for everything. She'd been huge in my life, I loved her, always would, but what else can you do when someone wants to go? The hurt like the pleasure would pass, it always did; the memory of Claire's goodness to me was already written into the heart's journal.

For a few weeks after saying goodbye to Claire, I drank every night. People liked to buy a jar for the actors and I let them do it. And there was always one pub where you could drink after hours. In some towns it seemed drinking only really got under way when the pubs closed. I knew I was feeling the loss of Claire but I never talked about it, I kept the hurt hidden, with the help of the drink, the late night company.

When I woke up next morning I'd have no memory of the previous night's carry-on. Later I'd be told I'd entertained the late night drinkers in the pub, that I'd sung and danced on the counter, that I had to be carried back to the digs. Sounded like I had some fun. Pity I missed it!

After that I didn't do much drinking for a few months, scared by the way my memory took a walk at times. Besides, I didn't have the money to drink the way I liked to drink once I started. If I left the booze alone I got along all right, knew I didn't need it as a stimulant where sex was concerned. And I was getting sex when I wanted it.

I studied Noel Dalton's acting, he'd been trained in London and he could be brilliant in the right part. It was not his fault he'd been playing everything except juvenile leads until I arrived. That was the way of it. You did whatever you had to do to get the show up and keep it going. Everybody accepted this, it was part of the lore of the touring show.

I was flattered that Noel bothered with me. We talked books, listened to afternoon plays on radio and he could be very amusing when he slagged formal education.

'I've been educated to a fucking standstill and what did it get me! I'm unfit to do anything except be a fucking actor. And any fool can be an actor.' He snorted a laugh in self-deprecation. 'And just the other day I heard someone say I spoke as though I'd just cut my mouth on a saucer!' He laughed heartily then, his eyes wild. 'And the scandalous thing is he was right, the bastard was absolutely right.'

I felt sorry for Noel, who never seemed in any way happy. He had genuine talent, he deserved a better life than touring Ireland. He never stopped moaning about how tacky it was on the road — he had a point, he looked down on the audiences we played to week in week out, by times he seemed to hate everything. And before long his discontent started to rub off on me. Like Noel I began to feel resentful when business was so good that the hall was packed every night. 'You'd think George'd throw a few pounds extra into the pay packet' became the moan inside me that didn't want to be silenced. There was a lot of this kind of thing on the show, dissatisfaction caused by resentment that George and Mae were making a few quid.

I was alone with George in his car one day, we were on our way to book a couple of dates for the weeks ahead. George wanted me there with him as part of my training. The way he put it, 'Some day when you have your own show — if you're not in Hollywood! — you'll know how to go about the booking end of it.'

He asked me about my own education and I told him the truth. George appreciated I'd be so taken with Noel Dalton. There was a fella, terrific acting talent, educated up to the eyeballs, full of knowledge about books, theatre, the arts generally.

'A real pity nature didn't give him a bit of common sense to go with all the brains.'

This sting in the tail of the complimentary litany told me George had a message he wanted me to hear. He asked me if Noel knew why we were out together in the car. When I'd told Noel I was going, his reaction was predictable. He urged me to remember that I was an actor and not a showman like George and Harry McCormick.

I admitted Noel had tried to talk me out of the trip but lied, telling George there was a story on the radio he wanted me to hear. Had Noel warned me about the danger of becoming a showman, George asked. He got his answer by the way I burst out laughing. The way he could read things never ceased to amaze me. It transpired that Noel, like a lot of people working in the fit-ups, had run his own company at one time. He had lost everything, so George said, because he considered himself such an artist that he gave no attention to the business end of things. That was why so many people on the road were resentful when business got good. They were mostly failed managers and never got over the fact it hadn't worked for them.

'And I've noticed,' George said quietly, 'since you got pally with Noel you quit sweeping the hall the way you used to. If I were you, I'd think about that.'

I knew he was right. He wasn't complaining. I swept the hall good enough for him. But what about myself? Was I sweeping the hall well enough to suit my own standards of how I did any job? I knew I wasn't. My standards had slipped because I had been influenced by Noel out of respect, and even envy, for his intellectual prowess, so that when he said you shouldn't have to do things like that, I took the flavour of that on board and the work suffered.

I knew I'd get back to cleaning the hall properly, remembering a man I knew used to sweep the streets of my milk round. He always wore a trilby and a blue overcoat, you'd never have guessed he pushed a brush for the Corpo! But that's what he did and he decided he'd be the best road sweeper he could be. Once he was doing that, doing his best, he knew he'd be okay.

I was writing something every day. I often tore up the pages that came through; like everything else writing had to be worked at, it had to be practised, and I'd never been afraid of hard work. Besides it was really what I wanted to do. As I spent more time on tour I found the predictability of life on the road boring. After a few months I knew every line of every play, all the gags, sketches, double acts, so there wasn't a lot to stimulate my imagination.

Month after month we toured all over the northern counties, we stayed for two weeks in tiny villages like Newtownbutler. Incredible when you consider the size of places like that, but by presenting a completely different show each night of the week, you could entice the same people back night after night.

The show wasn't just for the people of the town or village you were in. We catered to people who walked and cycled miles to see us. They drove horse carts and jaunting cars from the surrounding countryside, anywhere within a radius of twenty miles or so.

Along with the travelling circus we were the only form of entertainment available to more than three-fifths of the population of Ireland. National radio was still a part-time affair, television seemed light years away. Even electricity was not yet available in rural Ireland, wouldn't become so until 1956 which was three years away.

12

I left Showtime Parade during an afternoon drinking session in early December 1953. We were having a couple of nights off while the local hall was being repaired and I certainly drank more than was smart.

There was some kind of row, Yvonne was involved in some spat with Mae. I said something, someone else said something — who knows and who cares! I threw the head, and within an hour Yvonne and I were on our way back to town.

In Dublin later that same evening I put Yvonne into a taxicab to take her home to her mother in Kimmage. I wasn't feeling good after the drink I'd had earlier in the day so it wasn't hard to ignore the signals that she was sending my way. There was room at the house for me and her mother would welcome me, Yvonne knew she would. For a moment I felt a pang of guilt. She was a sweet, wonderful girl, but I hadn't just quit *Showtime*, I was on my way out of Ireland. I wasn't looking for a girlfriend.

It didn't hit me till weeks later that I'd been in a row that was none of my business. So, did I use the row to allow me to walk off the show without my conscience giving me a hard time after George had been so good to me? I never came up with an answer and I never asked myself if it would it have happened at all had I not been drinking alcohol.

Two weeks later I was renting a room in Kensington Park Road in London for two guineas a week. I had just started working a twelve-hour night shift in a factory called Rotax in North Acton. I was neither happy nor unhappy. The work was beyond boring; the long hours and the hike to and from the job made their physical demands, I was sleeping like a baby. My room was a small one, a cell really, but it had a washbasin with hot and cold water. Luxury!

George called me. He'd been up to Mount Pleasant and got the phone number from Ma. He hopes I'm coming back. What happened was just the release valve, all of us letting off steam. 'These things happen from time to time. It's never personal really!'

I told him I'd be in touch in a few weeks, lying, not needing to put him down, he'd always been a good guy to me. But I knew I wasn't going back to *Showtime*, back to home, back to anything.

Soon after this a letter came from Ma telling me Aunty Kay had died in St Kevin's hospital. I cried only because I couldn't help weeping. The poor love was never coming out of hospital, we knew that and I guess Kay knew it herself. She'd gone blind; on my last visit you could see her guessing which of the boys I was until I told her in a roundabout way.

Both her legs amputated, the blindness maybe caused by the years of insulin. Her bravery through all the injections given her by a kid who sometimes had to shut his eyes to drive the hypodermic into her arm. A remembered conversation then, my surprise when she said once how grateful she was to her sea captain who walked out on her.

'Me believing that he was waiting for me. That kept me going, Leo, especially that last ten months when my mother was in dreadful pain. If I hadn't believed he'd be there, I honestly think I'd have killed myself before Mammy died.' I could see her nodding her greying head, confirming in her mind that she meant what she said. 'So in a way, he saved my life, even though he wasn't being honest when he said he'd wait for me.'

On the bus to work in North Acton I felt my tears on my skin. Poor Kay! Our unpaid home help when we hardly had a chair to sit on. Poor Kay! Who couldn't cook potatoes! God love her and God love me.

The next letter from Ma told me Da wasn't at all well, a blocked valve to his heart. Really he should stop working, Ma said. Some hope! He'll never quit working. Not till the day the heels go first.

I was working seven nights a week in Rotax, saving over twenty quid every Friday. Not hard when you were going from bed to work. I had a count-up to see how much I'd put by. And I remembered a decent skin called Eddie Bohan who was in the wholesale end of the confectionery trade. Eddie told me one time that if I ever wanted to get into business, start a shop, he could help me get the right kind of credit. This meant you could get something going without having a lot of money up front.

I had £140 saved from Rotax, more money than I'd ever had in my life before. I was earning enough to add to this week by week for as long as it took to get some kind of small shop going for Da. I phoned Eddie Bohan and he said sure, nothing's changed, I can help you when you're ready. I wrote to Ma, told her what I had in mind. I would send money to her every week to put into the post office. We were going to have a little shop, something to give them a living without him killing himself riding a bike up and down the Pigeon House Road in all weathers. I told her I didn't want Da to know about the money till we had what we needed. But she was free to tell him I was saving some money to buy him a shop.

And so it began, the dream to help my father quit killing himself in the job that had saved his head some years before. I buried myself in the factory, mostly checking car battery stoppers. Every night I picked up 12,000 rubber stoppers. Each one of these screw-in stoppers had two holes in it. In my other hand I had a yellow card. I looked at the card through the two holes in the stopper. Once I could see two yellow spots the stopper passed muster and went into the Out bin.

For the next three months I did this seven nights a week, sent Ma another £220 to go with the £140 I'd started off with. We were well on the way to having enough to get the little shop started. Ma said he was calling it 'the chicken farm'. Any idea about writing had to go on hold. That was all right, I'd have all the time in the world to scribble. Unless somebody did something to make Da's life easier than it was, he wouldn't have much time at all.

In the job I turned my mind off as much as possible and I listened to a lot of night-time radio. The people I worked among were decent guys and I never had a single problem in that factory, if you forget the noise. What mattered was I didn't break down, I stuck to my target. I had no social life during that time and I didn't care. All I wanted was to save Da from the journeys up and down to the Pigeon House. I needed to do that.

Early in May I decided to go home, see Da, feel him out, hear what he had to say about the shop idea. To save the train fare I hitched from Hendon to Holyhead, taking the boat ride to Dún Laoghaire.

I got home on a Saturday morning tired, but feeling good. When I added the eighty quid in my pocket to what Ma already had in the post office, we'd have enough to get some kind of confectionery shop opened for him before long.

When Ma opened the door to me the blood drained out of her face as if someone had pulled the plug. I stepped in and shut the door, wondering what the hell was wrong. Jesus! Da hadn't died while I was on the way over on the boat?

Ma's eyes rolled for a second, flickering shut as she fell, fainting really, into my arms. I supported her, got her to the divan bed in the corner of the kitchen. Her eyes opened, she began sobbing, a terrified child trying to speak, to explain something, but I only caught the odd word like *forgive* or *Jesus help me*, stuff like that. You didn't need a doctor to tell you she was in a state of shock.

What was wrong? Was it Da? 'No, son, not your Da!' She told me in a short eruption: 'The money you sent home to your Da, it's gone, son, all gone and you'll have my life!'

I went into a state of shock of my own. Ma fell back on the bed, groaning in torment. I was taking deep breaths, trying to hold my head, not to let my mind run away with me. How? What did she mean? How could the money be all gone?

Ma nearly rolled off the divan as she twisted in agony, like a woman knifed. I bent to her, held her, she grabbed my left hand, clutching it tightly enough to hurt me. The story tumbled out of her. How she'd started to go into town on the bus to play Housey Housey in the Fun Palace.

The Fun Palace was an amusement arcade on Aston Quay in the city. You could go in and play this game in which a caller yelled out numbers chosen at random. You paid a shilling for the card and if your numbers came up you won twenty, forty times your shilling, depending on your stake. Before long this game would turn into Bingo.

And here was my mother telling me that all my savings for Da's shop had been gambled away in this fucking Fun Palace. I pleaded with her to be reasonable.

'It's not possible to lose the guts of four hundred pounds at a shilling a card. You'd have to play twenty-four hours a day to blow that kind of money.' I was so torn by what I was hearing that I didn't even think of the obvious answer until Ma told me. You didn't have to play for a shilling a card. Ma graduated to playing Housey Housey for two pounds a card without even knowing how it happened to her.

There was a sudden uprush of violence in me, for one awful moment I thought I was going to slap Ma's face. What I really needed was to get up and walk away from her, just go, just get out of there.

I knew I had to leave before my father came in off the night shift in the Pigeon House. Unless I did he'd surely find out what Ma had done, he'd want to take her life.

'I've got to go, Ma, before Da gets in from work,' I told her bluntly, sick to my stomach. Ma grabbed me, somehow rising from the divan bed, fear providing the energy, begging me, literally begging me not to go.

I crumbled, my legs going from under me like broken biscuits. I wept, crying uselessly onto the lino, pounding my fist on the floor, all the dumb questions pouring, all of them adding up to *Why Me! Oh Jesus Christ! Why me!*

By the time Da came in the door I'd pulled myself together. He gave me a hug and I felt the shared tug of the heart when he held me. I hugged him passionately, my eyes somehow dry as tears rained down on me inside. He tapped me on the jaw, swinging his fist gently in a short arc, and I knew there was no way he could ever hear about the Fun Palace. He took off his ESB-issue raincoat, looking me up and down, messing when he said, 'You don't look too bad for an actor!'

It got more difficult after that. We drank tea and I told Da things were tough in England, which wasn't true. I worked hard sure, but I got well paid for my time. I was building a bridge to get past the money I'd promised never materialising. He was glad to see me and that really helped. His face was grey, he seemed smaller but he was chirpy and still a Drumcondra fanatic even though 'They have no Billy Mulville these days,' naming a great half-back himself and Leo played alongside in the old days.

Football. His great passion in life. The family passion at one time, all of us able to play a bit. I played for Charleston Athletic in a cup final at St Patrick Athletic's ground. Scared that day being in a final, I bought whiskey and just before the game had two shots of Jameson Ten. I played a blinder. We won the cup along with three other trophies that season. After the cup final I never played again; without booze in me I couldn't make the grade.

Ma giving no thought to what her madness might do to Da or me: that kept coming back, I could hurt myself all over again at the stupidity of the whole thing. I got drunk both nights I was there and when I returned to sleep in Da's bed, I silently dared Ma to say one word. She lay mute on the divan in the kitchen, accepting the gap that was there between us.

Saying goodbye to Da on Monday evening was very hard on me. I wondered would I ever see him again. Not just because of his heart. I knew I really was going travelling, I might be gone years.

I'd barely seen Michael over the weekend. He was courting a nice girl, Betty Harris, he liked old-time dancing, was in a musical society, he needed my company like he needed pneumonia. Brendan was still a quiet lad, big and gentle, a guy who kept his own counsel.

Saying goodbye to Ma I didn't hide how I felt about the money. I couldn't, I just couldn't find it in me to act noble, dress it up as just one of those things. It wasn't just one of those things, it was a terrible thing for her to do. Not just to me, although I felt so hard done by I wondered would I ever get over it.

Soon after my return to England I dropped back to five nights on the job, slept less during the day, began scribbling again weekends. With the writing I didn't have to make a decision, it just wouldn't leave me alone even though I still couldn't have told you where it came from. It was just there, like the weather, every morning when I woke up. And as soon as I was sitting down with the pen in my hand, Redmond started to sound off again in my head. It was as if he came with the territory: Harry Redmond, the voice of the know-all, in there with the rest of me. A pal I had all to myself, reminding me I felt easier than I had done for months. Then it struck me — I was leaving Rotax and I was getting out of London for the summer.

After I left the factory for the last time, I was in Regent Street when I saw this sign in a travel agency: 'COME TO SUNNY JERSEY!'

'Where is it, Jersey?' I asked the man who came to serve me inside. He smiled and you just knew nobody had ever asked him that before.

'It's a hundred and fourteen miles from Southampton.'

'In which direction?' I asked in all seriousness.

Jersey was one of the Channel Islands occupied by the Germans during the last war. It was governed by French law but English was the spoken language. The island was emerging as the up-and-coming holiday resort, so the travel agent told me as I bought a ticket for the boat ride from Southampton. Jersey offered reliable good weather, very reasonable prices, good cuisine, top-class entertainment. It sounded as if it had everything going for it. And now it was going to have me as well. Look out, Jersey, here I come!

The weather in St Hélier was the kindest I'd ever known, really warm but not too hot, enough air around to keep you comfortable. I walked the little narrow streets, drank the local beer, Mary Anne, at sixpence a bottle. Forty bottles for a pound — imagine!

In two days I am working in the Pomme d'Or hotel, knowing I won't be there for long.

There are two nancy boys working with me, pearl diving, dish washing in the plate house, nice characters who adore each other. They have the disgusting room next to my disgusting room and while I never quite figure out who is punching who up the panties, they get through a lot of action in the two nights I lie on the other side of the parting wall. Apart from the heavy screwing they laugh a lot, they play pop music all the time, and I think they're just great. And, like me, too good to work in a place like the Pomme d'Or, French for Golden Apple. Golden Apple my arse!

During two days dealing with mini-mountains of dishes I sing a lot. I sing to stay free of how awful it is in that kitchen. Some of the waiters admired me for singing, Italians and Portuguese, other guys thought I was nuts and said so. And I kept on singing, because I was as free as a bird, getting freer by the hour, knowing my career as a pearl diver was coming rapidly to an end.

In the hotel bar, two Irish guys discuss this Dub nutcase who sings even if you can't see him half the time behind mountains of dishes. Johnnie tells me later, 'You were a legend the first lunchtime and we didn't even know your name!'

Johnnie McCusker, the night porter, and Phil Connolly, a barman, actually come visiting to gape at me as though I'm some kind of unusual animal the zoo passed on. They stand off to one side in the kitchen for a while before they say hello.

That evening after some hours bending the elbow, they still think I'm nuts. They've no idea where I'm coming from, like you have to be crazy to be a singing dish washer! I tell them if you do the job with a happy sort of heart, you'll be moved on to a better one. They wonder how could any other job not be better than dish washing.

Next day I'm in the hotel bar trying to cure a hangover you could photograph. Connolly is working away, not a bother on him. Johnnie McCusker is in bed, he worked all night after he left us. Denis, the head porter, comes into the bar, a nice fat fella I met the day before, asks me am I looking for work.

'As long as it's not pearl diving, Denis!'

He laughs. 'We could be talking porter, even cocktail barman if you have the bottle to go for it.'

In minutes I'm on the way out of there, the last words coming from Phil Connolly with the Clones accent. 'Why not go for manager while you're at it? Sing them a fucking lullaby!'

I take a cab to Mont Millais where the Olwyn Grove hotel sits on the high road looking down over the town and the sea, convinced I'll get the cocktail bar job. I know I don't want to be a porter, all those suitcases!

I know nothing about bar work and more specifically, even less about cocktails. Never mind. On the principle that fortune favours the brave, I walk into the fabulous hotel in my dark grey suit, my white shirt and plain red tie, with my pork-pie hat in my hand to make me look mature, and I ask to see the man in charge.

The receptionist comes back moments later followed by a thickset man with angry eyes and an aggressive manner. He tells me in a Birmingham accent you could cut with a knife: 'I'm Frank Newey, the owner.' I introduce myself and tell him I'd be happy to fill his barman vacancy. That his hotel has been recommended to me by a good friend of mine, Denis, who is the head porter at the Pomme d'Or hotel.

I deliver this in my best Laurence Olivier. This doesn't make me sound like the great actor, it does ensure people understand what I say first time, that my accent, overall Irish, is neutral enough to make it interesting. I'd worked on it by reading Shakespeare aloud to myself in the halls we played many an afternoon for months.

Frank Newey and I get into a question and answer session and I simply respond to what he asks me. Telling the tale is fun, and so far telling lies hasn't cost me a single job.

'Where did you last work as a cocktail barman?' Frank's speech grates on the environment while he stares at me as if he doesn't even trust his mother.

'That was the Isle of Man Holiday Camp last summer, Mister Newey.' Always hit *Mister* as though you're saying *Your Majesty!* It never hurts in an interview.

'And what have you been doing since then?' Frank Newey's faith in his ability to size people up is showing in his eyes. He knows so much nobody could con him! I tell him I've been at Trinity College studying for my degree in English.

Telling lies, or boosting your CV, seems to me par for the course. It's also important to be relaxed as you lie, so you can produce a face like a bereavement card that hasn't forgotten how to smile. And keep the eye-to-eye contact going at all times.

Frank Newey leaves me there by the reception desk, returning moments later with a white V jacket which he hands me. He tells me to try it on, I do, it fits perfectly.

He nods for me to follow him, we go into this beautifully decorated lounge, a long bar against one wall housing an array of drinks the likes of which I had never seen before, never even imagined. I draw a deep breath. Jesus! Maybe this time I've bitten off more than I can chew even with a mouth as big as mine!

I shift my attention to the carpet under my feet, which is deep, very expensive, just to take my mind off the awesome bar for a few seconds, get a breath, stay loose. I glance at the furniture, it looks to be genuine antique but what do I know. It's easy to see an awful lot of money had gone into achieving the overall effect, which is classy and stunning at the same time. I let my appreciation show, I let out a breath, I shake my head as though I can hardly believe it, aware that the man from Brum is delighted with my reaction to his baby.

There is a woman behind the bar, a white-haired lady with the sort of breasts you'd need to rest on the counter every few minutes. She has eyes like gobstoppers, the bulbous eyes of a serious drinker, but she likes me and I smile and give a tiny little bow of my head.

Her name is Sally and as she shakes my hand she is seriously ladylike, the way people are when they're putting it on. She holds my hand longer than a lady would, but it's motherly as opposed to sexy, and I give her all of my eyes as well as the juice I'm willing into my fingers. She smiles and when Frank Newey suggests a week's trial she gives me a private look suggesting *Don't mind him!*

Fortunately for me, Sally falls in love with me on the spot, as the son she never had, and from that moment on I am in clover. Even on an occasion later when Newey wants to fire me over a mistake, Sally saves the day. She now gives him a look that says *You can go*, which, to my surprise, he does. He nods, leaves the lounge, and I know I am in like Flynn.

Some weeks later I discover that the bar licence is in Sally's name. Frank Newey is the money but not the licence, allegedly having had to hurry away from Birmingham where he'd been a bookmaker. Enough said. Now Sally tells me that the hotel is fully booked for the summer, that we have about a week to get used to it all before the season gets officially under way. She assures me that I am most welcome and tells me she'll be back in an hour after she's had her lunch, then I can go and have mine. She shows me how to work the till, assumes I can do everything else, she is gone, I am alone in this amazing cocktail bar.

A minute later I'm on the phone to Phil Connolly. He laughs out loud when he hears I am running the cocktail bar at the Olwyn Grove while Sally is at lunch. He tells me to come down to see him when I get my afternoon break and he'll help me hold onto the job. 'Not that you need me. With that *open heart* of yours, if you lose that job you'll just get a better one, right!' He's laughing. I stand there shaking my head. This is going to be very tricky.

I walk up and down behind the bar. All the beer pumps are identified by a clip-on hardcover label. There is a cold shelf, a glass washer and three cocktail shakers. Behind me there is a display of coloured bottles like a design for a liquid peacock. I see names like Courvoisier, Parfait Amour, Napoleon VSOP, Grand Marnier, Crème de Menthe, Crème de Cacao.

Before I have time to have a panic attack an old lady comes into the lounge. She has the air of a woman used to being attended to, a real dowager. I greet her respectfully, no hardship since I like people generally and my manners were always good, came easy to me. I come around the bar and hold out a chair for her. She asks me for a half-pint of shandy, which, when you see the selection of drinks behind the bar, would be funny if I happened to know what a shandy was. I don't. I hear myself asking her how she liked it made. She appreciates that, replies half beer, half lemonade, no ice. I ask if she prefers a glass or a mug and she positively beams as she tells me a mug, please.

That shandy was the first drink I ever served in my life and when I insisted that it was on the house since I had just started work in the hotel, the dowager was just thrilled to pieces, leaving me a ten-shilling note as she went off to have her lunch a bit later on. Meanwhile a guy with a Scottish accent and a Brylcreem hairstyle came in and asked for Bisquit Dubouche. I pretended I didn't hear him and he said,'Brandy, Bisquit, please.' I had no problem finding the Bisquit bottle alongside the Courvoisier and minutes later this guy, who is from Edinburgh, picks up on the Dublin in my accent, shakes my hand, and tells me that he likes the Irish even more than the Scots. I have to restrain myself not to look up and say thank you, God.

I'm smiling to myself as I think of the spoof I laid on Connolly and McCusker about the open heart leading you to a better job and all that stuff. That had been off the top of my head, tap-dancing if you like, but it's happening that way in the Olywn Grove, whether I believe in it or not.

We had just those two guests booked in for that first week, so I had no problem with the bar. As I leave Sally to go and get my lunch she tells me I open the bar at six o'clock for aperitifs, drinks before dinner, I'm free until then. I don't ask what time we finish, how much wages I'm getting, nothing. I don't care. It looks as though I have landed on my feet and all I need now is some help from the Man from Clones!

Connolly would tell me some years later that he had never seen anybody concentrate the way I did as he gave me a crash course in being a cocktail bartender on that late May afternoon. For me it was the most valuable two and a half hour learning session I ever spent, and I went back to Sally confident I'd be grand until practice made me perfect.

13

In days I knew how to use a mixing glass, how to look as if I was at it a long time. I did a twist for a dry martini as though to the manner born, I could use a cocktail shaker no problem. I had seven or eight recipes for cocktails written on postcards I kept with me. Connolly loaned me his United Kingdom Bartenders' Guild book, which is a primer on the whole set-up of the cocktail business, including hundreds of recipes. Not that you needed that many. Basically you'd be asked for one of eight cocktails; once you had those off pat you were in good shape.

I memorised the recipes for Tom Collins, Dry Martini, Clover Club, White Lady, Gin Sling, Whiskey Sour, Alexander, Pimm's, Gimlet and a few more, and got familiar with the look and the taste of liqueurs. When Sally wasn't around and we weren't busy I had all the time I needed to study champagnes, sparkling wines. I didn't pinch any bottles, I bought the stuff I wanted to sample.

Sally was taken by what she called *my gentle way with women*. She was right, I loved women. For her I became a sort of tea cosy, keeping hassle away from her by covering her up with my stewardship behind the bar. The fact is she was very slow at the work, had no head for figures, and could never learn how to shake a cocktail. But she did have her name on the licence and that made her lady of the manor!

At this time I could think on my feet the way Gene Kelly danced, and I could keep all the tapes in my head, eight of them anyway, going at the same time while I was pulling a bird, organising the fiddle from the till or whatever. So I became Sally's minder in a sense and she loved me being there for her. I rescued her so many times when she got in trouble trying to fix drinks she couldn't handle that she made me look good about ten times a night.

I shared a huge room in an annexe at the back of the hotel with two waiters, Adalbert and Tino. I got along with them even though one was German and the other a crazy, lovable, hot-blooded, sexual satyr of an Italian, who, as he said himself, would fuck a hen! 'I would even fuck you,' he assured me in his passionate matter-of-fact way, and this was a guy without a really homo-sexual bone in his body. Like Brendan Behan, to Tino, *A block was a block!*

During that first week I found Tino in bed with a Swedish girl he picked up in St Hélier. Adalbert humped an English girl several times during a night when I didn't get much sleep because she groaned and cried out as if she was getting it from King Kong. I forgave them both for keeping me awake. It was refreshing to find we could be so open with each other, that some women weren't hung up about someone else being in the room.

And by the end of that week I met a German girl called Anita. Part of Anita's work included doing our room; when I got into bed Saturday, there was Anita waiting to do me as well. Up to this we had smiled at each other a whole lot, I helped her carry a Hoover, she read my little signal, no English necessary. I hadn't a word of German if you leave out Berlin and hamburger, but the guy who wrote 'You Don't Have to Know the Language!' had it right.

Anita and I melted, sharing a gasp of delight as I slipped into her, as we followed the way of the lovemaking. When my room-mates turned in pissed, we lay silent, till they slept. We fitted together as though my body had been made for hers and we came a whole lot of times before she left me on Sunday morning to start her day's work.

Jersey was like a huge store crammed with all kinds of goodies, all of them girls. Girls to knock your eyes out were everywhere, and so many girls went for waiters and bartenders, it was as if we were toys to them too. So we all played a lot with each other, and I thought it was about as close to heaven as I was ever going to get. You could buy brandy at a shilling a shot, Drambuie, Cointreau, the same price. Twenty cigarettes cost one and fourpence. So a serious smoker who was also a serious drinker could die a very happy death in Jersey!

The staff food in the hotel was good, compared to the awful Pomme d'Or. Even so I took Connolly's advice, gave the chef two bottles of decent wine, bought and paid for with the receipt handy in case I needed it. The little roly-poly Frenchman was in the palm of my hand after that, I ate like royalty. He got a bottle every Friday night. I never took anything from the hotel; it wasn't smart to mess with the stock, especially when you had a good fiddle going

The fiddle was part and parcel of any bar job. As Phil saw it, a barman enjoying a percentage of the bar take was important to the overall structure of the cocktail bar industry. Because everybody did it, Connolly explained, if there was one guy suddenly showed up who didn't do it, this would be noticed by the people running the bar, who expected it to happen to such a degree that nobody ever talked about it in concrete terms.

What did this mean, you overcharged customers or what? 'Or what!' Phil said emphatically, nodding his head, hard as a cannon ball under the sleek, black quiff of hair. 'You never rob the punters, well, not strictly speaking you don't!'

What Phil meant was *You didn't rob customers of money.* When it came to the drinks you served, it was part of the etiquette of cocktail bar work to keep back some of the spirit ordered by the punter. It stopped them getting stinko a lot of the time, which if you thought about it was doing them a favour really.

'With two barmen working together it's a doddle,' Phil said casually. 'On your own you always put ice into the glass before the whiskey or whatever you're serving. You use a spoon to do this, make sure you get a drop of water in there along with the ice cubes. Then you clip the measure a little. Unless you're serving some publican from the mainland, then forget it! He knows as much about fiddling as we do.'

You didn't take money out of the till, you left the extra for the house. Up to a point. In this way you built up a percentage above the legitimate return. You used the cocktails as a mask. This is where the bartender usually gets his own fiddle in the course of a week.

You pushed cocktails any way you could. With young women you introduced them to the White Lady or Clover Club, something gin-based, with maybe Grenadine, Cointreau or Citron Pressé — lemon juice, a hint of egg white to provide a nice clerical collar on top, and ice and whatever. You gave the first one free, a small one, and you made a game out of presenting it with a laugh as if it was a trophy. In the second week of their holiday you'd notice · how they came in and said, 'White Lady, Lee,' or whatever, to impress the new arrivals at the bar with their sophistication. It never failed.

Three or four girls together, you turned them on to cocktails, you renamed a drink in some female's honour, week after week. To prevent them drinking too much and spoiling their evening, you shared one measure of spirit between the four of them. With all the other stuff added, nobody ever noticed, and you had three measures of spirit to your credit in the stock. You had a great mind for remembering what you were owed, you took the money out of the till late at night always leaving a little bit extra in there for your oh so honest employers who knew nothing about such devious carry-on. My arse!

The basic pay for bartending in Jersey was about seven or eight pounds a week plus your bed and board. And you got commission on the bar takings, 2.5 per cent, a tidy sum when the season was going full blast. So, between my earnings and the fiddle, and the fabulous tips, earned by your ability to be an entertainer, I was making over two hundred quid a week.

The problem was finding a way to keep the money safe. I mean, we were all nice guys but you didn't want to put temptation in anyone's way. Basically I knew I had to get the money out of Jersey. I had a bank account in St Hélier, my first, I put my commission into it when I got my cheque but I couldn't go near the bank with the money I was making every week. My bosses would have heard about that in five minutes, I'd have been out on my ear, lucky if the law just threw me off the island. Jersey law was French law, so someone told me. There you were guilty till proved innocent, and I was far from innocent.

Frank Cunningham in Dublin, a lovely guy who put some bit of direction on my reading, to me he was the perfect person. I know that sounds a bit highfalutin', but Frank was the truest, bluest fella you could imagine, with a sense of humour second to none. He was no relation to my hero Michael Cunningham, now working in Essex, but what great fortune to be able to say those two guys were my friends. I wrote and asked Frank if he'd mind my savings till the end of the season.

Frank said sure so every week I sent two maybe three fifty-pound notes. With that little chore out of the way I was free to work without worry, attend to the women and the wine, loving the late night ladies and the early morning music by guys I knew who played evenings for the bread, all night for the love of the music. Halcyon days and nights!

You worked hard behind the bar in the season but I never minded the long hours. Jersey was my first real chance to earn the kind of money you dreamed about. On top of this you were meeting gorgeous girls all the time, laying them practically side by side. And you didn't have to kill yourself socialising, the girls came to you via the holiday companies sending them to the hotel, and you had all the lovely Europeans working alongside you as they learned the language and how to say naughty things in bed in English. It was an amazing time for me, getting my share of the new women who were bursting out of convents, colleges, corsets and constraints as the fifties crossed the halfway line.

By midway through the season Johnnie McCusker and I had become good pals. He was still working in the Pomme D'Or as the night porter — a very good job — and he was my breath of the Liffey. Like me he was born in Dublin, we talked a lot about the place even though neither of us felt we'd live there again.

So there I was spending every afternoon in the sunshine, as many nights a week as I chose in bed with one female or another, and earning more money than I had ever seen in my life before. I ate the best of well-prepared food, I was drinking fine drinks in a very sensible fashion, so why with all this going on did I sometimes feel sort of empty inside?

For all the excitement, despite practically overdosing on sheer sensation, I knew that all in all, Jersey wasn't much good to me, not unless I decided to be celibate and use all the sex energy for writing. The idea of picking up a rich woman who'd keep me so that I could just write did hit my mind from time to time. It was a joke, really. Whatever was wrong with me, I couldn't even let a woman buy me a drink. Some kind of macho thing, back to John Wayne and a man's got to do and all that. But one thing was certain, I had to find a way to keep on scribbling. And that was never going to happen on that beautiful island called Jersey.

Up to that summer in St Hélier I'd had more than sixty rejection slips for my short stories, articles, a few poems. But I made a decision to start writing a novel, even if I only got to write one page a day. I was never disheartened by being rejected, expecting it really, somehow feeling more like a writer, following in the footsteps of some great scribblers given the same treatment.

A page a day: you'd have a big novel in a year. Imagine that! A novel written, going out in the post to a publisher.

This fantasy was the cause of me thinking I might give the fit-ups another shot. Not necessarily with George and Mae — it didn't matter who I worked for — but so that I could decide definitely, one way or the other, if the stage was for me. And, more importantly, so that I could spend most afternoons autumn to spring writing, my savings from the season in Jersey subsidising my touring wages. The thought of finishing that first novel excited me so much, gave me a bigger buzz than I was getting from any of the girls I was coming with night after night. No matter what high I was getting, especially now with marijuana creeping into our lives, nothing gave me that kind of open healthy high as the idea of being a novel writer. As September arrived I was actually starting to get a glow just from thinking about getting back to what I most wanted to do. And just for once, I'm not talking about sex or booze or drugs.

I left the island at the end of September 1955, my first priceless season behind me. Within a fortnight I'm touring Ireland with a fit-up company, only this time, like Gene Autry, I'm singing south of the border.

This came about faster than I expected thanks to Eddie Bohan, the guy helping me set my father up in the confectionery shop until Ma lost the money playing Housey Housey. I'm only back in Dublin a day or two when I call Eddie. We go for a drink together and run into the guy who owns the Top Hat ballroom in Dún Laoghaire. Your man is from Glasgow, his name is Louis de Felice, and he's looking for a singer to front his band for the coming weekend. Eddie tells him I'll do the job.

I audition with the Norman Williams orchestra who rehearse on Friday morning, de Felice is delighted with me, and I run through some numbers with the band before I head off to meet Frank Cunningham. Frank, college-educated, quit the priesthood, admitting he didn't have the vocation. He was one guy who never told me I couldn't make it as a writer because I had no education to speak of. Which is probably the main reason I end some sentences with a preposition.

I didn't mention the Top Hat gig at home. If Ma had reacted 'Jesus! What's he doing now!' I know I'd have hit the roof. Her licence to comment or criticise went out the window when she gambled my money in the Fun Palace. We were all right together chatting about nothing; no more intimate stuff, not yet anyway.

Da was bearing up, never going to be really well again, but tough like a greyhound, and very proud of his job and the living he was earning every week. You couldn't but feel good for him after all the years he'd put in living on the breadline. He was a very good man and at times I had tears in my eyes when I considered how noble he had been. I stayed in the flat for his sake really. He liked having me there and it was good to be around him for the couple of weeks I was in Dublin. I gave Ma some money but she wasn't getting any heartbeats. I might have been ashamed to carry a grudge against her over the money, but I wasn't. My anger allowed me to justify shutting her out.

The singing gig worked out all right, my appearance at the Top Hat got some newspaper coverage including a picture in the *Evening Press*. In a day or two I got a visit from a guy called Bill Costello who had heard about me on the fit-up grapevine. He ran a touring company called Bohemian Players and he offered me ten pounds a week to join his show right away. We shook hands on it and in a matter of days I was out of Dublin, on the road again.

With one or two variations, the Bohemian Players touring show was just like *Showtime Parade* with George and Mae. The same kind of plays, melodramas running for about an hour, a variety show, a raffle, and a long laughable sketch at the end to send the punters home with a smile instead of a tear.

To my amazement Bill Costello, not a bad guy, played the leading man in some of the plays even though he looked like a giant toby jug, with a huge head, a badly fitting denture, and a beer belly you'd throw into bed before you climbed in after it. His missus, a woman who gave credence to the notion of having been 'vaccinated with a gramophone needle', said, 'He'd ate a stone a spuds apart from mate if ye give him a pounda butter and a bagga salt!'

Pretty soon the missus was complaining to me, 'He hasn't been near me for months so he hasn't. That bitch isn't far off, that's where he's headin' those nights soon as he's counted the money from the door.'

That bitch was her husband's mistress, word had it she'd borne a child for Bill and he'd set her up with her own touring show. The legend suggested she was never more than forty-five minutes away from the big man, who didn't like to drive for too long with a hard-on. He hated driving in the dark when what was on his mind was driving in, in the dark, if you see what I mean.

Big Bill had a daughter, Nancy, a blonde beauty with a very good singing voice. She and I played opposite each other a lot, we sang the odd duet together. I'd say we were probably a bit in love with each other, but there was nothing to it, nothing happened between us.

It was a fact of life that girls in the Irish Free State didn't go all the way sexually as easily as those wonderful lassies in the six counties. It was to do with birth control, something that was a non-event in the twenty-six counties. A girl could be going mad for it after we'd been snogging and petting late at night, many lassies were more than willing to go over the jumps with someone just passing through town, but they were terrified of getting pregnant. You couldn't buy contraceptives, French letters, in the twenty-six counties. In fairness to the girls there was the religion thing too, though when you did find one with an adventurous spirit, *Oh Sally Come Home in the Dark!*

I did my thing on the show, singing, acting, selling raffle tickets, taking my turn in charge of admissions. The bonus for me was working with a comedian called Clarrie Daniels, one of the funniest men I have ever known. Feeding him in sketches and a couple of double acts was a real privilege for me. And I enjoyed being friends with him and his wife, Flo.

Clarrie Daniels knew the after-hours pub in every town we played — one of the benefits of having been on the road for most of his life. He needed to drink, loved Guinness and was okay once he didn't touch spirits. Once in a while someone bought him whiskey, he'd drink it like an addict getting a fix in, and in minutes Clarrie, a good skin, became a major asshole. He got belligerent, a real Jekyll and Hyde job, and one particular night I had to knock him out and carry him back to the digs before one of the locals beat the shit out of him.

Clarrie was a sad case. He had the talent to make it in the big pond. Ruby Murray had done it, five records in the UK Top Twenty within a year of working alongside him on tour. But he lacked the something extra that you must have to get into the big time.

The really important thing was that I was writing something most afternoons for three or four hours. I got a novel started in the first month of the tour, and I blocked out the plot for what might turn out to be my first stage play. I didn't mind where we were performing. We were playing central Ireland really, Meath, Roscommon, Tipperary, small towns and large villages, places with no resident entertainment such as a picture house. The audiences always seemed to enjoy the shows and life was no hardship for me. I did find myself surprised though by how many people were still living without electricity.

I left in May, bypassing Dublin on my way back to Jersey. I'd written to Ma once a week through the tour, always sending her a couple of pounds, but I didn't feel like visiting Mount Pleasant. Da was going okay, but life was grey for Ma, sad. I couldn't handle getting too near it at this time. In Ma's company, following the script she wrote for both of us down the times of our distress and want, I'd been too sad, too mad, too often. I'd swallowed enough anger to last me for a lifetime. I was out of the cage, I'd keep flying for the minute.

Within a week I was tending bar at the Imperial hotel right there in St Hélier, a no problem situation because the manager was a drunk who knew it all, so the fiddle was a doddle, the season turning out very much like the first one. I made good money mixing cocktails for girls looking for guys, with bored publicans' wives from England dropping in for a drink and to hear this Irish bartender croon with the pianist. I got no pay for the singing but the tips went through the roof after I finished chanting for the night.

I was up to my ears in good-looking girls. Some nights you went with one girl for an hour, leaving her with the impression you were off to bed — which you were, but with someone else. Maybe some of those girls were doing the same thing. We were all just looking for the high in whatever we did. Sex and booze were the staples, dope smoking was providing a new kind of hit, especially for late night music listening, and we were starting to use speed to give us the energy to do things we shouldn't have been doing anyway.

Within weeks I was surprised to find I had slipped back into the same old routine in Jersey. A month and I hadn't written a page. I started to feel I was cheating myself. Really my life was wonderful, I was free. No Ma there moaning about drink and late nights and whatever. Except there was a voice inside me that seemed to have taken over Ma's role. It was as if some part of me knew I needed protection from myself.

Then a girl called Jean Allison arrives for a two-week stay and in a matter of days I'm wishing to Christ she had stayed at home in Fulham. I didn't want her, I didn't want any female coming into my life the way she did.

When she orders her first drink, tossing me that elfin grin she wore like a great haircut, I think *tasty*, nothing more. She gets a Senior Service cigarette going, tells me to have a drink for myself. Her two mates arrive at the bar, both glamorous and curvy, but Jean, who was just Jean, left them in need of a spotlight.

She was no Miss World, and I didn't need her, no way. So it was safe to flirt with her, play the word games at which she excelled. God help any guy giving this chick any routine that smelled even slightly of Bullshit City. She was ruthless with the put-down, dangerously quick with the repartee, and not afraid to get mean if a guy tried standing on her trip. I treated her like another guy and she looked for nothing more. Jean knew she was the equal of any fella anywhere and superior to most and she never hid that from anyone.

I found I really liked her. She was refreshing because she wasn't looking for anything, as far as I could work it out, she wasn't even looking to get laid. That made her almost unique in my experience of the two seasons I'd spent in St Hélier.

Within a few days I'm keen to take Jean to a movie, so keen I agree her mates can come with us. We trundle off, the four of us, but something is happening between Jean and me. Some nights she is there when I close the bar, we have a drink and a cigarette together, and I tell her bits about my life, my dream to be a famous writer. She has two brothers, a sister. Her twin brother, Peter, died at birth; she dreams about him frequently and he is beautiful. In time she wants a husband who will be true, a home and children, dogs, and she wouldn't mind if her man turned out to be rich and famous! This last allowance offered with a huge smile, the brown eyes twinkling, her mischievous way refusing to be hidden for anybody. Her parents are still alive: 'Mum's well-meaning and very kind, change scares her.'

'Change scares everybody, just about,' I told her, meaning it.

'I can't see you being scared of much.' She grins at me and I get the feeling she wants me to kiss her.

'Listen,' I say, 'I get the feeling you want me to kiss you.'

She laughs out loud: 'You're right. But you better wait till I tell you about my father.'

'I should hear about your father before I kiss you! Does this lady know how to grab a guy's attention, or is it only a rumour!' This in my rabbi accent, probably not very good, but Jean finds it funny.

'He's a Geordie,' Jean chortles away as she tells me the story. 'He's self-made in business, he's mean and moody and he hates the Irish.'

'I can't have a man like that for a father-in-law!'

'So that's it then, yeh!' Jean nods in understanding. 'So we won't bother with the kiss, huh!'

'Oh come on,' I put my arm about her. 'You came all this way, the least you should get is a kiss.'

So Jean and I kiss each other like kids playing a game and in a few moments we are wrapped up in each other's arms and the kiss had turned into something else. But the something else doesn't turn into bed and it won't. Not with Jean in Jersey. She is hot but she's not into casual sex; she came a virgin to the island, she's going home the same way.

Saying goodbye to Jean at the airport I was sorry she was going but on the way back to town there it was again, the relief that things had been taken care of, that Jean was on her way home, neither of us in bits, having agreed we'd have a drink when I hit London in September.

We'd given our attraction for each other a walk around the block, talking endlessly, laughing a lot. At times to my amazement Jean was even funnier than me. My God! That kind of admission must mean something, I tell myself. But what? Yeh yeh yeh, we hardly knew each other, so why did I feel as though we'd known each other all our lives? Answer me that one, Harry.

Her honesty, her couldn't-care-less attitude about being in love, was that what had me going on about her in my head? Jean was about the only girl I didn't have sex with that summer. So what happened? There I was, up to my eyes in beautiful women who liked sex as much as me, in walks this chick from London and suddenly I don't want to be with anybody else. To make it worse she doesn't really give a goddam. Oh she fell in love, she admitted that, had a good laugh about it, warned me of what a cheeky cow she was, and lots of other stuff designed to drive you crazy.

I could have quit my job, gone back to London with her. She never suggested it but she wouldn't have said no. What power there was in that ability to hold back, let me work it out for myself. I was too scared to move though, I couldn't run that fast even if I hated her leaving. I needed time to digest the chronic disturbance Jean had caused.

I had dreams no sensible girl would listen to outside of a holiday romance scenario. It could be different when we met again in London at the end of September. Part of me wanted it that way but whatever had happened, *Jean and me* was taking up enough airtime to kill that idea stone dead.

The night Jean left I went to a jam with musician mates of mine and I smoked some heavy shit, deadly pot from Afghanistan. I ended up with another English chick, a striking creature, an existentialist she called herself. I wasn't sure what that meant exactly, but I wiped out the empty feeling I had about Jean by sharing her bed for several nights, before she took off with a rucksack on her back.

Johnnie couldn't understand how I could lay other females when I was so disturbed about Jean. I left him with his reservations, not feeling any need to explain that sex was like alcohol, I had to have it. And that no matter how much I got, there was no way to get enough. If only I'd been able to listen at that time I might have heard the tom-toms of addiction beating our their warning. But I couldn't listen to anybody, not even to myself.

Just days later I was down at the docks to pick up my kid brother Brendan. I hardly knew him in any real sense but I was treating him to a holiday, wondering if I might be useful to him in some way. He was bigger than I remembered, a bit taller than me, powerfully made and handsome. Well, he was my brother!

Brendan loved this little car I'd bought the day before for twelve pounds, a 1933 Standard Nine saloon that ran perfectly once you gave it a push to start. It was so light I'd run alongside it, push, jump in and take off like the clappers. Talk about joy! Your first car and your first woman — you never forget either of them.

Apart from chit-chat about the trip Brendan didn't have a lot to say. He might have been shy, I wasn't sure. As we drove into St Hélier I got to feeling that my speedy way, my high-handed behaviour, wasn't sitting well with him. I'd have bet good money he didn't like people like me.

At the hotel, before he even got his case unpacked, he said he wanted to go back home, his tone yelling *Now!* The trip had been my idea, I'd paid his fares, and maybe I had just dumped it on him. Because I'd have been delighted to get a fully paid up holiday in sunny Jersey, I'd assumed he'd feel the same way. Wrong, pal! Brendan's mouth was as tight as a double gusset, no way was he the happy camper. Maybe it was just homesickness, maybe it was just being around me!

I shrugged: 'I'll make arrangements for you to go home in the morning. Nothing we can do this evening like!'

He was all right with this, possibly relieved I accepted how he felt without trying to change his mind.

'My pal Hans, the head waiter here, nice fella, he'll look after you for dinner, I'm working the bar. You have a shower and come on down when you're ready.'

I left him alone and I got the bar open for the aperitif crowd. By the time Brendan came down in fresh clothes, I'd made a phone call to a local girl I was pally with who had a genuinely healthy interest in the opposite sex. I invited her in to meet my gorgeous brother, assuring her that if she played her cards right I would fix her up with this amazing guy.

I poured Brendan a Carlsberg Special, he killed it no problem. Two more lagers he was laughing like everybody else, like a fella on his hollyers, and it looked as though going home was no longer a priority. When I introduced him to my red-headed friend Susan, it looked as though going home was no longer even an option! Susan was a fun girl, so passionate she could have lit a fire without matches, and though I've no idea what they got up to or down to, I can tell you that when the baby brother left Jersey — going home by plane if you don't mind! — he was flying in more ways than one.

When he left the island two weeks later, he seemed like a different bloke, though he wasn't that much different towards me. Brendan would always find me hard to take and that was okay. Giving him the holiday was my little bit of effort at being his family if you like, there was no law saying it had to be a huge success. What sticks in the mind about him at that time was that he was a really nice fella, very decent in his way, deep as a well, and likely to make some woman a good husband. When he was gone that was okay too. I felt good that I'd been his big brother the evening he arrived. He needed me for sure, that one fine time. Just a pity that was the only time. Who knows, given the chance, we might have gotten to know one another, might have become pals.

I wrote to Jean about once a week and she called me a couple of times during August and I was seriously troubled by my need to keep in touch with her. Even Johnnie, who accepted that I was some kind of sex maniac, came to believe I was serious about her.

He'd been a huge fan of Jean's from the moment they met. 'She's the sort of bird you take home to your Ma. No wonder she has you bothered!' He passed me the cognac, blew smoke at the sunshine, his malicious grin a question mark.

'I'm going to go to New Zealand,' I said, surprised by what I was hearing.

'It's a long way from Rathmines.' Johnnie took the flat half-bottle back. 'Any particular reason? New Zealand like?'

'To get away from Jean, and anyway I promised my brother Mick a post-card from the other end of the world.'

He smiled, giving me the warning finger. 'She got into you and she'll be with you wherever you go.' He chuckled, delighted with himself. 'New Zealand won't cure that. And it'll cost you a bomb to get there.'

'Merchant Navy! Work my way. Want to go with me?'

'Fuckin' New Zealand! Nobody *goes* to New Zealand.'

'I'm leaving here next week before the season ends. A million waiters go on the boats for the winter. I want to get in before there's a flood.'

'You're fuckin' crazy, y'know that, don't you!'

'Hey! If I wasn't this world'd drive me nuts.' I was grinning at him. 'I'll miss you, baby!'

'You're some poxbottle! You know fuckin' well I'm coming with you.'

'We have to go next week, Johnnie.'

He nodded, bemused. 'I was the brightest kid in our school. How the fuck did I ever get tied up with you!' He shook his high-domed head and I laughed, glad he was coming, relieved too. It was a scary thing to be taking on and I already knew the value of having Johnnie by my side. We were born to be great pals, we drove each other pineapple at times, but in the crunch we were there for each other in a way that brothers can't always be.

Johnnie and I met Jean in a submarine bar in Hammersmith, west London. She'd had her hair cut short, her smile would have lit up a dark room. 'I'm really glad to see you.' She sounded surprised. I was biting my tongue not to say, 'I love you, let's get married,' and God knows what else.

We did some drinking that first evening, holiday memories, small talk. Jean smoked one cigarette after another, I took the odd one just to keep my lungs in shape for dope smoking. We got fairly jarred, dropping Jean off by cab before Johnnie and I went back to our hotel in Victoria.

The next night I took Jean out to dinner, told her about the New Zealand idea. She was great about it, she knew about my dreams to be a writer, thought I should travel as much as I could. I told her I was in love with her, that my feelings hadn't changed in the six weeks since her holiday ended. She told me it was the same for her. 'And don't think I'm not surprised, by both of us,' she admitted. 'I thought, a fortnight and it'll be ships that passed in the sunshine.'

'Speaking of ships, I'm going to try and go the Merchant Navy route, work as a waiter, y'know, a steward. If I don't get a seaman's ticket, I'll be back. I'll take it as a sign I'm meant to stay in London.'

Jean gave me a wry grin. 'The only problem with that is, I can't see you not getting in, not if it's something you really want.'

It was great that she saw me as a fella who wouldn't quit. I got a picture of us together, *till death us do part*, a couple who would never quit on each other. That made me feel warm for a second before I went cold at the idea of being tied down, being responsible to Jean or anyone.

I let it all go. Just thoughts getting in the way, they could wait. First there was this Merchant Navy thing to be handled.

Next morning, wearing my staple dark grey suit, I went into the Savoy hotel and emerged in minutes with several sheets of their stationery in my inside pocket. The Strand Palace was my next stop. That same evening I dictated the character references we needed to Jean and she typed them up on the fancy hotel paper, doing her bit to help us get our seamen's tickets.

14

According to my dictation, Johnnie and I were first-class waiters and cocktail barmen, honest, upright, sober, with a keen intelligence. I varied the words, the phraseology, signing myself as Christian le Blanc, Assistant to the General Manager of the Savoy, and Alan Chater in the same role at the Strand Palace. All fiction with a third reference from an invention of mine called the Portmarnock Country Club Hotel, County Dublin, which did not exist at that time.

This reference was full of *And may God go with them on their journey through life* and this kind of thing. So it sounded Irish the way *The Quiet Man* sounded Irish, which is how the world seemed to think of us. Why not give people what they want, spare them having to use their intelligence! As if hotels like the Savoy, where waiters come and go like snowflakes on the river, would be typing up references.

Next day Johnnie and I go down to the Pool in the East End of London. This is where seamen do their business, like a union hall. The place is full of seamen, a lot of them rough-and-ready people who didn't waste too much energy on good manners.

In one of those curious moments that crop up from time to time I chance to look at McCusker as his cigarette literally drops off his lips. His great rheumy-looking eyes are hanging out the windows and I'd go so far as to say he was speechless. I turn around wondering is it a naked woman or what, and there on the wall facing me is this sign, writ large as the fella said, for one and all to see:

FALSIFICATION OF REFERENCES CAN LEAD
TO SIX MONTH IMPRISONMENT.

I take Johnnie by the arm and lead him over to where we can lean back against a wall and get a fresh cigarette going for him. I take a fag myself, more shocked than I let on to him. Smoking eases the tension, in seconds we're over the worst.

We have our application forms already completed, with copies of our birth certificates, the phoney references attached. We go to the grille, give the paper and our money to the guy inside. He gives the stuff the most cursory glance, stamps it, more or less dumps it in a drawer in front of him under the counter. He tells us to come back next week. And that's it.

Johnnie is ready to take off. I nudge him back to where we'd been standing backs to the wall. I smoke another cigarette, trying to use it to help me think. I can't answer his question why are we waiting. I just know that something tells me to stick it out, stay where you are.

A few minutes later, twelve thirty on the dot, our man behind the grille is relieved by another guy who seems equally disinterested in his job. He sits down on the stool behind the grille like a man wishing he was somewhere else.

'Give me the cigarettes and leave the talking to me,' I tell Johnnie. He nods, hands me the John Players and follows me back over to the counter.

I wait for the guy to look up, to give us the time of day. He takes his time, this is his power point, he's got to get what he can out of it. As he finally decides to honour us with his attention I'm taking a cigarette from the packet, I say hello to your man, holding the pack out to him as though it's my second nature. Looking a bit surprised he takes the John Player, when we're lit up I tell him why we're paying him a visit.

'We left in all the necessary papers, references, the lot, last week. The guy here told us to come back today, pick up our cards.'

I inhale smoke, deeply. Jesus! Am I totally mad or what! I can't answer myself but I'm very grateful for the cigarette. 'He said the stuff would be in the drawer there.' I take the risk, just going with the flow, trying not to let the guy see I'm holding my breath, not able to look at Johnnie, who is probably wondering how we're going to survive six months porridge.

The guy is smoking on the cigarette, he opens the drawer, his eyes screwed up as he leans over a bit to avoid the smoke. He comes up with our papers, which are sitting right on top of whatever is in the drawer, gives them half a glance, nods to himself.

Fifteen minutes later, I swear to this on all that's holy, Johnnie McCusker and I walk out of that Pool with our Merchant Navy membership cards in our pockets, like a couple of mongrels after a steak dinner. Your man behind the grille is a tenner better off, and we are now free to go and offer ourselves for hire to any of the shipping companies along the Royal Albert Dock.

Again, as it happens, the first sign to catch my eye reads NEW ZEALAND SHIPPING COMPANY. I nudge Johnnie, point at the sign, he simply barks out a laugh, saying: 'You're spooky, d'you know that!'

September 1956 Johnnie and I sailed out of Southampton on the SS *Ruahine* headed for Auckland. We were going to be at sea for 31 days, a bit longer than the 114-mile overnight to Jersey.

While I threw my bags into our cabin Johnnie walked the ship, coming back to tell me she was the length of a football pitch, that she weighed 22,000 tons, carried 400 passengers, a large crew and God only knows how many tons of cargo, including the slow-slow heavy mail that you can't slip into a letterbox.

We're sharing a four-berth cabin with a straight English guy who was bent as hell about older women, and a very gentle, good-natured, screaming faggot who looked absolutely sensational when he dressed up in his Spanish costume for an Iberian evening.

I was unpacking when this very good-looking queer guy came in and draped a valise across one of the top bunks. His eyes lit up when he saw me and his mouth took on a smile that was probably a mortal sin.

He held out a girl's hand, with no more than three or four rings on it. I shook it and told him my name. He cooed so naturally you just knew he didn't know any other way. 'Well because you're so gorgeous and so very civilised, you can call me Katy.' I burst out laughing, he stepped back exclaiming dramatically: 'My God, I'm sharing a cabin with a *Straight* thinks Katy is funneee!'

'It's my mother's name,' I explained, not wanting him to think I was making fun of him. I was also wondering what Johnnie would think of sharing a cabin with a serious poof. Why didn't they put *them* together in one section?

'Well dear, I could be all kinds of things to you between here and Auckland, but I'm too young to play *Mother*!' He unzipped his valise and threw a huge suitcase up on the bunk as though it was a handbag. 'I don't suppose you're queer, are you?'

'I wasn't the last time I looked. Is that a problem?' I said it lightly but decided I needed to be very clear about things. 'As long as you don't get any ideas about me, sharing is okay.'

Katy was just one of many homosexuals on board, and with no females available for social or sexual intercourse, you could understand why poofs went to sea. When Johnnie realised we were sharing with a *bleedin' poofter*, we had a laugh about it. It was all part of the same adventure. And anyway, Katy was a nice guy.

The day started at five forty-five when the second steward, a little bloke pushing fifty, woke us up by opening the cabin door so hard it slammed back against the bunks. He yelled the usual Rise and Shine stuff that can turn you off a person very rapidly.

'Imagine being *him*! ' Katy shuddered, tumbling out of her bunk with natural agility. And so my first day as a Merchant Navy Steward, A Seagoing Waiter, got under way.

The work began with the stewards carrying crates of beer up to the bars two decks above. This was forty minutes hard graft before you served two sittings of breakfast in the saloon, the dining room.

I had seventeen passengers for each sitting and I had to wash and dry my own silverware as I went in and out of the galley carrying this oblong plastic tray that would take two large plates side by side.

In the galley you yelled your order, two breakfasts went onto the tray, you covered them with solid lids, two more plates went on on top of the lids, you put dishes of hot breads sitting on top of this lot. Keeping one hand free to protect yourself at all times, you slammed through the door into the saloon.

While you were waiting for your food order at the galley counter, you were washing and drying the cutlery already used and you had to be on your toes or somebody gave you a bollocking. There was no please and thank you in the galley, you were expected to get in and out fast without ever rushing.

When the second sitting of breakfast ended, you had to scrub out the area covered by your tables. You needed a bucket and a mop and some cleaning product to do the job and I asked the head waiter if he he needed anybody to give out the buckets and that. As a matter of fact he did and I got the job.

I'd twigged that some stewards had what were called Locker Jobs. One guy handled the jams and marmalades locker, somebody else the cheeses, and so on. With these jobs there were two bonuses: you didn't have to do Scrub Outs, and you got two extra hours overtime a day, just for putting out the stuff as it was needed and putting it away when the work was done. There was a third advantage: you were excused from serving Afternoon Tea, which was a pain in the behind, especially when we got into the tropics and you could lurch on deck in the sun after lunch, have a swim in the crew pool, unless you were serving tea.

Johnnie went mad when he heard my news. 'You jammy bastard! Locker jobs? I never even heard about them. How did you hear?'He was even more furious when he realised I was excused Scrub Outs and Afternoon Teas and we actually threw a few punches at each other in the cabin. And we were only at sea three days!

On top of the early beer carrying duty, two servings of breakfast, lunch and dinner to seventeen passengers each time, adding up to 102 people daily, who ate like insatiable gannets throughout the trip, we had to do regular Fire Drill and regular Boat Drill. This ate into your leisure time and the crew bitterly resented it. But it was Captain's Orders and you have to understand one thing when you're at sea: The Captain is God, the President, the Prime Minister — you go against him and you lose. So you hit your Fire Station on a signal and you went through the drill, a lot of the guys making jokes, which made you wonder how many stewards would be there for the passengers if there was a fire. Would you be there yourself?

Boat Drill was something else altogether. You were out on deck, the ship would be clipping along at fourteen knots which meant if you went over the side you would have real problems. I thought it was all for show, to obey regulations, keep the passengers happy, like training soldiers to shoot blanks at dummies. Like, if there was a real crunch some day, the women and children would have to hurry to the lifeboats, to get there ahead of the catering staff.

Every evening I scribbled for an hour or two. It helped keep the mind off Katy, every night the high heels, stockings, the works. And Katy looking my way all too often. She'd offered to *do my dhobi* — wash and iron all my clothes for the entire trip — if only I would sleep with her. It just wasn't my scene. Not even after ten days at sea when heteros are allowed to give one of the girls a punch up the panties.

You couldn't post a letter till we docked in the Dutch West Indies. That didn't stop me writing to Jean every evening. Yeh they were love letters, though I didn't want to be in love. Trouble was I couldn't get her out of my mind. At the same time I was torn, glad the trip was a month each way with two months spent on the coast of New Zealand. Four months should help me get anybody out of my system. I mean, four months was for ever.

The closer we got to Curacao the more I wondered would I hear from Jean. Before we left Tilbury I'd sent her a mailing list so there could be a letter waiting for me at our first port.

Curacao in the Dutch West Indies, our first port of call. I felt a real thrill being there and again I was aware of how kind the weather was. Like Jersey only warmer, with deeper colours in everything and the water so blue. A few feet under the surface with a snorkel that first afternoon I was in another world, with all kinds of technicolour fish around me as I swam.

There was a letter from Jean waiting for me. And I make no bones about my heart jumping in my chest when I read her handwritten pages. She felt the same as I did. She hadn't been looking for me when she booked her holiday in Jersey, now she couldn't wait for January when the *Ruahine* would bring me back to England. Our letters mirrored each other's. Neither of us wanted to be in love but we were up to our necks in it.

That night I drank three or four local rums that hit very hard, so that I was half-jarred before the night really got under way. We drank a lot, Johnnie and me and a couple of other guys we were pals with on the boat. So that when somebody suggested taking a swim in the Caribbean, I wondered why I hadn't thought of it myself.

'To come all this way and not have a dip would be sacrilegious,' I heard this drunken Irishman say before I realised it was me.

'Are there sharks here?' Johnnie asks this black girl he'd laid earlier in the evening, standing up apparently.

'Fack me gently, baby, it's the Caribbean, got sharks okay. But the lagoon got a shark net to protect swimmers.' She sang when she talked, she laughed a lot, her eyes were like ads for joy.

In minutes I swim out to the diving board erected against the shark net. I'm mad with drink, climbing up on the board, yelling like a madman in my naked-ness. Johnnie and some of the others are swimming towards me. I am so excited to be so far away from home, bursting with a kind of manic energy that I feel I could fly. I go soaring through the air, tearing my shoulder on the barbed wire, so drunk I don't know whether I'm inside or outside of the fucking shark net!

The pain in my left shoulder blade as the salt water hits the wound is an experience I know I won't need to repeat. Mercifully, I am inside the net. The salt in my wound powers me the fifty yards to the shore. When I fall onto the beach I pass out.

For the next three weeks I have to work through the tropical heat with a dressing on my shoulder. The bleeding is minimal but it never quits because of the heat and the hard work. Through the Panama Canal, on down to Pitcairn Island in the Pacific, I have this shoulder wound, paying dearly for my night of madness in Curacao.

You don't go ashore at Pitcairn but the descendants of Fletcher Christian and the other mutineers of the *Bounty* come on board selling souvenirs. One guy gave me a whole rake of stuff for the jeans I was wearing. They all had huge feet, any trace of their Englishness buried in their Polynesian features and their colour. As we left they were there in the swell created by the *Ruahine*, bobbing up and down, someone playing a squeezebox while they sang 'We Shall Meet on that Beautiful Shore', sounding like a very good Welsh choir. And why not — the ship that Christian took out from under Captain Bligh had set sail from Bristol.

In Auckland I had to go to a hospital. The doctor who stitched the wound told me this should have been done the day after I got hurt. I'd known this in my heart but the ship's doctor, a pompous bastard if ever there was one, dismissed me with a dressing. I asked the hospital doctor for a note to this effect but he demurred, shrugged his face. 'Let it go,' he advised. 'In the Merchant Navy you have no prayer against the doctor. He's a Ship's Officer and you, my friend, are just flotsam.'

I knew he was right. It galled me to accept it, there was nothing I could do. Maybe I was being punished for the way I'd behaved in Curacao. For the first time I had an idea that a pattern was emerging. Like, every time I did any real drinking I got hurt or into some kind of trouble. Not the odd time, or some times, every time.

This sort of nebulous scratching on my mind in search of common sense might one day produce something, but not in Auckland. We'd been at sea for seventeen days and I needed drink, lots of drink, and a good-looking woman to help me forget how lonely I was.

Before I joined my mates for a booze-up and whatever, I found a shop selling postcards and wrote one to the brother, Michael. Just to let him know, 'If I go any further than this I'll be on the way back!'

The females I met in New Zealand were a real find. The Maori women were so generous in their lovemaking I practically became an addict to one girl who picked me up in a movie house while I was having a soft drink with Johnnie and a shipmate from Surrey, Jeff Denton, during the interval.

Some guy was bothering her, she said, looking at me as though there was nobody else around. Could she sit with me for the second half? I said no problem, she goes to get a soft drink. Jeff looks at Johnnie and me, shaking his head in sheer disbelief. Johnnie just laughs.

When we go back inside, Toni finishes her drink in about eight seconds flat, she turns to me in the dark, waits until I turn to her, kisses me on all cylinders, and bam, we are into a four-day sex thing that makes it hard for me to get back to the ship on alternate nights, which is the drill while we're shoreside in Auckland.

Jeff Denton and I were two of ten stewards picked to serve food at an International Grasslands Conference at Palmerston North, quite a way from Auckland. There was some tie-up between the shipping company and the people running the occasion. We didn't give a shit, we were chuffed; it meant more money, time away from the ship and the docks, a chance to meet new people, whatever.

When we check our bags into Massey Agricultural College, we call a cab and head for the town, see what the place is like. We're going to be free every evening of the week once we serve dinner and we want to know what's available to a couple of thirsty sexual maniacs.

With careful camerawork you could have shot a Western movie in Palmerston North. A dirt street, wooden footpaths, swing doors on the saloons. Part of me believes there were hitching rails but I'm not prepared to swear to it. As Jeff and I walk along there is a guy coming towards us, his mind elsewhere so he does not see me.

In an instant I'm back in London, working at Lyon's Corner House weekends to earn a bit extra. There's this guy from Christchurch in New Zealand that I get friendly with, a nice fella, John A. Gordon. We go to see a few plays together, have a beer now and then, whatever. And when he is leaving London to go home after his world tour, I say to him in that bullshit way you do, 'One of these days I'll run into you down in New Zealand.' We have a laugh, say goodbye and that's it.

And here he is, John A. Gordon, walking towards me on a wooden footpath out in the middle of fucking nowhere in New Zealand.

'Hi John!' I say casually, pretending to walk on by.

He practically staggers back away from me in shock. His eyes bug out, he laughs nervously, am I imagining this! Then we are hugging and shaking hands and all Jeff can say is: 'I don't fucking believe this. I'm here, I'm shaking your hand, mate, I hear the story, I'm in the fucking movie, and I still don't believe it!'

To add a twist into the tail of this tale, it turns out that John A. lives in Christchurch, he is only in Palmerston North one day a month selling beer. I'm there because I got into the part of ship's waiter so well I'm picked to do the gig at the college. Just running into John A. was the miracle of the trip. That and Michael's postcard from the other end of the world.

A phenomenon from those same days was Elvis Presley coming into our lives. When we left England in September I'd never even heard of the guy. By the time we get to New Zealand he has two records in the Top Ten and along with Bill Hailey and the Comets he has lit things up brilliantly Down Under.

Jiving, which became rock 'n' roll, was something I could dance as though I'd been born to do nothing else. It was a fantastic time, as we all seemed to be trying to burn ourselves out. There was no satisfying the sensation buds — the more we got the more we had to have. By December when we began the trip back to England I felt sexed-out. Towards the end I'd been going to bed with girls just because that's what you did.

The truth is I wasn't free to be with those ladies. No matter how I tried to lose it, shake it, blot it out, the fact was I was in love with Jean back in London, and though I kept hoping for a reprieve on the thirty-one-day voyage back to England, the better part of me couldn't wait to see my Jersey girl again.

As I picked up my pay and my seaman's book at the end of the trip I was given a handwritten offer of the assistant head waiter's job on the next trip to New Zealand. Very nice if you wanted more trips to sea but all I could think about was seeing Jean, there was no way I could have committed to another four-month trip. We hardly knew each other but Jean had my heart in her handbag the day we docked in London.

Johnnie was having a good laugh at my expense. 'Don't worry, son,' he patted my shoulder in commiseration. 'I'll get you through it, I'll be your best man!'

15

Early in May of 1958 I'm on the knowledge of London. You may well ask what the hell that is. A year earlier and I couldn't have told you, but we live and learn. And I'm learning that the first fella with the streets of London burned indelibly into his mind is already through the Golden Gates and put sitting close to the right hand of God. Through Jean's older brother, Frank, I got to know that you could make wonderful wages behind the wheel of a regular taxi. Terrific, sure, but to be legally allowed to push one of those droshkies around, you first of all have to get a licence and a Green Badge. Which I was determined to do if only to prove Jean's father wrong. Dick Allison hated the Irish, he certainly couldn't stand the sight of me, and he had said to Jean that I wouldn't have the guts you needed to survive the knowledge.

To do that you have to complete this course *The Knowledge* and if you make it even halfway through, you know why the job is a high earner. Because just by doing the Knowledge you have earned the right to make oodles and have it tax-free, you should live so long!

The fella who said riding a bike is a pain in the arse, he had it right, but I had to risk it, seeing pedal pushing as the only way to take on the Knowledge. I felt I needed a slow-paced approach if I was to take in all I needed to know. A lot of guys used mopeds but since when did I ever do anything the easy way!

Going on the Knowledge is the only way to learn where the streets and avenues and hotels and railway stations and public buildings are, which streets are one-way and a hundred other things you need to know to earn a crust behind the wheel of a black cab.

The whole trip starts at the Public Carriage Office in Lambeth Road just south of the Thames. Here you're given a list of 480 possible taxi rides by a Public Carriage Officer. The way this guy looks at you tells you he doesn't give a shit if you never come back again. You soon learn that about 80 per cent of the guys signing on for the Knowledge give up before they even put their arse on the saddle.

Just to start you off as they mean to continue — treating you lousy and giving you the bare minimum at all times — the people running the Public Carriage Office give you just the street name at each end of the 480 journeys on your list. To help you build character you have to work out the rest for yourself. 'Jesus Christ! No way can I get this together. No chance,' until I thought of Da Allison and his opinion of me. I knew then I'd never give up, that whatever it took, I'd find it, show the old bastard I had guts to burn.

So I do what all the other Knowledge Boys do, I buy a large map and some sewing needles. I stick a needle at the beginning and the end of the first cab ride on the list, which reads 'Manor House tube station to Gibson Square'. I tie a length of cotton thread around the top of each needle, pulling it tight to get a straight line. Now I write into the jotter that will be my Bible for the next few months: 'Leave the tube on the left on Seven Sisters Road, left Holloway Road . . .' And so it starts, with me writing out each street name following the straight line of cotton. Then it's on yer bike, mate! For three runs a day including lefts and rights, landmarks and potholes!

In my case I have to work out one extra run. This is to get me from my room in Barons Court, west London, to Manor House tube station, which is so far north you expect to meet Eskimos. As I set off I seriously wondered if I could hack it. Was it even possible? Or was I just so in love I'd lost my reason entirely? In love with Jean, who was decorating her own apartment in my heart; in love with the dream of being a writer. Making a crust from the type-writer at my own desk in my own home, not having to go out to work. Smoking a pipe. All lovely stuff, stuff a fella could write about, but Jesus, I had nearly 500 taxi runs to write out, ride around, learn off, and then I had to get examined once a month for God knows how long by guys who hated every fella ever went to look for a taxi badge. Dare I suggest that reality can at times add new dimensions to the notion of unkind?

Sticking the doubts to the back of a drawer I'm never going to open again, right, I allow myself a year to complete the course. This marks me down as a total optimist because some guys take two to three years to earn the Green Badge. Forget even two years — I know I won't last that long. I'll ride over three runs every day, do my *Call Overs* with Jean most evenings before I hit the Dorchester on Park Lane to work as a banqueting waiter to earn the rent.

So Jean sits with my book in front of her in my little room in Barons Court and I call out, 'Call over . . .' the names of the streets and roads and avenues I've ridden across earlier in the day. I always start with the first three runs, working my way through to today's harvesting, a bit like an actor learning lines. I begin burning London into my mind. I enjoyed being on the bike once I got used to the volume of traffic everywhere, though it was no fun when it was raining. I hated wearing the waterproof cape, but as spring turned into summer I was out there in shorts and a T-shirt.

Obviously the course involved seeing all the sights from Tower Bridge to Kensington Palace and the Albert Hall, but I wasn't interested. And I can't put my apathy down to the weather. That summer's very tasty problems were women and girls in skimpy summer dresses, long bare legs everywhere and no shortage of come-on smiles from so many gorgeous English females.

What annoyed me was that I didn't feel free to smile back. Every time I did flash the come-on my guilt deepened as much as my tan was doing. Jean and I were engaged, so I wasn't supposed to be drooling at the sex parade coming at me in battalions as if some God with a wild sense of humour was trying to drive me nuts. I was like a mongrel on a *nice doggie* training course. I was on a lead and I wanted to win a prize as sweetheart of the trip but at times I ached to eat up some terrific-looking chick on the street. Somehow I stayed straight but just the workings of my head, mind and libido hand in hand, made sure I was getting no peace. *How are you going to cope with being married, till death us do part and all that*, was the constant question.

Most of me wanted to be straight, faithful, or I would never have got engaged. With Jean as my missus I could make a life, get time to write, find out if I had anything worth bothering with scribblingwise. But when the judge passed sentence: *No Other Women*, it created a lot of turbulence in my mind and I couldn't talk to anyone about it. I certainly couldn't have discussed it with Jean. Whatever Jean did she needed to be number one and that applied double where I was concerned. So feelings that seemed just as real as the noble one to love, honour and cherish and all that, those feelings got buried deep, out of sight, but this didn't stop them corroding my well-being. In a way I was back where I started, hiding my less respectable truths, not from Ma now but from Jean, who thought that the sun shone from the part of me that was getting more saddle-shaped by the week.

I rode just over 8,000 miles on that old bike of mine. Sometimes when I got home to the little room in Barons Court, I would fall down on the bed and sleep for an hour until Jean came in, bringing me some tasty sliver of Camembert, a slice of strudel, from the River Club restaurant where she worked as cashier, and all of it best welcomed by an appetite that wouldn't quit. I was always hungry, hardly surprising when you find yourself so far east of Charing Cross that you expect Poland to be the next stop.

I was in Wood Green one day, a long way from home, when I saw a trolley bus that was heading for Enfield. Seconds later I'm following the trolley. Joe lived in Enfield with my great sister-in-law, Eva — well, they lived there seven or eight years ago, the last time I saw them. Thank God they were still at the same address, the Granny Rogers gone for her tea, nobody weeping about it when it happened which seemed about fair. Not a nice woman. Neither was the Granny Dunne, so how come I loved her to pieces, sick that I was at sea when she kicked the oilcan, probably gone looking for the old moneylender who had passed on himself while he still owed her a few pound. As I turned into the street where Joe lived, the front wheel of the bike buckled under me and I did well not to hit the deck. All those years of riding imaginary bucking broncos while we were making films in the street hadn't been entirely wasted.

'Well good gawd! What a lovely surprise!' Eva threw her arms around me and in minutes Big Joe was there shaking my hand, calling out to me as though I was across the street: 'You little bleeder, taking so bleedin' long to pay us a visit.'

I felt a huge wave of surprise flash through me. Joe was so clearly glad to see me, and he looked well and happy in himself, which hadn't been the case when I'd last met him. I remembered how miserable, off colour, Joe had been during my week's visit some years before.

'What happened to him?' I said to Eva as though Joe wasn't even there.

'Got his gallstones out, Leo, stopped being a miserable git right away. Made a new man of him so it did.'

Eva was right. Joe was now a huge, jolly guy who would do anything for anybody. He overhauled my bicycle overnight, got me a new wheel, new ball-bearings for the back wheel, new brake pads.

'I'll have to get this yoke insured after all this,' I said, playing the old soldier, asking him with a deadpan mush: 'How much do I owe you?'

'I'll get the camera out before you go,' Joe came back with a chuckle. 'Get a few pictures of you I can sell when you're rich and famous!'

'I wouldn't mind going on the Knowledge,' Joe said on his thirteenth potato as we had our dinner. My niece, Janice, and my nephew, Michael, had already finished eating, they were long gone from the table. My brother and Eva were tucking in to second helpings, like a pair getting settled in for the night. I could eat but Joe and Eve were just amazing.

I felt good to see them at ease with each other, having fun, and I was double glad I'd followed my madness and the trolley bus without any second-guessing. Joe was very interested in what I was doing: 'I turn a bleedin' lathe,' he said as if he needed to spit. 'So if there's money in cabbing,' he broke into a huge grin at the very thought, 'do put me in, old son, I've a strong desire to have some money in pocket Mondays!'

In time Big Joe would become a cab driver, using my books and routes to do the Knowledge, and I will never forget the sight of him on a moped — more like an elephant riding a two-wheeled pimple. 'Fourteen pounds, six ounces at birth,' Ma used to say. Seeing him on that motorised push-bike you couldn't but believe her.

When you're working on the Knowledge you go back after twenty-eight days for your first oral exam. I was nervous, washed and scrubbed and trying to look like a choirboy that hadn't discovered hand galloping yet. You know from other guys that the least thing out of line and the examiner will shaft you and enjoy doing it. So you play the game, yes sir, no sir, three bags full sir, fuck you, sir, doing what you have to do to get what you want, the way you did with other arseholes to get other jobs in other places.

You make five or six appearances and if you're answering the questions well you're told to come back in three weeks, then it's down to fortnightly exams. By this time you're fit enough to be a jockey and why not! You're riding in your own personal Grand National, hanging onto the pommel as you begin to dream of the home stretch, the badge as the finish post.

One day you're through with the bike work, you put Trigger out to pasture, listen to your ass singing as the message filters through that this is goodbye to the saddle days. While you're on fortnights you get a job that will help you be a red-hot driver for the special test all cabbies have to take. The message from my cabby mates is that you take the test driving like an angel with balls, you don't even blink in case it's a traffic violation. Then, when you've got your badge, you get behind the wheel and become the controlled lunatic every other driver will hate even in the short time before the Nobby Stiles, piles, come back to remind you that it's no fun sitting on your bum all day.

I was washing and refuelling cabs in a garage owned by Jean's family. Her brother, Frank, had given me the job, telling me the old man was against it. This didn't surprise me, Dick Allison had no time for the Irish. Driving cabs up and down ramps, parking on a sixpence, I felt like a cowboy breaking in horses, glad I was able to romanticise a pretty shitty job. I had to stay up in spirit, I was so near to the Holy Grail, the licence, the green green badge of freedom.

Finally Dick upset Jean so badly she asked me for a Time Out, a few weeks of space. 'Maybe Dad's right.' Jesus Christ, was the old bastard hypnotising her, or what? She wondered: 'Maybe we're just infatuated,' and more of this kind of thing. I was stifled by the fear I'd already lost her to the old man. She was going to Somerset for a couple of weeks. We'd talk after that. And then she was gone and I was unhappy without being sure why. Was it just missing Jean that made me so miserable or was it because the man I hated more than anybody was getting his own way?

Wherever the misery came from I used it as an excuse to give myself a present that went in and out in all the right places. A waitress I knew gave me a night and the next day playing Mammies and Daddies. It was really enjoyable, and I felt good to know I could still pull. My ego and my guilt were a right cocktail as I got to Piccadilly Circus tube station. I had just sixpence on me, the fare to Barons Court was eightpence. I slipped through the stile without a ticket and when I got off the train I handed the Uniform my tanner and said 'Knightsbridge' although I'd got on two stops earlier. 'That's not possible, sir,' your man told me in a tense Irish accent to go with his serious, priesty face: 'We've had special checks all day at Knightsbridge, impossible for anybody to get on without a ticket.'

'Oh sorry,' I said, 'it must have been Piccadilly, yes, that's it, it was Piccadilly.' I moved to pass on but he held my arm like a guy who had done this before.

'I'm sorry, sir, I'll have to take your name and address.'

I didn't make a show of myself though I was pissed off and seriously distressed by what was happening. In the last weeks of your efforts to get a taxi badge, the Public Carriage Office went through your record with a fine-tooth comb. If you had any blemish, anything suggesting *Bent* to your name, you would be punished for it. One really decent guy I knew on the Knowledge, he was kept waiting an extra year for his badge because he'd stolen a bicycle as a teenager and got fined in court. And another thing — what if Old Man Allison found out about this? He knew everyone in the Carriage Office. They were mostly ex-cops. Dick was a long-time Freemason. Those guys all had a hard-on to wear the apron and all that. I'd given them the ammunition to neuter me, no problem. All for 2d!

When I got back to my room in Barons Court I wept when I fell down on the bed. Of all the stupid fucking things to do, all over tuppence, the price of the fucking *Dandy*. Jesus! And no Jean coming this evening with some titbit from the River Club. I felt so alone that I shook. My suede boots had got soaked on the wet walk from the tube to my room. I put them standing against the square surround of the electric ring on which I'd sent Heinz shares soaring over the previous nine months. Then I did another stupid thing, I fell asleep through some subconscious desire to just shut out the whole fucking miserable world for even a few minutes.

The smell and the smoke created by toasting chukka boots woke me up rapidly. When I mention smoke I'm talking about engine room when the ship is sinking sort of smoke and I opened the window so fast the old frame nearly dropped out into the backyard.

When the room was clear again I lay down like a guy saying you can carry me out to the firing squad cos I ain't walking! The chukka boots looked like cinders on toast, pretty much how I was feeling. Bruised blue was the colour I felt, like an indigo ache feeding off itself to create an even deeper shade of the meanest colour known to man. I felt so sorry for myself that if I was a movie I'd have been weeping at me. Not so bad I wanted to kill myself exactly but more than willing to go for my tea if some loving god would just be a little responsible and put me out of my wretchedness. Some day!

I didn't help myself in the Carriage Office by being high-handed when the examiner, a fifty-year-old haemorrhoid with eyes like dartboards, threw my tube train fine in my face like a fella having a good time.

'Yes, sir,' I said, trying to touch the cap but not making it. 'That was very unfortunate.' I told him straight: 'You can't say anything to me I haven't said to myself, sir.' Thank Christ I remembered the *sir*!

He jumped all over that. 'You broke the law, you stole from London Transport. Perhaps that's *unfortunate* in your land of saints and scholars but here in England it's a criminal offence.'

'Yes, sir,' I said, touching the cap now, all my principles flung out the window. If this stopped me getting my cab badge I really would slit my wrists. Jesus! To be so close and blow it!

'You can be grateful', he said, 'that Dick Allison and myself are old acquaintances.' And so as I got my hard-earned badge I was sick as a pup that I owed any part of it to Jean's father. Last time I saw him in the garage he'd waxed enthusiastic about my obvious willingness to earn my pay: 'You have to hand one thing to the Irish, they do work better than the niggers.'

Jean had a good laugh about the whole thing, looking better after her break. But then I hadn't said anything about the possible trouble at the Carriage Office, or that if I'd been riding my bike instead of my waitress friend, I wouldn't have needed a tube. I said nothing because I wanted to marry Jean, who was back on me now that she'd been down to Somerset to take another look at this guy Gerald, a farmer that her family wanted as her husband. Jean liked him a lot, and he'd carried a torch for her since they were teenagers going around together during summers gone by. As I hid the hurt I felt that she had gone at all, I had to allow that she was giving her old man something, anything to shut him up. She was right but it didn't help me one little bit when I faced Dick Allison. Somehow he seemed to read me, and I always came away feeling he had won.

New cabbies are called Butter Boys. When you're new to the job, hungry to earn after the long haul of the Knowledge, you don't just want to earn your daily bread, you want butter on it. In my case I wanted jam and marmalade and preserves, Jean and me having decided to get married in a year. We would have our own home, I would have a stable life and a place to write. Jean was behind me all the way. She thought I had all kinds of talent. I was giving her my earnings to stash for us, so now every time the old man put me down he made me look even better than I was.

Because I was earning well, saving real money every week, I was stronger around Jean's father. I no longer felt threatened by him so I was able to put him on the back burner in my head. All my energy was now given to the long hours on the cab, my writing on hold till we got married. I made a point of not seeing much of Jean's parents. They didn't bleed or anything. Dick didn't pretend, he was barely polite to me, about the same as he was to his wife, a decent old girl who could slice roast lamb so fine you could read the newspaper through it.

From time to time things got a bit rocky in Jean's mind thanks to her father's drip-drip refusal to just give up and leave us alone to our nice little romance. She'd been in love before, she'd remind me. How often she wondered what it meant really, being *in love*. She could sound so offhand about it, I've asked myself over the years what would have happened had Dick left us alone to get on with our in love scenario. Poor Dick hadn't the wit. He wanted his way and he went after it like a dog with a sore prick. Because he imposed so much misery on what was a good time for Jean and me, he created resentment even in the heart of his more than loving daughter, scattered stardust on the ordinary, practically forcing us into a touch of the Romeo and Juliets.

Jean and I, we became each other's heroes: me and Preparation H working my arse off to save money to get a home together for us, Jean a queen standing up for me against the main man. Dick and me faced each other when we had to — a pair of shit slingers really, ready for the Gunfight at the Fuck You Corral. Come on! *The Girl* was on my side. I was *The Chap* in the script. He was her *Cruel Father*. My life was a total cliché and it was so attractive, so seductive, no wonder I wanted to get married even though the road signs in my head screamed No Entry! After Ma and Da who could blame me wondering about marriage.

Wondering didn't stop me getting hitched to Jean in March of 1959 in St Paul's church in Hammersmith. As I stood there at the altar rail with my best man Mick Cunningham, waiting for Jean to arrive, I felt sort of happy. Only *sort of happy* because I was troubled by the number of drinks — 'a right few brandies', Uncle Jimmy said — that I'd imbibed through the early morning to get me into the role of bridegroom. It just didn't seem right and me going to marry Jean. I shrugged off the criticism, though I knew I shouldn't be drunk, which I was.

Uncle Jim Rogers — Jimbo — had stayed the night with me at the house Jean and I were buying. A serious booze-up the night before had left the pair of us in need of repair, or maybe it was demolition. Jimbo was the man given the job of looking after Ma, who was doing a fairly good Lady Macbeth about me hitching up in a Protestant church.

This was a joke really, Ma throwing shapes after a lifetime of token cap touching to religion. It had never meant anything to her beyond its worth as a creator of some kind of social order. But nobody went to sleep when Ma was *on*! Jim handled her no problem and she allowed him to take her to a pew. He was getting on in years but he was still a mighty kind of a man, with a huge baritone voice and a great live and let live attitude. Smart in a quiet, low-key way, a guy that never read a book in his life. With Ma down off her high horse things were grand — quieter but grand. I laughed as I remembered Alfie Heffernan: 'You should do well with the acting all the same, with your mother like!' Jean loved that story.

My sister Rose didn't get to the wedding though she lived not that far away in Berkshire. She'd begged me some weeks before not to marry a heathen. I swear to God! In my room in Barons Court while her two small children looked on, me asking Rose to take it easy, she might scare Gillian and Paul. I didn't give a damn what Rose thought or said, but I'd do a lot any day of the week to stop any kid being frightened by stupid adults.

Jean loved me on her wedding day just as I meant it when I made all those pledges at the altar. We danced the legs off each other as her family did us proud with a reception to remember. We stayed in our own little house on our first night, both of us so tired, Jean tipsy, me three sheets in the wind. But no harm, we were in our own home, in each other's arms, and by the time our honeymoon in Cornwall ended, I felt we were in each other's hearts for all the time that was left to us.

Our house was pretty good. Terraced, built about 1880. It came with a sitting tenant in the ground floor flat. Jean and I had a huge lounge, one bedroom, kitchen, bathroom, with everything we needed to enjoy a very comfortable life. And it really was *ours* since we'd worked and saved to buy it. We had a mortgage of course, but since it cost just £1,800, we expected to pay it off in no time.

As I stacked my books on the shelves in our lounge I felt good that they had a permanent home. I still have those copies of *War and Peace*, *Anna Karenina* and *Crime and Punishment*, bought for sixpence each in a junk shop above Kentish Town, not far from Highgate cemetery where I used to go and pay my respects to Karl Marx, who actually wrote *Das Kapital* in London.

Right from the earliest days in the library on Rathmines Road, my reading had been voracious. Later, thanks to Frank Cunningham, I got some idea of *necessary* reading if you like, books that were a must and writers that certainly deserved many a visit. Frank was a great Somerset Maugham fan, 'A master of the English language,' so he said, 'without being too heavy.' I loved Maugham's *Cakes and Ale* and *Of Human Bondage*. I wasn't looking for messages or anything, just reading. I remember yet how he took me down the alleyways of south London to the hovels and the grovels of the kind of people you'd only meet in Impressionist paintings.

Frank recommended the work of A.J. Cronin. How right he was. The *Keys of the Kingdom* had my heart in the palm of its hand from the opening pages. The priest in the story was a great man and I believed in him all the way, glad to meet him, a Christian being so unlike the clerics of my early days. Nevil Shute grabbed me with *A Town Like Alice* and *No Highway*. Behind them there was one long list of writers I admired. I found Hemingway, wonderful John Steinbeck, the great Thomas Wolfe — *Look Homeward, Angel*, my God, to write like that! F. Scott Fitzgerald and *The Great Gatsby*, maybe the greatest American novel ever. I've never forgotten 'where ashes grow like wheat into ridges and hills and grotesque gardens', the tragic waste of Jay and Daisy's chapter of the American Dream.

To me reading was as simple as eating, it wasn't something you had to work at or study or whatever, you just had to do it to live. I got a list of the classics, recommended reading, and I worked my way through like a fella doing some kind of educational Knowledge, minus the bike and the piles. Reading *Madame Bovary* was like having surgery with just a few aspirin for the pain, but you kept this to yourself, not wanting to appear dim or un-sophisticated. There were many more *great* books like this that did nothing for me in any sense. Then again something as simple as *The Catcher in the Rye* could grab you, hold you, without you ever having to wonder what the hell am I doing reading this. I can still see the cab driver's face when Holden Caulfield asks him about the ducks when the pond in Central Park ices over. I laughed at that man's expression: 'Now I have heard it all!' I think that along with Salinger's book, the stories of O. Henry, Dashiell Hammett and Raymond Chandler were a great help to me.

Later, Ken Ware, a writer I worked for at the BBC, gave me Elizabeth Smart's *By Grand Central Station I Sat Down and Wept*, saying something like 'We should live so long!' This was a milestone book, prose poetry beyond my wildest ambitions, written by a magnificent woman I would get to know later around the Queen's Elm on the Fulham Road. Another book never to be forgotten called *A Day No Pigs Would Die*, written by a guy called Robert Newton Peck who loved his 'Sharer' father even more than I loved Da, and wrote about it in a way that I could only dream of. So many, so many books to live for.

Jean was a good reader herself. She thought *Anna Karenina* was a greater book than *War and Peace*. I went back and read them again, coming to like Anna K the more, tasting the sexiness of that doomed love affair so beautifully carved out of Tolstoy's Russia, the echo too big and vast and powerful for an individual to make, the voice like the rumbling tumbling tone of the universe itself filtering through before the writer died in the stationmaster's shelter at a Russian railway station.

Mark Twain was another one, his writing so simple, capturing so perfectly the idiom of his time and place, the rhythm of his environment, if you'd read him you'd been there and lived there so that you'd never forget all Samuel Clemens (his real name) shared with you, without ever trying to be a writer. He just told you the story, making it seem so simple. Which of course it is, once you remember not to confuse *simple* with *easy*. Colette did the same thing, you just knew you could write like that, till you tried it. Learning later that she worked her buns off to deliver her tales in that easygoing style.

Carrying my first ever typewriter home from the shop, tasting the glory of getting something I really, really wanted, excited to the point where I couldn't wait to get stuck in, get the stories out before they choked me. So with a copy of *Pitman's Teach Yourself Typing* on the kitchen table, I went to work one Sunday at ten in the morning, spent the first half-hour just returning to the home keys, following the instructions from there like a good little altar boy, and I swear to God, by ten o'clock that night I was touch-typing — slowly, sure, but typing with all fingers without looking at the keys. Achieving this, and it was to me a great win altogether, it gave me a buzz I've never forgotten. Writing in longhand was fine, it just wasn't fast enough, I needed more speed to punch down the words that were fighting to get out.

So I began to write each evening after work, having picked Jean up from her job on the way home. We passed on the early evening food quite a bit because we were making love every time we looked at each other. Jean was one lady who never had a headache! When we did have dinner, we'd eat at our kitchen table — Jean was a gifted cook. I'd work on the portable there once we'd got the dishes out of the way. Within a few months we bought our own taxi, more responsibility yeh, but you could earn more, and we intended getting a driver to use it when I was at home writing. Jean's idea more than mine, she was the practical one of the family.

A while after this I saw a letter in the *New Statesman* magazine from a guy called Maurice Girodias who ran the Olympia Press in Paris. He was interested in receiving manuscripts from English writers, 'preferably tending towards the risqué'. I didn't even have to think about it. I was so full of sex, I loved doing it, thinking about it, talking about it, reading about it, and I was so convinced it was the reason for everything, I knew I could write a horny book no problem. So I took ten days off the cab to knock out a book called *Hell is Filling Up*. It was about a guy arriving at a house, waves lapping the rocks below, to ghost-write a book for the sexy lady owner who has a couple of man eating daughters. Not too intellectually demanding, you understand, the romance of it appealed to me, wishful thinking clearly the genesis of what turned out an entertaining, sexy thriller. It was the first book I ever finished and I sent it off to Girodias in Paris, not knowing he had published Brendan Behan and God knows who else, often under pen-names since his company name was synonymous with pornography.

About six weeks after this I have a leaking gas pipe in the front hall of the house. An engineer from the Gas Company arrives and rolls back the lino inside the front door to raise the floorboards and deal with the leaky pipe. He does the job, puts the lino back in place and takes off. Next morning the smell is still there. The guy comes back, I decide to hang around, my presence designed to help the soft prick do the job properly this time. When he pulls the lino back there's an oblong envelope lying there on the floorboards. Obviously the letter came through the door the previous day, the guy hadn't noticed it and just put the lino down over it. And it might be there yet if I hadn't felt snotty about his attitude to his job.

The letter was from Maurice Girodias accepting the book and asking me if I could write him another one straight away. He would pay me $600 advance against royalties, he enclosed a contract which seemed extremely generous to my innocent eye. It didn't matter. I'd have signed my life away to get a book published, even one I wasn't ready to put my name on. I told myself I was keeping my name for my First Novel, if you don't mind. But really, I just didn't think it was a good idea to put my name on what the Americans would call A Hot Book, maybe even A Dirty Book! So for that first story I used the name Peter O'Neill.

Jean was very impressed, my mates were very impressed, let's face it, I was very impressed! I mean the first book I'd put together, in ten days at that, and this guy was willing to publish it and pay an advance. And he wanted more. Believe me, I didn't think it was the sequel to *The Book of Kells* or *Ulysses* or anything like that. It was a potboiler, a train ride, plane ride book, all action and sex and violence with the kind of snappy dialogue you got in some of the old movies with Cagney and George Raft and Bogart. What mattered most was that a professional, someone who made his bread publishing books, was saying *You Can Write*.

I called the second book *The Corpse Wore Grey*, the big twist being that the dead guy had been stuffed into a suit of armour which stood there while everyone was running around like blue-arsed flies until inevitably the hallway began to smell like a Gorgonzola factory. Anyway, Girodias bought the book and asked me for another one.

While this was going on Jean produced a miracle of her own, our first-born child, a girl who to this day warms my heart just by saying 'Hi Dad!'

Sarah landed on my heart on 31 July 1961. I held her in my arms in a beautiful kind of joy but awestruck and just a little scared at the same time.

Jean was pretty well wiped out, she didn't even want to talk about the labour, telling me in a whisper that she didn't think she'd ever be able to have sex again. I let that go by, thrilled more and more by every second of holding our daughter, and without trying I managed to move Jean to tears when I said, 'Thank you for our baby girl.' Moments later she snorted down her nose at me like a horse as I asked, 'Can we call her Cassidy for Sean O'Casey?'

'No we fucking can't,' Jean warned me. 'We're calling her Sarah. Cassidy Dunne! Jesus!' You could have bottled her derision. 'Who'd do that to an unfortunate child!'

Tired though she was Jean was already very naturally into the role of mother with Sarah, who was making noises in search of the nipple. Jean seemed so easy about it all, as though she'd been doing it for years.

In my own demonic way I was determined to be involved with Sarah from day one. I shared the caring, the night feeds, nappy changing, the lot, leaving out the breastfeeding. I wanted our baby to know that her father was there for her too. I thought that might be good for a child. As usual, my intentions were the best once I wasn't out on the street starring as Jack the Lad.

About a year after Sarah was born Jean took an evening job to get some time out of the house. The money she earned took some of the responsibility off my shoulders. I was still driving days on the cab, writing most evenings. Now I willingly looked after Sarah while Jean went off to the El Cubano, a trendy restaurant in Knightsbridge. I loved feeding her and changing her and just seeing that she was comfortable. Those times were among the best I'd known in my life, when just for a change I wasn't looking for anything, only wishing to be useful and loving and reliable.

Meanwhile I'd met a guy who hopped in the cab one day on his way to commit sin. His name was Jack Connell in those days and we made such a great contact that when I got my six author's copies of *Hell is Filling Up*, he just had to get one of them — whether he wanted it or not! Jack was a well-read guy, bright, street smart, used to rubbing shoulders with all kinds of brains and bullshit in his job as manager of Finch's pub on the Fulham Road, for me the all-time mecca of pubs. My going in there probably changed the course of my life, and not for the better.

Jack introduced me to everyone as the Gabby Cabby. Through him I met writers and painters and sculptors, musicians too, seriously bohemian people who worked hard and played hard and thought that rules were for the children of a lesser god. So you might say I'd landed on my feet!

I'd been two years married, my daughter was lighting up my life more and more, and I still believed I'd never want any woman but Jean. I spent all my time at home, rarely went anywhere except to work and down to Craven Cottage to watch Fulham play, or to Stamford Bridge to watch Chelsea. In my heart I was a Man United supporter but I only got to see them a few times a year. I went to football with Tony Hillier, a cab driving mate I wrote songs with, songs that went nowhere. Tony was a Fulham fanatic, a guy who only saw eleven players instead of twenty-two. And he always said, 'May the best team win,' leaving out the words 'As long as it's Fulham!' Two or three years after Tony and I quit writing together, he won the Eurovision Song Contest with 'Kisses For Me' sung by his group Brotherhood of Man. What can I tell you!

I liked having a home, being married, and now that I had a daughter I was happily a home-bird. What drinking I did, and it could get fairly heavy on weekends, I did it in Jean's company. Johnnie came by when he was home from the navy, Phil Connolly, my mentor from the Pomme d'Or in Jersey, would drop in. We usually played poker late into the night, and drink was never scarce. Connolly was a fierce drinker, never social, always looking to get pissed. And I was never behind the door when it came to bending the elbow. But even so there was none of the mad carry-on that inevitably led to promiscuous behaviour on my part. Not until I became a regular in Finch's pub.

Meanwhile, Girodias in Paris sends me a sample chapter as a guide to *how hot* he'd like the next book to be. These pages are designed to raise the blood pressure, a book like this would probably sell very well to guys about to spend a year on a whaler. I'm not sure about this, it's not the route I planned for myself, but I start to work on a story that could have carried a strong sexual theme. Maybe it doesn't have to be as sexy as Girodias wants it to be. The first evening I knock out about twelve pages before Sarah begins to whimper in her cot. In a flash, I have her out of there, I make sure she's dry and burped and not in need. She's ready to go back down but I sit with her in my arms for a while, just enjoying the weight of my baby girl, the gentle sound of her breathing. There's something on television but I have the sound turned down. I don't need to be entertained, I'm quietly happier than I've ever been, flattered by the total trust of my daughter. Fanciful? Maybe. But that's how I'm feeling and later, when I do put Sarah back in her cot, I tear up the pages written for Girodias. Why? What difference! I just know I don't want to write gratuitous sex for the man in Paris. Which is how the first leg of my writing career comes to an end.

16

In Finch's pub I met a girl who was working on a television series called No Hiding Place. She brought me a copy of the script in rehearsal at the minute. I read it and I knew I could write better than this. Once you could see the right spot to get your natural breaks in, you were halfway home, provided you had a story. And I had hundreds of stories running all over my head.

I called this first TV script of mine *Who Killed Cock Robin?* My friend read it. She made a point or two, I agreed, did the retype. She felt it would probably help if I put her down as co-writer. I didn't feel at all happy about this, it was my script, but if it meant getting in the door, I would go along.

The script was bought by Rediffusion, it got reviewed, not that usual for a run-of-the-mill cop show, and it got reviewed very well indeed. The TV guys wanted another script, but my friend now believed we were co-writers. She would say this to people in my company, it wasn't true, and I couldn't be around it. So we parted company, Penny and me, the TV company and me. Good or bad, I wasn't going to be anybody's co-writer!

At the BBC TV studios in Wood Lane, Shepherd's Bush, I met a story editor called Ken Ware, a real human being. So I opened up to the guy, told him about my dreams and all this energetic talent that seemed to be bursting out of me. Ken Ware took a chance on me, gave me a commission for a script, introduced me to some other guys who were okay. That was Ken. If he couldn't do you a good turn he'd never do you a bad one. He and his wife, Liz, were never less than decent to Jean and me.

Thanks to Ken people started to mention my name in the television scriptwriting world and during the next two years I wrote for many of the current TV shows, things like *Taxi* for Sid James (who later died while working on stage at the Victoria Palace), I contributed to *Callan* which starred Edward Woodward, *Vendetta* starring Neil McCallum, *Troubleshooters* starring Ray Barrett. I also wrote some television plays, comedy scripts, and got a commission from Patrick McGoohan for a *Dangerman* episode that never quite reached the screen. I was sorry about that because I thought the series was superb.

In 1962 Jean and I moved to a bigger house at Hertford Avenue in East Sheen, halfway between Putney and Richmond. The house was mock Tudor, semi-detached with a garage for the cab, the avenue was tree-lined with Palewell Park at the top of the road and not much further on Richmond Park itself, which was magnificent. Jean and I were the envy of our mates but what really mattered was that Sheen was a great place to live in, our kids would get a better start than their Da got.

Our son, Peter, was born in our bed at the house in Sheen, on 3 July 1963, literally popping out of Jean as I came back into the bedroom with boiling water. Peter came in as a wonderful fella. Sarah had been a lovely baby, easy on us in every way really. But our first son, we didn't see the colour of his eyes for six months! He took the diddy like a gentle carnivore, he dumped like King Kong, but for the most part, well, as the man said, he slept like a baby.

A couple of weeks after Peter arrived I bought a twelve-album pack of classical music from Reader's Digest, I also purchased *Encyclopaedia Britannica*. I was going to read it to my children, playing the classical music in the background. I would always be available to them, I would never dismiss any single question they asked, and I would never say no. Other parents said *No*, not me! I'd say *Can We Talk About This?* I would be their friend as well as their father. Such were the dreams I took into fatherhood, a child myself who hadn't yet discovered the difference between being childlike and childish. Had I even set foot on the long hard road to that particular discovery? I'd no idea.

Jean had taken on my friends, so Johnnie and Phil Connolly, Pat Glasser and Jeff Denton spent a few days with us to wet Peter's head. We played poker, sang, I cooked for all of us while Jean took it easy, we had a good time. Jean never cared how much I drank once I was at home. But from our earliest days she worried about me and pubs, especially when I had taken the cab with me. And especially when I went to Finch's!

Through a connection I made in that pub I was getting acting work in TV commercials, starring in several, one of them for Harp lager which was made by Guinness in Dublin. I was cast as *Leading Drinker*, the advert was shown in Ireland and of course Da loved seeing me on the box. His remark to Ma that he was 'glad all his time in boozers wasn't wasted!' was typical, cheering me up because it meant he was still full of piss and vinegar, lots of life in him. Thank God for the TV work, the daytime traffic had become murderous on cab drivers, and I felt miserable just thinking about going back out into the nightmare day after day.

By this time I had broken my marriage vows with a passenger one late night in the cab. A blowsy woman who made no bones that she would like to get laid with me, her street sound turning me on like a light switch. I got in the back of the FX3 with her, pushed everything else out of my head and threw whatever standards I'd been hanging onto out the window.

I'd been tempted before this in Finch's, where there was a certain bohemian attitude to sex. Here you could find women wanting a good seeing to who didn't give a damn whether you were married or not. I got to thinking that my battle to stay straight made me more attractive to the Finch's ladies. It must have done because once I put my spurs on in Fulham, I spent more time in the saddle than Roy Rogers and Gene Autry put together.

Finch's, the Queen's Elm, the Salisbury in St Martin's Lane were great pubs by any standards. Because they were used by actors and writers, painters and journalists, females more than willing to go over the jumps flocked to them. Not the kind of place any sensible, sincere married man should be doing his drinking in. But I couldn't stay out of them.

It wasn't all sex, there were plenty of laughs too, amazing characters, some famous now, others on the high stool in the sky. I got a glow from being part of that wild time — there was more to the 1960s than the Beatles — proud that I could hold my own as a storyteller with the best. Pride of course, as the man said, goeth before the fall. In Finch's loo someone had written on the condom machine *This machine will soon be out in paperback by Lee Dunne!* I laughed at this along with my mates but it hurt. Even though I believed totally that there was no such thing as bad publicity, I had to admit to an awkward grudging need for respect in the eyes of others.

The adultery scene was getting to my guilt, but a few jars could help me kid myself it was all right. I was a writer, different to average blokes, I was some kind of artist, I needed the stimulation the forbidden fruit provided. There was no limit to the bullshit I could come up with, I could have alibied murdering somebody in those days. But inside where you hide the stuff you can't deal with, there was no kidding the fella who lived in there. It took many another drink to blot him out for a while, to forget him entirely, him and everything that might get between me and what I wanted. Not that I wanted that much. Just real fame and a fantastic fortune, a rock-solid marriage, the love of my wife and children, and the freedom that artistic people needed to indulge in extramarital sex and lots of boozing, without the wife or anybody else giving them a hard time.

By 1964 I was leading a very busy double life, as though there wasn't enough work, pain, responsibility in playing one part in a huge live-in soap opera. I was working the cab nights, earning some money, not enough because I drank and met women and got laid. Sometimes I'd be with a woman for a couple of days, my taxi parked somewhere, God alone knew where. Often I could be found wandering around Fulham, Chelsea, Hampstead, looking for the cab, no memory at all of where I'd left it, or when. I never set out to lose my memory, I never intended to drink enough for that to happen. But once I got one or two drinks into me, common sense deserted its post, I wasn't there any more to look after myself.

It's no lie to say that when I had drink taken I could turn into a madman. Not a bad guy, but a mad guy, a had-to-be-glad guy, sometimes a sad guy. If I said I just lost control, more bullshit. I threw away any wish to be in control, and I was guilty of this in some situations where I might well have lost my cab badge, put the tin hat on my marriage. Thing is you knew this at the time. You know a certain scene is crazy, you should leave it alone. But there's this mongrel looks like you and he wants to walk the wire, and you go with him because he's more fun than you are. Or so you tell yourself.

Like the night in Finch's, this redhead who claimed her reputation as a nympho with a throaty laugh that sounded like a happy orgasm. She was structured to commit every shade of mortal sin known to man, good-looking with it, and so overt in her way that all you had to do was stand in front of her. If she fancied you that was it. And this night in Finch's, St Jude finally came through and she chose me.

We get out of there and in the back of the cab which is parked just around the corner in Gilston Road we are getting vulcanised at the mouth. She is crazy to have sex but she is not as crazy as I am, since I am willing to go right there in the cab under the street light. She tells me to take her somewhere, anywhere, so that we can strip off, do the thing properly.

At this time I'm buying my fuel from a guy with a private garage off Draycott Avenue. He has a diesel pump, you fill up, sign for the juice on the honour system, you pay him monthly. He has a two-car garage, mostly only one motor is parked there, so I hurry around to the mews. I'll drive into the space, shut the doors and just trust St Jude to keep me alive long enough to remember what this amazing creature is going to do to me, God bless her!

Wouldn't you just know it — this night both spaces are full. Not to worry. People were used to seeing cabs come and go to fill up. I park right outside the garage door, I'm into the back of the cab, find the lady wearing only perfume, shed my gear, dive into the moment. In no time it's like being in a big sack with a bunch of rattlers. I can't say how long we're glued at lip and hip, I am so buried in the proceedings that when I hear a fairly rugged knock on the window of the cab, I think I'm imagining things. There it is again! An urgent rap on the window of the cab. My heart almost stops beating. If this is a copper on foot patrol, I'm in serious trouble.

The cab's steamed up like a Turkish bath, there is another rap on the window that sort of scratches across my brain. I rebel. Fuck it! I'm not going to shiver over this. I'm not going to beg or plead or any of the rest of it. I'm caught redheaded, and like it or not I'm getting the chance to live up to my motto — *Do what you like as long as you're willing to pick up the tab*. More bravado, sure, but I could be like that when something got up my nose. I move away from the lady, who is lying back, her amazing breasts looking right at me as I haul down the window.

Standing there is a guy wearing a cab badge. As he sees beyond me to your woman in her magnificence, his eyes come out on stops. I'm not even sure he's breathing, it's as if he's hoovering into his memory bag as many shots as he can get of the finery nature's bestowed on my redheaded friend.

If fried bread could talk it would sound the way he does when his voice comes through: 'Excuse me, mate. Sorry to disturb you. Could you move your cab up a bit, I need to get some diesel.'

I'm so relieved I want to kiss the guy. I'm so happy I get out of the back of the cab, forgetting I'm in the Jeyes Fluid, get in the front, start the cab, shunt it up five or six yards. I salute the other driver as I return to Red. He looks as though he's having his envy cut out with a hacksaw. Thanks to his appreciation of my Adam and Eve act my reputation as a raver went right through the roof — every cabbie in town heard about it.

I always went to work on the cab well dressed and well aftershaved. It was a habit more than vanity, though I was very vain as well. I'd worked in hotels, around food and drink and people who expected you to look right and smell right. This was a big help when it came to pulling women on the cab, and before long I introduced a gimmick that attracted females like flies to a light bulb. I discovered that the driver's cabin on the FX3 taxi was like an echo chamber; when you sang up front it could be heard back through the six-inch gap the sliding window allowed. So I'd moved on, no longer needing to be jarred to cheat on my marriage vows. When I went out to work, I went out with the intention of having any woman who wanted me. I felt entitled, telling myself this was how I was.

This was early 1964, I was working nights. London was a twenty-four-hour town; sometimes in a few hours at night you could take more money than you'd earn driving around all day. And you got *Mysteries* hailing you during the dark hours. Mysteries were women of the night, not prostitutes, though we got a lot of business from them, but girls who worked as escorts, nightclub hostesses, sometimes waitresses interested in a buzz after doing an evening shift in a hotel. And married ladies who'd had a few jars and could be very interested in a bit of rough on the side before going home to hubby.

To facilitate my new scenario, I dropped some Three in One oil into the channel housing the sliding window in the partition between the driver and the female passenger in the cab. After midnight I only picked up ladies. When the fare told me where she wanted to go I made sure she saw me shut the sliding window, knowing when I made the first left turn the window would slide open. You slowed down for right turns because you didn't want the window to slide shut again. Then I'd sing. I'd sing Sinatra, standards, love songs, all those lovely lyrics coated in self-pity, and whether I did his voice or not, I knew every inflection from endless listening to *Songs for Swingin' Lovers* and just about every other album he ever recorded.

This was the most successful gimmick I ever came up with for making time with women. One night a Mystery got in the cab, I started singing, and in three minutes we were making love. Sometimes on a weekend you could touch for six or seven different passengers. I swear to God, if Frank Sinatra had known what I was doing with his songs he'd have charged me royalties!

So I was drinking too much, sexing too much, not working on the cab enough, but I seemed to be getting away with it, thanks to Jean who was working away at the El Cubano, our Spanish au pair girl Conchita looking after the children. Yes, I seemed to be getting away with it until one morning I woke up with a very severe rash all around my genital area. My Man, John Thomas, was in the clear which gave me some relief but it looked as if I was in serious trouble.

I spent a week in Princess Beatrice, the hospital in Earls Court where Sarah was born. Remembering how I first held her in this same building did nothing to alleviate the shame I was stuck with. Nothing was working; all the medication, the creams, the lotions and the potions, they were a complete waste of time. They took me by ambulance to a hospital specialising in skin diseases. I was very depressed by whatever was happening to me. All the blood tests had been negative, thank God, but I was still very sore. The hospital was a long way from where we lived in Fulham so I saw Jean just once a week. She didn't have a lot to say to me — we talked about the kids, day-to-day things. She was glad my tests were negative, so she said, but overall, she didn't seem all that interested in me. And I couldn't blame her.

After a couple of weeks this young doctor took a long look at my problem. He asked me if I was doing anything that was making me feel guilty. I didn't admit anything and he seemed to understand that. Then he said in a gentle, man-to-man way: 'Allow me put it this way. If you are doing anything to make you feel guilty, you either stop doing it, or you stop feeling guilty about it. Understood?'

I thought about what that young medic said to me and I decided I would stop playing around. I would pull in the horns and if I got rid of the rash I'd never be unfaithful to my marriage vows again. Whether I was kidding myself or not, I meant what I said, and I repeated it like a prayer all through that same evening. Next morning when I woke up in the hospital bed the rash had disappeared, and within days I was discharged and sent home. I didn't keep my promise to monogamy, and I didn't consciously decide that I wouldn't feel guilty. But the rash never came back and I often wondered was I brain-damaged or what? Like, even the psychosomatic process gave up as though it decided I was a hopeless case.

In September that year I sat down to write a story. This was a short story I needed to write, a nagging idea that wouldn't go away. It was based on how I felt morning after morning for three and a half years as I rode down the hill past McGrath's pub onto the Ranelagh Road going to work in the insurance office. The hundreds of times I'd said, choking on the vehemence I felt: 'Some day I am going to say goodbye to this fucking place!' wishing something would happen, something, anything that would help me get me away from the flats and another Mount Pleasant Monday. In six weeks the short story had written itself as *Goodbye to the Hill*, the novel that would change my life.

Jean loved it, it was dedicated to her, and she was a bit proud of me. I showed it to a couple of mates from Dublin, painters both, Joe and Kathy Magill. They said it was wonderful, maybe a bit horny for the Irish censor. I didn't care about that. I had no interest in Ireland. I had no intention of ever going back there, even for a visit. As far as I was concerned Ireland should be given back to the leprechauns, with apologies!

The Magills said, 'Try Hutchinson's, they published Brendan, maybe they'll go for this.' They were talking about Brendan Behan, who was a big mate of theirs. I'd had jars with Behan a few times, I didn't like the way he put people down. But he was *a name*, so I dropped the manuscript into Hutchinson Publishers, in Great Portland Street, trying with all my heart to write it off for at least six months. This didn't work. From that moment on, no matter where I was or what I was doing I was wondering would they go for the book.

Three weeks later I'm in the Queen's Elm just down the Fulham Road from Finch's. I'm fairly jarred, not happy, feeling as though part of me is missing. Maybe my better part, Jean, who is at home with our two children being the good mother she is. Then Jean is there beside me and she hands me a piece of paper. 'A guy rang about your book. This is his phone number.' She is trying to be friendly but she is hurting, her face saying: 'What do fucking pubs have that your wife and your kids and your own home can't give you!'

'It can't be about the book, Jean. It's only three weeks since I dropped the manuscript in.'

'Suit yourself.' She looks at me. 'I'm going back home.'

'It can't be,' I say, knowing it can't be about the novel.

'Fuck you!' Jean storms away from me.

I go to the phone and talk to this fella Anthony Masters, a writer of short stories, who earns his living in publishing and reads manuscripts in the evenings for publishers. A published writer with a good reputation, as I find out later. He telephoned to tell me how much he enjoyed my book. He was not supposed to call writers, but was so taken with the story he wanted to say hello, to tell me that he would be recommending the book for publication. When the phone call ends I stand with tears running down my face, then just for once I do the right thing and get a taxi to take me home to Sheen. I want Jean to be the first to know the news, that somebody in the business thinks I have written a book that ought to be published.

When I get home Jean is not there. Conchita has everything under control, so I walk down to my local, the Halfway House at Priest's Bridge, and proceed to tie one on in a quiet private celebration. Well, the book is over the first hurdle. A while later Jean arrives in. Conchita has told her where I am. I buy her a drink, she tells me she's been talking to her pal Betty Clarke, asking her is this the way marriage has to be. 'Because if it is,' Jean says, emptying her gin and tonic, indicating more, 'then I don't expect to be married to you till death us do part.' She sniffed back her tears. 'And when we got married, that's what I wanted. So I'm just letting you know. I've been on your side, positive all the way, even with Dad. If you ever turn me off enough, that'll be positive too. You remember I said that.'

I promise her the sun, moon and stars, wanting to mean that I would never stray, never not be there, all that it would have been good for a woman to hear if she could believe it. I don't know whether Jean does or not, but she only needs a halfway fair shake to let go of her anger. We make love that night, but we don't melt into each other the way we used to. Having her cigarette afterwards Jean says, 'Congratulations, you bastard!' I let that one go and for a while after that things are a little better between us.

Hutchinson want to publish the book! I am knocked out. I mean this is not Olympia Press publishing Peter O'Neill. This is one of the world's largest mainstream publishing houses and they love *Goodbye to the Hill* by Lee Dunne. I swear, if I hadn't been sitting down I'd have had to ask for a chair. This young editor says to me: 'It's autobiography of course.' I say no, it's a novel. He's surprised. 'Surely it's just your life story.'

'Are you serious!' Now I am surprised! 'I couldn't write my life story. If I told everything my mother would skin me alive. What's the most auto-biographical part?'

'Where the younger brother, Larry, dies of tuberculosis.'

'I never had a brother called Larry, never had a brother died from anything. If you don't believe me you can ask Ma.' I sit back, knowing he believes me, that I amn't lying. 'Thousands of kids died from TB in Dublin in the forties. Larry was for them. I wrote him for them, the ones nobody knew about except their relations. I cried when I wrote that. Poor fuckers!'

So Hutchinson would publish the story as the novel it was, I signed a contract, they gave me £50, the first third of my advance, and I walked down the street to where I'd parked the cab feeling so light I thought I'd float away. On the way home to Jean, I found a shop and made a copy of the cheque, knowing the original wouldn't see the weekend. There was some serious boozing due to take place and I would be at home with Jean, who was now pregnant on our third child. Just this once I wouldn't go astray.

My son Jonathan was born on 17 May 1965, an amazing little guy who would scarcely cease to be less. With fire in his belly and a touch of the mad laugh in his mind, he would light up all our lives, a rebellious little fucker, like his Da! I was knocked out by him, as I had been by Sarah and Peter. To truly enjoy them, feel such immense love, really want to be there to see them grow up, take life on, the thought thrilled me. What a pity it wasn't enough to still the madness that could run rampant through me when it wanted, all my decencies cast aside when the moon inside me was full.

Jean had turned quiet on me during her pregnancy, she was very fed up with me, and I kept looking to the publication of the book in October to relieve things. What I really meant was I was hoping for some kind of miracle with the novel, a runaway best-seller with a huge movie deal, nothing Mickey Mouse about my dreams. I was looking for the book to rescue me, rescue my marriage which was surely slipping away from me.

As the year reached halfway I was drinking more; the drink led me to another bed, another couch, another hump with another woman I would never get to know. There was no end to the promiscuity. But no matter how much you indulged, you could never get enough.

Where I fell down as a husband I tried to make up as a father. I did play the classical albums in the background while I rolled around the floor with Sarah and Peter, I did read bits of the *Encyclopaedia*, I sang to them with the backing of my old three-chord trick on the guitar, I recited poetry and nursery rhymes and generally tried to be good for them, in short bursts. Jean was there for them all the time.

Sometimes, on good mornings, all four of us in the big bed, we'd play this game where I was a lion who couldn't roar. The kids would tease this lion, do things to make him roar in annoyance, the lion would wind himself up, really go for a big mean roar, which would emerge from his angry mouth as a whimper, and the children would die from laughing. To an outsider I had it all.

I had a play happening, another novel, a big idea for a television series, and I was still getting a commission for a script here and there in television. We would have been all right financially if I hadn't been drinking so much.

With all of this going on, including the rows resulting from Jean's demand that I work a proper day on the cab — 'At least earn enough to pay our way, is that too much to ask?' — I could have justified my drinking by asking 'How could she talk to me like that!' Jesus! I was trying to get rich for both of us, using the talent that had already shown up. And I kept on working at the keyboard. No matter what else was going on, I was writing most days of the week.

Jeff Denton was driving my cab days. This helped but it wasn't enough to keep us afloat so I placed a parcel of manuscripts on the desk of a bank manager in Hammersmith, told him I was going to be the new Brendan Behan and asked him to back me for a while. The man agreed to take a chance on me, impressed by the approach. I got a £2,000 overdraft limit, which was a lot of leeway in 1965, if you'll pardon the pun! So I paid all the bills, gave Jean money, told her I loved her, kissed the kids with a see you later, went out for one drink and didn't get home for ten days.

Despite this kind of horse shit pouring through my head I'd no idea I was sick. I knew I was wild, which wasn't a bad image. I sang 'Call Me Irresponsible' in pubs and at parties all over London, with such heart that people thought I was great. But I was ailing because I could go against all I held dear, all I believed in, just push it aside, indulge the scumbag side of my nature with its ever-ready appetite. For a bloke who knew everything, I didn't know lust couldn't be satiated. And I mean upstairs and down, bed, brain, mouth and mind. No matter how much they got, *much* always wants *more*. And on and on for ever and ever, amen!

Jonathan was three months old when I got a phone call from Ma saying Da's back in hospital, that things looked very bad for him. Meaning he could die at any time. I was shattered. For the past year or so I'd been so busy with my own trips, my own hang-ups, my own addictions, that I'd hardly given Da a thought.

To make matters worse the bank manager had frozen my overdraft facility. Too many of my cheques were made out to pubs and clubs and he wanted to talk seriously to me before I could draw any more money. I had only managed to deposit one cheque in the past year. Not good enough.

Jean's brother, Frank, loaned me the £200 I needed to get home to Dublin. He barely spoke to his own father by this stage. I'd seen this coming, how they were moving in opposite directions, when I first got to know them. This early impression festered in reality, Frank dropping Dick entirely, refusing to even go to Dick's deathbed, no interest in a last goodbye to the old guy who'd never quit adoring the son who couldn't stand the sight of him.

Frank had already asked me to work with him in the cab company the family owned, promising me a lot of money, with the chance to be a millionaire in the not too distant future. I didn't doubt this for one second. Frank was going to make all the money in the world. But I couldn't kid him, I told him: 'My heart's in the scribbling, I have to give it a go. I take your offer I'd be cheating you, giving you the front, not the back. It wouldn't be right.'

He tried to talk me around. He needed me. There were certain things that had to be done in business, it needed family members, people who could be trusted to keep secrets, and a lot more between the lines stuff you didn't need to be an Einstein to understand. Still I said sorry, I was going to be a writer, and he accepted that. He was a pal to me, never more so than when he gave me that loan to go and see my father.

The minute I saw Da, I knew he was dying. There was no fight left in the terrier. The years of struggling to and from work with a blocked heart valve, and its complications, had done for my father. I hated to admit it, but as sure as God, Mick was going for his tea. I hurt so much when I sat with him, I felt such pain in my heart, I can't even remember one thing I said to him. It was the same ache that was always there when I had to accept I wasn't able to do anything, not for him, not for anybody, not even for me. Finally, I had to go to the lavatory, get into a cubicle and cry my eyes out as quietly as I could.

I was in Dublin for two days and I drank like someone determined to be dead by the end of the session. I slept in Da's bed wanting to be there in the smell of him, crying myself into some form of drunken sleep, so torn that even my libido seemed to have given up the ghost.

As it happened Da seemed to perk up and a doctor told me he could live for a good while with the right rest and care. I left the proof copy of *Goodbye to the Hill* with Ma, leaving it to her to decide when he might be well enough to take a look at it. I went back to England, vowing to return home in a week or two. I'd be more in control of myself, swimming a bit instead of just drowning in self-pity.

A few days later Ma called. Da had died: 'He passed away in his sleep, a peaceful death, son, be grateful for that.' I curled up inside, cursing his going, not even wondering how Ma might be feeling, as I went drinking for a week. When I surfaced I felt as though I was carrying a large septic boil around inside me. To have him pass on just six weeks before the book was published seemed so cruel. I'd needed more time than Da had been granted. Time to find the guts to say just once *I love you, you fucker!* — even if it made him laugh and ask me *Are you some kinda cissy or what!*

Early in September Giles Gordon, my editor at Hutchinson, calls me: *Goodbye to the Hill* has been chosen as a Green Title. This meant it was one of 50 books picked from the 400 they published annually for special advertising. This was good news, until I found out this special treatment meant three or four ads instead of one or two, with the book jammed in a block advert with God knows how many others. Which meant it had little or no chance of being seen, of gathering any attention. I didn't think so, thank you very much.

After getting this far, I wasn't going to watch the book disappear just because the publishers wanted to keep it a secret!

I mentioned this to a mate of mine who's connected in Fleet Street. A few days later he introduced me to a journalist, a colourful guy, all 'Jolly good show, old bean!' But behind the bullshit, the handlebar moustache, lurked a sharp and devious mind, a thirst needing constant support and a bookmaker who insisted on being paid. In other words, I met a man who would do anything for money. His name was Charlie Dee.

I explained to Charlie that my novel was being published on 4 October. I felt it needed help since Hutchinson were being very conservative about advertising it.

'Cheap plonk in the Cheshire Cheese', Charlie speculated on the launch, 'will get you about as much coverage as a Presbyterian church meeting!' He quaffed a half of ale, one gulp, no problem, held out his mug to me. 'One swallow never made a summer!' He chuckled: 'Attend the launch, little or no publicity. Obvious alternative. Don't turn up for the fucking launch! Publishers with egg on their faces, how jolly! Chagrin in their pox-riddled eyes, splendid! Hatred in their horny hearts, majestic! You get exposure for yourself and your dreary Irish novel.' He hollered at my reaction, 'Relax, old chap! Haven't read it.' He killed the other half-pint, whoosh, like a Hoover. 'All Irish novels are dreary.'

Charlie lit a cigarette, any minute the snuff box is what I was thinking. 'For every picture of you that I get into a national, you pay me fifty quid. A hundred quid against the first two pics in advance.' He smiled grandly, impressed and delighted with the proposed scenario. 'How does that sound, old bean!'

I met Charlie again about a week later. He had me drive my cab down to the Embankment, he had a photographer with him. He pulled two nurses who were walking by, talked them into glamorising the picture we were going to take. The girls were more than happy to get their pic in a national newspaper and it did appear the next day, with me as the smiling cabby, his book being published in October by Hutchinson. So we were on the way with the press, but I had another idea to help the book along.

I found a printer who told me the most eye-catching combination of colours was black on yellow. I wrote out the wording for a regular-size poster, ordered 250 plus 2,500 of a cut-down version, a flier you could hand to people. Featured along with the book's title was the claim *The Publishing Event of the Year!* which it certainly was for me.

The week before publication my pals and I planted the posters in pubs and clubs all over London, in shops where we were known. The fliers were being handed out by cab drivers to passengers, with the verbal plug that it was 'an amazing read by a working man with real talent'. I handed out a lot of fliers myself on the cab, giving the passengers the same spiel without even a blush, admitting with a laugh to the one or two who asked me that I was the author.

On Saturday, 2 October I said goodbye to Jean and went down to the Halfway House for a drink. Jean wished me luck, knowing she wasn't going to see me for a few days, again behind me even though she had some reservations about me disappearing.

I met Caspar John, who was actually Sir Caspar John, Admiral of the Fleet. He was the son of the late, great, ever-horny Augustus John, who was still rogering females at eighty-three years of age, so the legend went. Caspar and I were drinking pals, alcoholic acquaintances as opposed to great friends, but we knew each other all right, enjoyed ourselves together. The way Charles saw it, if Sir Caspar John was the last man to see me before I disappeared, that ought to get some attention in the papers.

I spent a few hours with Caspar in the Halfway House, we left the pub with a few other piss artists and went back to the Johns' house, with me leaving at about half past midnight to go home. All normal enough, we'd had many a good night in that house in Barnes. Caspar and Mary John's parties attracted the most talented and the wildest and the most bohemian, their friends let nothing get in the way when they were having a good time. Even though he was the top sailor in England, Caspar was his father's son.

As we knocked back the booze that night I kept remembering the big instruction from Charlie: 'Leave before you fall down, get a cab from there and take a train to any place, first train available, find a B&B, get into bed, and stay offside until after Monday morning's launch.' I followed the man's directions, the last thing I distinctly remembered was telling a cab driver to take me to Victoria station.

The next thing I know, I am in a scene that comes out like a clip from an old British movie. A guy is looking at his feet, which are shoeless. *Into the Frame* comes a pair of shiny black boots with big round toecaps, blue serge pants touching the top of the laces. *We Pan Up* along the pants to the jacket, which has shiny buttons on it, a heavy belt supporting a truncheon, up to a chinstrap and a helmet. We hear a voice say: 'Oi Oi! What've we got here then!'

'Where am I?' I ask. This is a totally genuine question, I have no memory of anything from the time I took the cab to Victoria.

'You're in Brighton, sir,' is the reply from a policeman, who turns out to be a real sweetheart.

'My God! How did you find me?'

'I was having a cuppa in the box there, sir,' he indicates a police box, 'and I heard you singing.' He smiles: 'Always liked "Danny Boy".'

'What day is it, Constable?' Coming back to reality, I'm starting to throw shapes.

'Tuesday, sir, five in the morning.'

I am so stunned my legs start to go, the policeman grabs me and half-carries me into his box, which is like a tiny room with phones and things. Suddenly my feet are hurting badly and there is a terrible smell in the box. Just before I ask where the hell the smell is coming from, I pass out cold.

When I come around the policeman gives me a cup of tea. 'Been having something of a piss-up, mate!' I sip the tea as I realise the smell in the cabin is me. I apologise to this decent man and he tells me no problem, smiling as he playfully opens the door a little wider. I chuckle along with him though my hands shake and I'm so frightened by what's happened I feel as though my brain is weeping. 'Can you call me a cab? I have to get back to London.'

I spend two days in bed cold turkey. I can't take a drink to help me ease the pain, the torture of withdrawal. Leon Heffler, my doctor and a great friend to Jean and me, gives me some vitamin B12 and stuff, but time was the only friend I was going to find in the next few days.

Jean feeds me soup, shaking her head, silently asking was it worth it. And she doesn't even know I blacked out so completely that I lost the plot.

17

While I'm recovering Jean tells me what happened while I was out of the game. Giles Gordon at Hutchinson had called the house when I didn't turn up for the launch of the book in the Cheshire Cheese. His boss was very upset with me for missing the launch and not at all happy about my posters stating that *Goodbye to the Hill* is *The Publishing Event of the Year*! Jean told Giles it was, as far as she and I were concerned. Other writers weren't happy about it, so he said. Good old Jean. Never stuck for words she said: 'Well, let them put out their own posters, we won't complain!' Giles was amused by that and very decently hoped privately to Jean that I was all right, that nothing bad had happened to me.

Two days later the publishers didn't hate me any more because the book was selling very well thanks to all the coverage we'd had. A few weeks later I got a note telling me it had sold amazingly in excess of what they expected from any first novel. A few weeks after this they got an American hardback sale with Houghton Mifflin of New York and Boston, and shortly afterwards Ballantyne's in New York came in for the paperback rights.

Meanwhile I got a phone call from the Brighton policeman, whose name turned out to be Fred Smith. Fred told me he'd found a B&B place where I'd checked in early on Sunday morning. There was a copy of my novel on the bedside locker. I paid in advance, went out for a walk on the seafront at breakfast time and never came back. I told Fred I'd like him to have the book and I wrote him a letter of thanks.

I paid Charlie the money I owed him and I never saw him again. Hutchinson wanted to know how the new book was coming, I said all right, that they could have a manuscript in six weeks. I didn't have a word written but the next story was fairly set in my head.

Jean relaxed a bit about me and I continued swearing I'd tone down the lunacy. I'm not saying she believed me but I was giving her an option, and I could see her settling for that, for a time, anyway.

Things with the bank manager were cordial again, thanks to the US advances. I began giving copies of the book to story editors in television. Why not, was how I saw it. Every story editor I ever met wanted to be a novelist, they were more likely to commission a script or two now that you had a story between hard covers. So thanks to the book I got quite a bit of TV work and I tried spending more of my free time at home with Jean and the children.

Jonathan was still a baby but Sarah and Peter were mobile enough to keep a team of au pairs fit and trim and slim. Especially Sarah, who was a live wire in need of constant attention. She fired questions at you like bullets, wanted stories and more stories to give her overactive imagination a workout. She got to reading very early. I wrote a word on a card, told her what the word was, what it meant, and she had it in one.

Before she was three Sarah was reading little stories. She had said her first word, 'Fuck,' at a year old, in front of her grandparents, who didn't get it because they couldn't have imagined a child that young saying anything, never mind the F-word. She pulled herself to her feet in a playpen on St Valentine's Day, which was just over six months after she was born. I remember it well because my brother Brendan and his wife, Martha, staying with us on their honeymoon, had bought her the playpen, and they were there on the spot when Sarah decided to stand up.

By the time Sarah was five I was taking herself and Peter swimming on Saturday mornings. Peter was such a gentle boy that my heart ached for him in the world about us. Sarah was a tigress, she'd be fine, Peter, oh God be good to this kid! Already he seems too good for this fucked-up planet. I loved Jean too, but it was middle-distance now, we were no longer crazy about one another the way we were that first year or two. We were still having sex on a regular basis, but we'd quit making love. She must have known I had other women but she never asked. Not until I came back from New York in 1966.

Houghton Mifflin put me up in the Algonquin while I'm in the Big Apple to do publicity for the book. I know about the Algonquin, I've read about the Round Table, I could name the great writers and the great lunatics that sat around it making sure people knew they were different to the rest of us. Thanks to Logan (Jack) Gourlay who wrote a showbiz column in the *Sunday Express* in England, I've got some people to see who might be able to help me in some way. Physically I feel terrible, my vaccination has hit me as I arrive, I have some kind of fever, the summer is scorching. So, though I want to be there, I'm lonely, lonely for my family, my kids more than my wife, feeling very alone.

I have some radio broadcasts and a public television show to do on the second day there and I go well. Michael didn't christen me Piggy Gabby for nothing, the gift of the gab comes in handy now I'm getting the chance to sell my wares through the media. Later, on Fifth Avenue, I'm having my picture taken in front of Doubleday's window — my book is up there on a stand — and instead of just enjoying the moment I find I'm angry, angry that it didn't happen years ago. I'm thirty-one years old, coming from nowhere, I'm published in America by a very reputable house, and I'm bitching inside while I smile for the camera. I feel disappointment in myself, sadness that I'm such a fuck-up.

That night I'm feeling a little better, getting over the vaccination sickness. I go to see Patrick Bedford and Donal Donnelly in Brian Friel's *Philadelphia, Here I Come!* on Broadway. Paddy Bedford was always a decent guy, he'd do anything he could to help you. I had very little money and when my time at the Algonquin ran out, he put me up in his apartment on West 45th Street.

I experienced immense kindness at all levels. I was drinking well, not too much, but gently pissed all the time, and I was seeing just about everything through pink glasses. I met Otto Preminger thanks to Logan Gourlay, Jerome White who was business manager for Rodgers and Hammerstein, a terrific woman, Allison McGrath, with contacts to burn, and a lot of other people willing to help me. But I wasn't there when I should have been there, I missed appointments because I had no memory of making the arrangements, and though I gave a lot of people a lot of laughs — Tom Murphy the playwright called me a world-class raconteur — I didn't do one thing to help my career as a writer.

The truth is I got onto the freeloader circuit in New York, where you're invited to everything if you've had your name in the press recently. I went from party to party being introduced as Ireland's latest literary export, stuff like this, with no shortage of late night whiskey in Downey's great saloon and the bar Jimmy Ray ran on Eighth Avenue. Jimmy Ray was a total sweetheart, a pal to me, even before I got addicted to his clam chowder!

Need I say there was no end of sex, so that despite falling in love twice, it was bedtime with dozens of women, most of them connected in some way with that whole theatrical, literary milieu. Basically I was out of it while I was in Manhattan, living like a single man, hooked on the booze and anything available in the drug line, lying to Jean whenever I called her, telling her I was doing all kinds of publicity for the novel, all the while burning up my life in the shambles that I considered to be the best time I ever had.

Initially I had gone to push the book for two weeks with Jean's blessing. When I finally got out of New York, I turned it all into a big laugh. Coming home after thirteen weeks, saying 'Imagine, I missed my plane. By eleven weeks!'

Jean picked me up off the plane from New York. As we started the journey home to East Sheen she asked me straight out if I'd had an affair while I'd been away. The lie arose, automatically you might say, but I didn't speak. Suddenly I was deflated in the bullshit department, I had no energy to tell her any more lies. After a few moments I said no, I hadn't had an affair, I'd had several, plus one-night stands. I confessed I'd been in love twice, having left one lady feeling that her heart was broken. No, right now I didn't want to go back to her, be with her, and I didn't want a divorce or a legal separation, I just wanted to get home, see my children, see if I could pick up a thread of decency from wherever I'd lost it, and see about getting back to my work and hopefully start to earn some money.

Once I started to tell the truth it wouldn't stop coming until all of it seemed to have poured itself out of me. Jean didn't go mad as I would have expected, she didn't react in any way big. As a matter of fact, she was calm enough to suggest she didn't give a damn. She didn't say this but she admitted it was a relief to know. I didn't press her for details, I was just glad she hadn't dumped me out of the car. But if I hadn't been so consumed with myself and the *I Confess* ordeal, I might have noticed that Jean's relief, coupled with her lack of anger, probably added up to an emotional involvement of some kind. But I didn't read the signals and it would be another three years before the situation would be spelled out so that even I got the message loud and clear.

We went on sleeping in the same bed, just living like mates, like reasonable people giving each other their own space, and we got along all right. We'd quit having sex, quietly moving in different directions, the main worry now being money, money, money. So much so that at times I privately wished I hadn't surrendered my cab badge. This was something I didn't have to do. When you earn that licence to drive a taxi for a living in London it's yours for life. But I wanted to give it back, because being a know-all, I just knew I would never need it again.

Wrong. I needed it as 1967 came up on the roller. I had to find a way of earning money. I needed to get the pressure off the writing, it was crazy to expect the scribbling to produce the groceries and stuff. To be able to write is a blessing, but you can turn this universal gift into a curse by expecting to make money from it. I was now guilty of that as well as so much more. Even as my father died I added pressure to the pain by beating up on life for taking him before he saw my picture on the back cover of my novel. I never asked myself why I needed to prove to Da that I'd made a mark. I never asked myself why I needed to get drunk over it.

Meanwhile my brother Michael was earning great money on the old FX3 I'd bought for £600 in 1960. He was a great worker, he was saving, himself and Betty were going to get some business of their own going before long. He'd always been good with money, he wasn't going to be poor any more, they were a couple who'd be well off long before they hung up the retirement sign. Big Joe and Johnnie were two more guys who made the hard-earned green badge pay off. Unlike myself and Pat Glasser from Clare. He had about as much heart for the cabbing as I had. Breeding horses around Kilrush was what Glasser talked about. We were destined to be lifelong friends, dreamers both. Of such stuff are the lunatics and the losers and the shapers made, and you need a lot of time, a lot of pain to see clearly enough to release the fear of just being an ordinary man.

At this time an agent, Jonathan Clowes, had taken me on thanks to the reviews for *Goodbye to the Hill*. His name alone was a good calling card, an introduction to producers and story editors in the TV world. He helped me earn money writing in the early stages of several series that never actually made it to the screen. So Jean and I weren't paupers but we were always strapped for money, because my drinking was now like a drug habit and for the first time the word alcoholic was thrown at me in a fit of anger over unpaid bills.

She relaxed a little as I finished the new novel for Hutchinson. It was called *A Bed in the Sticks*, based on my time in the fit-ups, and to tell you the truth, I didn't know whether it was any good or not. As it happened, Hutchinson liked it, with me thinking thanks be to Jesus! Then I took this gratitude down to the boozer. I'd given thanks, so now it was time to celebrate.

In August of 1967 I was so shattered by drinking and how's your father that I was desperate enough to say to Jean, witnessed by Johnnie who was there in the house at the time, 'I'm not going to drink between now and Christmas.' Jean gave me a look — a Dobermann sizing up a dachshund — but she said nothing. It wasn't her way to put you down, not if you were having a go.

Christmas arrived and I'd stuck to my guns! No booze of any kind since my insane declaration of sober intent the previous summer. Jean was so impressed she thought I was cured, that I could now go down to the Halfway

House, get drunk for the holidays, then just stop the way I did a few months earlier. I didn't even think about that. I felt pretty good about myself. Not only was I sober, I was earning money as well. Money which would help us have a happier holiday with more than enough left to pay the bills that would be there like the weather in the new year. So already 1968 was looking good.

This money I was earning came from writing an Irish radio soap opera called *The Kennedys of Castleross*. The gig had come my way through an American called Mark Grantham, a studious good guy I'd met years before in Finch's on the Fulham Road. He'd created the show years before, he'd written too many episodes, found himself in a writing cul-de-sac, he wanted out and he'd recommended me as his replacement.

Mark had helped me once before, soon after Jack Connell introduced us in London. He got me a scriptwriting commission from the Danzigers, Americans, who could produce a TV programme in a shoebox during lunch-time. A day and a half after Mark gets me this gig I go around to his flat in Putney not far from where I lived. He thinks I've come with the outline for the script, I've written the script itself. Mark reads it, finds it more than okay, passes it to the Danzigers, comes back to me in a day or two with my cheque for sixty pounds, which was the stunning fee these millionaires paid for a twenty-six-minute television script. I'm not complaining, I was just glad that my ability to produce a script on demand had registered with Mark Grantham.

Which was why I was taking over the writing of Ireland's long-running serial *The Kennedys* — hence this meeting with producers at Irish radio's office in Bond Street. I'd never heard the show, I'd been away from home too long. The producer, a gentle, artistic New Zealander called Willy Styles, played me several taped episodes right there in the meeting. I gave it a good listen, said I could write it, he was relieved and I signed up, agreeing to write three scripts a week, the first writer to take on the expanding format.

The soap job hadn't anything to do with my dry period up to Christmas. But the regular money coupled with my teetotal trip made for a peaceful home life, and I had no problems with the scripts. Willy Styles liked my work, which I delivered like clockwork. That was my way when I was being paid to write.

If it wasn't exactly a happy time, it was a period when it was easier to act as though you were happy, if only because I felt more entitled to breathe now that I was earning the grocery money once more. I was having some good days with my children too, I was again taking Sarah and Peter and a reluctant Jonathan to the swimming pool every Saturday morning along with Doc

Heffler's kids, Katy and Anna, and any of their mates wanting to come with us. This ritual brightened those winter Saturdays. I cooked pancakes for all the kids when we got back from swimming, throwing the crêpes towards the ceiling to the delight of the children, while Jean and Conchita got a lie-in.

On Christmas Eve, Johnnie and I headed for the pub and the guys waiting to welcome me. I didn't intend to go mad on the drink. I was looking forward to a real family Christmas. I was thirty-three years old, happy with some simple birthday presents from Jean and the children, ready to drink sensibly, sing a lot of songs, and hopefully behave myself. Johnnie was very supportive, never even hinting he knew this particular song backwards from hearing me sing it so many times.

The guys had the drinks lined up for me, and the general vibe was *Here he is, now you'll see some drinking.* In a flash I was really annoyed that I appeared so predictable. Was it really so bad that guys were making bets I wouldn't see straight for the next two weeks? I ordered a Coca-Cola, drank it, wished everyone a happy Christmas and went back home. I felt a bit delighted with myself, even if I wasn't sure why I felt like that. And Johnnie was so surprised he came back to the house with me.

I stayed on the dry into the new year. Jean had plenty to drink during Christmas, no better woman. We had parties that went on for days, all our pals came and went like snuff at a wake. I poured a river of booze, plenty for everybody, and I never touched a solitary drop. I joined in the fun, did my share of singing and poker playing. I had a very good happy time with the kids, enjoying their joy over their presents, really buddying up with them through the excitement of all the visitors that enlivened our days as 1967 came to an end. It was the best of times, that Christmas without a jar.

In January I tap out a soap episode a day for two weeks. I'm not sure why until I realise there's a play I need to write. *The Full Shilling* has me scared from the off. It's writing itself right onto the paper, and I feel as though I'm on a high wire, scared but excited like the first time swimming out beyond my depth in the sea at Williamstown. When you don't know where it's coming from and you don't know where it's going, you get gripped by being part of the action and you're lost to whatever is going on around you. It's a brilliant thing to happen to you, amazing. And like half a page from the finish you've no idea how it's going to end — that is really something!

Two days after I finish the play I'm back to work on *The Kennos*, very glad to have the pay cheque arriving, seriously considering the luxury it must be to earn regular bread even if it's all sliced up before you even take a bite out of it.

Early in February 1968 I get a phone call at about nine o'clock one morning. My head is clear, I'm a full six months on the wagon, so I know I'm not imagining things when this man with a strong American accent tells me he wants to make a movie of *Goodbye to the Hill*.

For a moment my heart skips a beat then I promise myself I will kill whoever is on the other end of the phone line taking the piss out of me. Trying to hear whose voice is hiding behind this very good accent, I ask 'What was your name again?'

'Daniel Haller,' the voice tells me, 'I'm calling you from LA.'

I'm in a quandary. Like the call has to be a joke. One of my mates busting my balls. Not Johnnie — he could never hide his sound from me. It might be Glasser? Kinger? — someone from Finch's pub, maybe even Jack Connell? Things like this just don't happen, yet this little eensy-weensy part of my mind holds out for the possibility, the very slim and utterly impossible possibility, that this is an actual genuine overture from a film producer with the hots for the film rights of my novel.

What I need is a line, to protect me from ridicule if it's a gag, that at the same time allows me to keep things open just in case I am on the receiving end of an early 1968 miracle. If I just jump in and say yes please and the guy goes 'Na na na na na! Happy New Year, Schmuck!' I will want to die. Not that I'll give my last gasp until I've strangled the bastard, whoever he is.

If you're willing to believe that a film deal right now would give me a lift like a rocket ride, you might understand why I give myself great credit for the words I drop into the phone.

'Well, Mister Haller, I'm afraid I couldn't possibly sell the film rights to a man I don't know.' Are you kidding? It's two years and four months since the book was published. By now I will sell the rights to Lassie, King Kong, even the Danzigers.

'I'm flying around the Pole to London tonight. May I call you when I get in tomorrow, meet you in the afternoon?' the man calling himself Haller asks me, and I say sure, that would be nice.

Two days later in my agent's office, Danny Haller and I sign contracts. He's bought the film rights of the novel, in a separate deal he's hired me to write the screenplay. I call Jean to tell her the news. She's thrilled, we both are, but she has news for me too.

Jean tells me *The Pale-Faced Girl*, my forty-five-minute screenplay, has been bought by a London producer, to be made in Dublin in May. They need to know I'll be available to help with casting. I tell her to reassure them. I will be in Ireland writing *Goodbye — The Movie —* while I'm tapping out three episodes per week of *The Kennedys*, apart from which I won't be all that busy!

We share a laugh about the change in our fortunes. I mention that Haller is taking me to dinner, that I'm going to have a drink with him right now. Jean says: 'Go for it, you bastard! If ever anybody deserved a drink, you do. I'm proud of you for sticking to your word. I didn't think you had it in you.' I heard her inhale smoke from the Senior Service cigarette that lived in her hand. 'I mean, let's face it, Lee, you could piss-up for Ireland!' We shared a laugh on that, the pair of us close, chortling with each other. So that just for a few seconds we were really tight, the way we were one time all the time.

I join Danny Haller in the hotel bar, feeling all the better for being solvent for the minute. I have a celebration drink, my first drink in six months, like a toast to my first Hollywood screenplay. Amen!

In the early hours of the following morning I fall up the stairs of the house in East Sheen. I get into the narrow bathroom. There is a built-in cupboard under the washbasin, the door of the cupboard is open. I see this as I take a heavy fall. My chest hits the open edge of the door. I go on falling, my face slides along the length of the outer edge and I go out like a blown light bulb.

A few hours later I come around, haul myself up from the floor. As I see myself in the huge mirror on the wall, my left eye is swollen shut and there is a cut on the top of my cheekbone where the blood has congealed. On my left chest I have a small hump of blood stuck to the inside of my shirt and a lot of pain in that area. I can see right away that if when I fell the points of impact had been reversed, I'd have lost my eye for sure.

My God! At any time while I'd been lying there in my own blood, any one of the children could have come into the bathroom. I'm horrified, really scared, and bitterly ashamed. All I can remember is meeting Danny Haller, a very civilised man, having a few brandies before sitting down to a rib of roast beef dinner in the Carlton Towers. I have no memory of anything after that until I get home in time to fall over, hurting myself more than any fight on the street had ever done.

The Doc, Leon Heffler, never told me I should give up the booze. He would say 'Pace yourself, you're in a tricky business.' I said sure, and got on with writing *Kennedy* scripts one-eyed while I got over the fall in the bathroom.

What drinking I did was done at home. I told the kids I'd had a fight with ten guys who were beating up an old man. I played it up and we got a laugh out of my fantasy. Really, I needed to be there with Jean and the kids at that time. And of course, I didn't want anybody to see me during my black and blue period.

I drank a lot of beer, so thirsty at times I thought of Aunty Kay. The diabetes. Jesus, could I have it? You never know. Jean never cared how much I drank when I drank at home. It was the wandering off for a week or ten days that shattered her. Hard to go on loving someone who comes home from a marathon drinking bout looking as if he's been pulled backwards through a rifle barrel. She'd been well aware of the other women for years, hard not to see the lovebites and the scratches all over me after some of my forays into darkness.

Mid-March 1968 I was in Dublin, renting a flat at the top of a house in Upper Gardiner Street, north of the Liffey. Of course I saw Ma, who was wearing well; when I hugged her it was a genuine embrace, not some little bit of ritual designed to convince her that she still mattered. No matter what had happened she would always be very important to me, even if I wasn't always ready to show it.

She was wearing a nice-looking dress with pink and amber roses on an off-white background. Her shoes were real leather, Cuban-heeled, and her stockings had never known a ladder. A far cry from not-so-long-ago days when a pair of silk stockings was beyond a dream. 'Nylons,' Ma said. 'Nobody's wearing silk stockings these days. Nylons from the States, though they're making them here now. Factories working full-time.' She was amused by my innocence, as she handed me a cup of Bewley's full roast coffee, topped up by hot milk. 'A cuppa Bewley's is your only man,' she tells with a laugh, taking a Gold Flake from me as if to the manner born.

Ma had some little pension, Da's legacy, from the Electricity Supply Board, I still sent her money every couple of weeks, and I know that some of the others weighed in with a few quid. Some of this money was on the floor, a square of good carpet covering the lino in the centre of the kitchen, a new china cabinet where Michael used to keep his turntable balanced on the shoe polish box. The television set dominated the wall next to Ma's divan bed. The bedroom was empty since Da's death, she had never slept a night in it.

She gave me back the proof copy of *Goodbye to the Hill* that I'd left for Da, witnessing my eyes as they registered disappointment, that *He* hadn't read it, and she said quickly, 'Oh he read it all right.' She was at the stove, giving my demanding look the elbow.

'Did he say anything about it? Did he like it, hate it, what?'

She faced me now, the fried white pudding going on the toast, while I salivated patiently. 'He said it was great, he enjoyed it.'

'There's a *But* in your voice, there's a *But*, Ma. What else did he say?'

'He said, let me see now . . .' Ma gathered the words to get the meaning right. '"That Leo is a sex-mad little bastard!"'

I found myself laughing with tears in my eyes, missing Da something awful in the moment. 'Eat the puddin' and me after fryin' it for you,' Ma said. The moment passed. Ma sat facing me, gone back to sipping her coffee, knowing I needed a minute to get myself together. I tried to focus on the rich, spicy flavour of the white pudding. Da had read the book. Then I said to Ma, 'You never told me what you thought of it, if you read it.'

'I read it,' Ma said, exhaling smoke thoughtfully. 'I wouldn't argue with the reviews you sent me from England.'

'It got the "Book of the Week" review slot in the *Evening Standard*. Did I send you that one?' Ma was nodding as I spoke. 'So, what?' We both knew she was holding back.

'I just don't see the need to write books like that. Letting people know our business. I suppose privacy, even other people's, that's what writers deal in, isn't it!' She had no approval for me, she didn't like me much then.

I felt a dart of anger, like a little cut in the heart. I wanted to chastise her, admonish her for being ignorant, remind her that the book had been published by one of the best houses around, that the reviews were brilliant, and that I must have done some fucking thing right. Of course, I said nothing, it wouldn't have been fair, but I felt badly let down. To my mind it was a minor miracle that the flats had spawned Connie Smith and me.

I moved the snack to one side, no longer hungry. The place mat had a country motif. I found the hint of a defensive smile. Someone must have given Ma the mats as a present. She'd never have bought *Country*! As I used to say to her for a laugh, 'If you go south of Dún Laoghaire you get a nosebleed.'

My agent had sent some publicity material to the Irish papers so I was met at the airport. Getting coverage in the papers was handy for late night drinking if nothing else. I could get into Groome's hotel run by Patty, wife of politician Joe Groome, not a bad skin. When he was *In* you could drink around the clock. When he was *In Opposition* you got turfed out by 2 a.m. This was hardly breaking the law since you were only drinking for three hours beyond the law!

All over the country people were drinking their brains out, to see people jailed was commonplace. The government turned a blind eye, tolerating this risk to the nation's health because 11 per cent of the national budget was going on booze. You can imagine the tax! Did they ever think of the man-hours lost at work because people were diseased from boozing on too many mornings every week?

The Irish were also eating out more, most of it done in pubs. This was unheard of just years earlier, when getting a decent sandwich in an Irish pub was like cordon bleu cuisine. Most pubs now had serious food on offer, many more were running talent contests over several weekends, guaranteeing jam-packed evenings. As one guy said to me: 'A talent show and the place is jammed to captivity!' He didn't register the malapropism but the crush in some spots actually made it difficult getting out, especially when the first prize could be £1,000. There was now a strong circle of professional artistes providing cabaret entertainment seven nights a week, with stag gigs on Sunday mornings, no holds barred material allowed to help the lads relax after the rigours of attending Mass!

Ireland, which already had a serious drink problem, was also turning into Turn-On City, the warning voices of the few with foresight not being heard. Not by those who could have done something about the incipient drug disaster that would sweep the country, and certainly not by the many thousands of people addicted to Valium and Librium, which of course were all right to take since you could only get them with a doctor's prescription. It was a bit like Disneyland on LSD.

Divorce Irish-style was making headlines, separated people sharing the marriage home because they couldn't afford to run two places. They lived together for the sake of the kids, leading separate lives, and it worked well enough until one of them fell in love. Thousands of applications for legal separations and annulments piled up in law offices and the Archbishop's Palace in Drumcondra, people who could afford it going to England to get a divorce, while girls who had not been careful in their newfound freedom took a plane ride to London or Manchester to terminate a certain situation. We had just about everything by the mid-1970s except the Single Parent. They were still called Unmarried Mothers! Childbirth outside wedlock was still one hell of a social stigma in the Land of Saints and Scholars.

Two days after I arrived in Dublin, I began to write my first Hollywood screenplay. I'd seen Ma, visited Da's grave, bought in the groceries and the drink, so it was time to start work, begin earning the money I'd been paid up front, with more to come as the pages gave Danny Haller the movie he wanted to shoot.

I connected with Vincent Smith, an actor pal in Dublin. He was *resting* so he was sound about keeping me company during the early days of scribbling away from home, especially while you're dealing with the effect of the previous night's drinking. I could be a bit paranoid in the mornings, Vincent's presence helped me realise the walls were not moving. He was a much-needed friend in those times, since no day passed now when I was more than half-sober, or less than half-jarred. Without even seeing it happen I'd crossed another forbidden line the day I had my first drink with Danny Haller.

I began the day with coffee, a brandy and a Purple Heart, then went to work knocking out a *Kennos* script. Nobody knew it except me but Hollywood had to wait while I made sure Ireland got the latest episode of its favourite radio series. I kept the show written six weeks in advance, which allowed the actors to get time out for work on a film, hospitalisation from drink, whatever. It gave the producer time to get his scripts copied, and do all the other things the public don't have to think about while they listen to the show. It took me just under two hours to knock out an episode, then I drank several coffees laced with brown sugar and brandy, and began the screenwriting job.

Vincent stayed in the flat, reading quietly while I worked. In a week I had a good fist of work done, the screenplay was happening. I sent the typed pages off to Danny Haller in California, asking him to let me know how they landed on him. That day Vincent and I had a lunch that lasted for about a day and a half.

During this mini-celebration in Jammet's, one of the very *in* restaurants, I met a woman with a gamey eye, we became lovers, she being a collector of talented sexos. We'd go on to become good friends in the years ahead. She was a well-off married lady who sang her own lyrics, lived like a single person when she felt the need, her husband so busy doing his own thing he didn't mind. She stood late night on her head, long after closing time in the foyer of the Shelbourne until the night porter gave in and brought us champagne. Vincent Smith and I stood admiring the best legs in Dublin, my ego purring at the idea that for the moment anyway, they belonged to me.

This was a far cry from the Dublin I'd left in the early 1950s when the movie *Bitter Rice* drew such an 'If I catch you near that fillum, I'll break your bleedin' neck!' warning from Da that my brother Michael and I ran into each other in the queue the next night. As Ireland headed for the 1970s she was rearing up on her hind legs. Foreign investment was helping create employment, grants were being given to companies opening factories and plants, and there was the feeling that everybody had a few pound in his pocket, something so new to me that it took a bit of getting used to.

I was very surprised when I found it hard to get a taxi at times. This was amazing in a country where for ever and ever only the well-off used cabs. The day Alfie Heffernan drove me to my life as a touring actor, that was only the second time in my life I'd hired a taxi. So Mother Machree was getting a taste of honey at last and the women who'd been held down for so long were starting to throw shapes, some of them even standing on their heads in hotel foyers.

Young women in nightclubs were getting into *abandoned* as a way of behaving. They could come in like beautiful virgins but a few drinks and they were snogging guys they'd just met, and though some of them stuck to the *I don't go all the way on a first date* there were others who thought that was very corny. No doubt about it, if you could show a girl a good time, and you had a pad to take her to, you could enjoy yourself in Dublin in a way that had been more than scarce up to the time I got out.

Up to my ears in females or not, I phoned Jean every night. We were being very nice to each other, surely a bad sign in a marriage. She was taking the kids down to Somerset for a break. It was like home from home, without the aggravation. I said fine, glad she wasn't in need of anything from me, since I was already taking home a different young woman every night unless I had a date with the married lady I called Anna, after Anna Karenina, a hint of literary licence, literally.

Danny Haller's telegram arrived from California telling me 'Wonderful stuff, keep it going!' Within three weeks I'd mailed the complete first draft screenplay, written to run for just under two hours.

Meanwhile I worked with Francis Searle, director, and Bob Gallico, producer, on my movie *The Pale-Faced Girl*, starring lovely Fidelma Murphy from Cork, with a very talented Limerick actor, Kevin McHugh, playing me, and me playing a randy Dublin bus conductor! The short film got made without too many problems and I waved bye-bye as the cast and crew head back to London.

I moved out of the Upper Gardiner Street flat, rented a house in Glenageary on the fringe of the city. This had four bedrooms, which would come in handy should Jean bring the children over for a visit, something I'd been looking for.

My family were back from Somerset. When I talked to the children on the phone, one name kept cropping up, Gerald. If my kids were warning me I didn't get the message.

Jean would bring the children over during that summer of 1968 but she brought her mother too, which made for a hard time. Thinking about it later I came to believe she was bothered by Jean's interest in Gerald, and of course she'd stopped liking me because I had turned into the kind of Irishman that no sane woman wanted her daughter to marry. All the same I tried to show them all a good time even though I was working my buns off. To be honest I hurt so much when the kids left that I began to understand why some guys never saw their children any more. They just couldn't stand the pain at the end of each holiday.

A couple of weeks later Danny Haller calls from Los Angeles. He tells me he is sending a script editor called Frances Doel over to work with me on the new draft of the screenplay. By the end of May I have rewritten it, typing on the dining room table in the Glenageary house, with Frances sitting across from me, taking the pages as they come. She's worked in Hollywood a long time as part of the Roger Corman organisation, which spawned Jack Nicholson, Francis Ford Coppola and many other startling talents. Roger has given Danny Haller the money to make the film of my book, and while he is notoriously careful about budgets, nobody can say he doesn't get movies made. And in the crunch, that keeps a lot of actors and writers earning, which is the dream of every freelance that ever lived.

Danny is a man who wants to get the job done in the cushiest possible way, which leads to my only reservation as to how he is approaching the movie. Through Frances I'm told I have to update the story, meaning that as we're making it in 1968 it will be *set* in 1968, not in the 1950s, as I'd written it in the novel. I seriously question this, I let them see I'm not happy about it. I'm told it's about budget. Nobody wants to spend all that money just to shoot it back there. The message is, we set it now or it doesn't happen. This was a major lesson for me in the art of the film-making business. Your original ideas, characters, just about anything and everything, can be subject to change at any time.

Then, out of the blue, we have a problem about Donal McCann, our leading man, who will play me in the film. Before Donal committed to our project, he had signed to do a play that was expected to run three weeks. To everybody's surprise, the reviews come good, the play is hot, it's booking out.

Danny Haller, who has arrived in Dublin by now, asks me to see if I can sort it out. He also asks me in Groome's late night hostelry if I will play Harry Redmond. His lugubrious manner is in place, the man is serious. I ask him to talk to me about it next day when we're both drinking coffee! The next day he insists he wants me in the part. I have to say no. If it was somebody else's picture, maybe, but it's my first Hollywood writing job, and I've got enough on my plate.

Milo O'Shea finally takes the role and suddenly I see what Danny had in mind when he asked me. I am a big Milo fan but he was never right for that part, and when I sat through the finished movie, I knew two things — I was right to turn it down and Danny had made a mistake in casting Milo. He was just too middle-class, too comfortable, too rounded to be believable as the Street Arab, Harry Redmond.

The film unit was based in the Intercontinental in Ballsbridge and I had a room there where I was chipping away at the script, me and Frances. Danny Haller has now hired me as an associate producer, I'm being paid a weekly fee, already earning it by helping with the casting and finding locations. I'm looking to rent a pub, the ideal place is just outside the back gate of Glasnevin cemetery. Forget it, I'm told. Mister Kavanagh who owns the Gravediggers never rents the bar out for film work, not for love or money. He's something of a free spirit the same man, opens and closes the pub when he feels like it, suits himself down to the ground, which I personally learn to my chagrin when he tells me no way. 'And that's final, Mister Dunne.' He bangs the counter to emphasise his message as if he needed any help.

I buy another drink wondering is there anything I haven't done that would get us a result. At that moment I hear the signature music for *The Kennedys of Castleross* come on the radio.

Mister Kavanagh lights up and gives all his attention to the soap. I sit there quietly as he soaks up the episode. The other drinkers know something I don't because nobody looks to be served while the show is running. As it ends the boss man turns down the wireless, releasing a big sigh of appreciation. I comment on the fact that he seems to have enjoyed it. He waffles about how great the programme is and I let him have his head for a minute before I say as matter-of-factly as I can: 'I wrote that episode in a flat in Upper Gardiner Street.'

Mister Kavanagh's eyes open as though a sadistic proctologist has rammed a brace of sturdy fingers up his bottom. 'Are you — ? My God! It's you, you're the man writes *The Kennedys*?' His hand comes across the bar, takes my glass, slams it under the optic, puts a large whiskey into it and gives it to me in my left hand so that he can shake my right as though I'm a village pump and he needs water in the worst way.

'Well, glory be. I live for *The Kennedys* you know. I never miss it. And I want you to bring your film here. But on one condition.'

I look at him as though he's stepped out of a fiery chariot and I say fervently: 'Anything, Mister Kavanagh.'

'You'll have the pub free gratis and for nothing. I won't take a penny from you, and that's final.' I shake his hand, throwing a silent word of thanks to the patron saint of scriptwriters. Then I'm saying to myself, Wow! With this kind of luck going for us, how can anything cause a ripple on the pond of our production?

I'm bursting to tell Danny Haller the great news as I get back to the Intercon. He's waiting for me and rides over my enthusiasm without any foreplay. He's finally had to accept that Donal McCann is in a hit play that will run for months. The film is off, he himself is leaving as soon as possible for the States.

Talk about a body blow. I have to take an eight count just to get my breath back. I look around the circle of the film's personnel. Disgruntled wouldn't cover it.

'Well shag this for a game of soldiers,' I tell Haller. 'At least give me the chance to show you one more actor. You owe me that.'

Fair play to Danny, who's really fed up, he agrees to leave things on hold until I get back in an hour. When I return to the hotel I have with me a young actor called Des Cave. He's been given a crash course in the lead character Paddy Maguire, which he needed, because he was something of a middle-class boy.

I always liked Des Cave as an actor, and he was smart along with his talent, which worked for us when we stepped into that hotel lounge and Des said 'Hi there!' His smile would have illuminated a neglected cellar, he was fresh, and pretty well designed to have girls all over him like a rash, plus he had this unusual blend of innocence in his way, which was the perfect picture of Paddy as I saw him.

Tamara Assayev, who is now co-producing with Danny Haller, is the first to react. 'Oh yes.' Tamara gives Des an appreciative handshake. 'Oh yes, indeed.' She winks at me —*well done* — turns to Haller: 'What do you say, Danny?'

Haller is nodding his head, slowly his grin opens up his face. 'Des looks just about right to me.'

'Of course he is,' I say. 'I just hauled him out of the Abbey to bring him here. I'm not going to offer you a schmuck and lose my first film, am I?' I laugh, knowing Des is in like Flynn.

'Make the deal, Tamara.' Danny shakes Des by the hand again, chuckling in relief as he goes to take a shower.

Now that we've sorted out our casting problem, I hit the bar in need of a medicinal drink that will double as a celebratory imbibe. I'm elated, no other word for it. That moment when Haller said the movie was off was among the worst of my life — from a dream to a nightmare in a moment. You earn every penny you get in this life.

This stunningly beautiful woman is walking in through the other door of the bar as I order my drink. Our eyes meet, we both stop. I can't believe it. 'I know you.' My heart skips a beat. 'You're Lynn, Lynn Tyler.'

'I've never forgotten you,' she tells me, wearing her mileage like a suntan. 'You never came back for another dance.'

'So you do remember me?' I'm knocked out. Such a long time, yet some-how, now, like yesterday.

As the film began shooting, Lynn Tyler and I fell madly in love. I hadn't seen her since she was this beautiful teenager back in my Four Ps days. We'd had one dance together, a disaster for both of us, she terrified by my savoir faire, having no idea it was booze-induced, while I took her to be a stuck-up cow who thought that what dropped from her bottom in the mornings was coarse-cut marmalade.

Lynn never mentioned her husband of six weeks from that first moment in the bar at the Intercon, but some people around town knew she was married, so there was a breath of scandal connected with us right away. She lived in America now; our meeting while she was here alone on a visit to her mother was some kind of coincidence. 'We had to meet again,' Lynn smiled knowingly. 'How could it have ended in the Four Ps?'

Our affair was fun, but Lynn knew I had a wife and three children. She knew that from the moment we met after all the years. I had never suggested we were going anywhere. She was wonderful, we were terrific together, she seemed to need my high-handed ways, we were tremendous lovers for each other, who could ask for more than that?

Besides I was so busy with the film, the publicity, writing the radio show, considering a couple of other serious offers, with a new novel being published in hardback in September, I didn't want to talk about anything as serious as separation. I didn't need it. What I did need was another drink, more speed, a joint of good shit, a pound of Acapulco Gold.

How could I deny how exciting it was to be in the eye of this agreeable hurricane, your picture in the papers all the time, publishers trying to poach you from your present involvement, your agent wanting you back in London to talk to TV people, an excited film producer wanting to talk a movie deal on *A Bed in the Sticks*, even though he'd read just an outline.

Only the odd time now did I get very drunk, but I was rarely, if ever, sober. This was due mainly to keeping an eye on the level of my intake, topping myself up with the skill of a survivor. I was taking a belt of brandy one afternoon on location in Dalkey when the stills photographer on the film, John Dolan, came to take my picture for a film magazine. I offered him a drink from my hip flask, he said not for me, thanks. Later that week after I'd put Lynn on a plane to the States, I ended up having dinner at Dolan's house in Blackrock. This happened through coincidence. Is there any such thing, I ask myself.

What happened was this — I met someone who happened to be staying with the Dolans. This was Ruth Phillips, who worked in film publicity. A beautiful woman with the blue-black hair of a Greek, passion-dark diva eyes, someone who knew she turned heads when she walked into a room. She certainly turned mine at the Intercon.

Already at the Dolans' dinner table were Danny Haller, Frances Doel and Tamara Assayev, and Judy Comwell, a friend of the Dolans', who was playing a major part in our movie. So it was a busy bread board, exotically adorned you might say by Joan Dolan, the hostess, who was sitting there in an outfit of iridescent colours, shades on her eyes, while she wore a live mongoose on her shoulder.

Joan Dolan was a crazy blonde lady, heiress to something like four hundred million dollars. Her daddy was one of the main men at a huge conglomerate in the United States. John was her second husband, she his third wife, and they didn't drink booze of any kind. Joan had to be *up* on something, she was so high-pitched, yelling a lot as though we were all deaf. Besides, if a woman wearing fur at dinner might seem eccentric, when the fur is breathing and moving about, the kindest mind in the world would surely allow that the lady is not the full shilling!

John was low-key but a real man, and though Joan was the source of the wealth that allowed them to live in luxury, I soon came to know that he wore the pants in that household. Like a lot of rich people, Joan wanted to be something, do something, rather than just have money. So she was all over the film crowd, I mean these were real live film-makers. And when she discovered I was a published novelist as well as the screenwriter of the movie, I became, in about three seconds flat, her new best friend. And I have to say I liked her right away.

That was how the Dolans came into my life though it would be a while before I'd realise just how important they would be. Ruth, too, became a friend; she lived in Fulham and there was always a bed for me if I needed a place to stay. Two new friendships in one evening, both of them designed to be enduring.

While I'd been in Dublin I'd been dropping in to see Ma fairly regularly, bringing the cast and a host of others to meet her. Luke Kelly, maybe the greatest ballad singer that ever lived, was a good mate, and he liked to come up to the flat with me. Katy used to feed him white pudding on toast which he loved, and Luke would sing a song or two for her.

Before I'd left Ireland for those far-off hills, I hadn't heard what you'd call ballads sung around Dublin. Dubs wanted Radio Luxembourg not Radio Éireann. Ma said only culchies, country people, could put up with the doodle-ee-do music, and those songs that went on for ever. Now, ballad groups were entertaining people all over the country, Luke Kelly being part of the Dubliners — a band that actually got a recording of 'Seven Drunken Nights' into the Top Ten in the UK, something you couldn't have imagined a few years earlier.

Showbands were another phenomenon, big bands with lots of singers and impressionists, touring all over Ireland, playing to packed dance halls. Lounge bars were becoming more and more upmarket and luxurious, as if they were in a contest for the Mostest drinking spot in town. There was a lot of money afloat like a drumbeat saying that for the most part the Irish weren't that bothered about tomorrow.

The most fashionable bars were full many nights a week, serving drinks to people who had bought their own homes, or were buying them on mortgage, homes with every modern convenience in them. But not enough to keep many a householder and his wife, or his girlfriend, by the fireside with a glass of beer. Home and hearth were losing out in the battle with bar and booze. Or so it seemed to me.

Before I headed home to Jean and the children I spent an afternoon with Mister Gallagher, the giant Corkman who rescued me from the damnation of

St Mary's on Richmond Hill. He lived in Mount Merrion with his daughter and her family. I took a bottle of whiskey with me for my visit, and the pair of us bored a large hole in it, sitting in the back garden of his home.

Seeing him again after twenty years brought back the memory of his kindness to the kids lucky enough to study under him. This didn't mean he was any kind of pushover, you stepped out of line you got punished. But he was always fair, so that when you did get twelve of the best, six on each hand, you had no bad feeling towards him afterwards. He'd always encouraged me to read and to keep up the standard of the handwriting. 'Good penmanship is like riding a bike, Leo, no load to carry.' Something of an old man by now, Mister Gallagher smiled, nodding his head under its white thatch. 'Your essays were far and away the best ever handed to me. But to be published in London by Hutchinson, and in America, my goodness! I could never have envisioned that for you, Leo.'

He had read my book, admitted being very impressed that I had reached such a height. But 'I was shocked by some of the sex, the very bad language, Leo.' He never adopted my change of name but he let me pour him whiskey. 'I had no idea you were hungry during the afternoons while I was trying to teach you the three Rs. How could I have been so obtuse, so insensitive?'

He was a fair man, a good man, settled into his role in life, not trying to go anywhere, just working to do the best job he could do. He knew we most likely wouldn't ever meet again and his handshake was the equivalent of a lot of hugs his generation couldn't deal with. I was truly glad I'd seen him, knowing I'd think of him every so often, the great and gentle man who helped me become someone who, regardless of how long I might live, would die a student.

Leaving Dublin, I called John Dolan. He asked me to come and stay if I was back in town, I thanked him, said I was hoping to see him again before long. I needed to keep in touch with him. I'd no idea I'd already made the all-important contact, made the connection that could help me pull my life out of the *merde* it had sunk into.

18

I was back home just a matter of days when I realised that the reason things were nice and quiet was because Jean really didn't care any more. I didn't mention this if only because I didn't know what to say. I weighed in with every penny I earned, less whatever I spent on drink and speed and a bit of smoke now and then. Jean hated the very idea of dope, she wouldn't touch it with a bargepole. No big deal, we weren't doing anything together, though we shared a platonic bed, for the sake of the children.

The children were terrific, Sarah seven, Peter five, Yo-yo as we called Jonathan was suddenly a three-year-old. I went back to taking them to the swimming pool on a Saturday morning, back to making the pancakes, back to trying to be some kind of father, feeling, if not knowing, that I was losing them along with their mother, that I was losing my grip on the things that really mattered. And however crazy or wayward or stupid I could be when I fed any of my addictions, my children mattered most, even when the behaviour gave lie to that particular claim. Yet, even in this state of confusion, nobody could have convinced me that I was a deluded person. Talk about being lost.

Just after I got back from Dublin I got to meet Dave Allen, the brilliant Irish comedian. I was excited. This guy was a household name in England and he wanted to play the lead role in my play *The Full Shilling*. He turned out a nice man, the part of Ted had him drooling, he assured me. The only problem was he hadn't got a free night for the next eighteen months. Would I wait that long? Maybe I should have said yes but I didn't.

Shortly after the meeting with Dave Allen, I talked on the phone to the film producer who wanted to make a movie of *A Bed in the Sticks*. I liked the sound of this man as he eulogises about the picaresque quality of the story, the writing, the setting of the touring show, so reminiscent of Priestley's *The Good Companions*. He mentioned a quick trip into hospital for a check-up. He'd like to meet me in a week, get a deal signed so that I can get on with writing the movie.

A week later he was dead. When the medics opened him up to see what was wrong with him, the cancer had already staked its claim. It was awful and I felt very sorry for him. But, being honest about it, I felt even sorrier for myself. To be that close to a movie of my second novel before it was published and then lose it, Jesus! And this happening right after the talk with Dave Allen. What was wrong with me? What was I doing that was so terrible? I couldn't answer my own questions but I was hurting as I asked them. I felt cheated and I was angry as hell. Guys I knew were making fortunes without half my ability — why was that?

This kind of thinking could send me out on the batter, I could get lost for days, not have to think about any of it. The odd time I'd seem to get a clear view of things, remember how I'd longed for the life I was now having. The dream had been to get off the cab, write at home for my living, making enough for a good life, building a future based on my ability to peddle a dream on a piece of paper. I had that life now and I was as miserable as a mortal sin with the punishment easier to identify.

Somewhere in my head I knew I should be enjoying the life, but it wasn't happening. I hadn't got enough success, enough money. That was it. If I had a bit more, well, a lot more, I'd be fine. I'd try working harder, be a bit more disciplined, with luck everything would work out. I'd make it happen better than it was happening right now. It was up to me, and if I could dig myself this far out of the shit, I could go further. It never occurred to me that a fella who can dig his way out can end up with enough shit in his eyes that he can't see the point where he starts digging himself back in.

A Bed in the Sticks was published in September 1968. It sold very well right away, easily going to number one in the Irish hardback best-sellers while *Goodbye to the Hill* topped the paperback list at the same time. English sales were excellent, Arrow bought the paperback rights and it seemed like a story that would get a movie deal. I was more than happy at that stage in the book's life.

I now shocked Hutchinson by telling them I didn't want to have any more books published in hardback, they cost too much for ordinary people to buy. I said it wasn't fair, I wanted *my people* to have the book on the same day as people who were better off.

This was tantamount to taking your fledgling career, dumping it into a deep hole, diving in after it before pulling the earth in on top of you. My friends thought the drink had finally scrambled my brains, but I shrugged off the derision showered on me by those who knew better. I *was* going kind of crazy, though I couldn't admit it, and I think this gesture was my socialist offering for the decade.

In November I agreed to rewrite a movie for a Hollywood producer, Phil Krasne. A pal of mine, Mike Ruggins, had signed to direct the film, and he asked me to come in and write him a script he could use. We'd worked together at the BBC, and I liked him even though he was a far-out kind of person. Phil Krasne was real Harry Hollywood. On our first meeting I seriously wondered how the hell himself and Ruggins ever got together. Phil was a bread-and-butter picture maker, he had to have a beginning, a middle and an end. Mike knew about these three elements, he just didn't see them in this particular order.

I went to work on the script at home in East Sheen. Mike and Phil came down to the house that evening and I handed them twenty-nine pages. They read them there and then. When Krasne was through he stood up, shook my hand and said with real Hollywood heart , 'Mister Dunne, welcome aboard! Now, I need to take a piss.'

Just after Christmas 1968 I'm back in Ireland, staying at the Intercon again, about to start working officially on Phil Krasne's script — working title 'I Can't, I Can't'. The way things are turning out has me buzzing again. A new film deal seems like a pretty good way to kiss in the new year of 1969.

I was given an office at Ardmore Studios but I couldn't work there. It was gloomy and I didn't like the way Krasne's partner, Lee Davis, kept putting his head in the door. From day one I felt the guy had read a book *How to Be a Successful Movie Producer*. Okay, he wasn't mad about me either.

By working in my hotel room, I could avail of room service. By now I needed to keep topping myself up, there was no way I could go two or three hours without booze of some kind. And by not being at the studio I didn't have Ruggins and Krasne in my hair all day. It would be a miracle for them to finish the movie together. I saw them every morning for a breakfast meeting, they came back to read the day's pages at about seven in the evening, which was about as much of them as I could take, professionally.

The day after I finished the rewrite Ruggins and Krasne came apart. A blind man could have seen it coming. I tried to get Mike to see reason. 'Make the movie, show the industry you can control a unit for eight weeks.' He said no, that he couldn't stand being around Krasne. They were totally incompatible. So my work was finished but Mike was gone. The movie would be made, screened as *Wedding Night*. It would be a mixture of my work and that of the guy who wrote the original story, and we shared the screen credit which was fair enough.

I was glad to be out of the movie, and I took a few days extra in the hotel. I saw my mother a bit, walked my Dublin, meeting some old mates, had a little holiday for myself. A pilgrimage to Charlemont Street, with its Corporation flats alongside the tenements like a row of old postcards drying up in the sun, the breaking balls of demolition ready to start the rebuilding that the city needed.

I spent some time with the Dolans, the only people apart from Frank Cunningham and his wife, Dolores, to invite me to their home for dinner. As yet the Irish hadn't overcome the public house culture. People, dying to see you, met you in a pub, you went on to curry in an Indian restaurant. Pakistani food really, even better than Indian. Along with Chinese food it was eating into the traditional fish and chip business.

The Dolans were both in the Alcoholics Anonymous fellowship, John dry for twenty-seven years, Joan on the wagon at present, though still out of it some of the time from smoking joints that should have carried a health warning. They were both good to me, very tolerant, especially during a lunch where I drank a couple of bottles of wine, followed by brandies, a callous piece of behaviour when you consider why they didn't drink alcohol. Later I could see that it was a sort of last hurrah on my part, bravado, as though I somchow knew that by the next time I met John and Joan, there would have been a major change in my life.

And so I headed back to England, Jean, the kids. Sadly I drank a lot on the plane so I have no memory of how things were when I got home. More sadness that need never have been because I decided to have just one drink for the flight. One drink that went on for ever.

One night in late spring, I pull some titled lady in Finch's. She is a real looker, but her name doesn't stick. The booze and my memory suit themselves about what they hold onto. Makes me wonder is it true that you blow ten thousand brain cells every time you get drunk!

Three or four days later I give Jean a cup of tea in bed and for the first time in about a year she makes it clear that she's interested in having sex with me. I am more than surprised, knowing I've pushed her to the edge of her endurance.

Shortly afterwards I know something is wrong with me. In an instant I remember an older man on board ship talking about VD, the way he said, 'You never have to look for it, son, if you've got it, you know it right away.'

My insides lock in fear. Sweet Jesus Christ. If I'm right and I have it, have I given it to Jean? I have to go and lock myself in the bathroom to try and still the panic that explodes inside. Jesus Christ Almighty, help me, help me through this, please don't let Jean be infected and I will change, I will change, I swear it on my children's lives. The useless prayers of the militant agnostic when he is in deep shit. I am demented as I drive up to Hammersmith to the hospital which has a VD clinic. Not that I need a doctor to tell me I've got a dose.

The doctor tells me yes, I've got gonorrhoea. I feel an instant crush in my gut, as though it's caved in down there, a stomach pain to bend you double, then it's over, and suddenly it's as though relief is pouring in through some hole I didn't know I had. It sounds crazy, I know, but hearing the very last news I'd have volunteered to hear, the weight that has been lying on my heart for so long seems to be lightened.

Driving up to the clinic I was hoping desperately that I was in the clear, that the swelling and the discharge I was experiencing was just some strain from too much activity. Yet when the result of the test is given to me, it seems that this awful punishment has, to some degree, set me free.

Gonorrhoea earns you a jab, just one injection, and some pills to take for a week, that's all the treatment you need. By the time I get home I can already feel an improvement in the condition, so physically it's no big deal. Mentally it can do a real number on your sense of well-being, but as I drive back to East Sheen from Hammersmith, I am trying to be calm. Telling Jean the story is going to be tough but it has to be done. She has to be seen by the doctor in the hospital as soon as possible.

'Don't look so worried.' These are Jean's first words when I tell her the bad news. 'You're no different today than you've been for God knows how long. You just picked up a little pox this time. I'm amazed this is the first time.'

Jean gets her injection and she takes her pills, at no time does she attack me in any way. I half-expect her to put a knife in me, who could have blamed her. But she does nothing and she is more than civil in the weeks that follow. When she gets the all-clear she decides to take the children down to Somerset. I say nothing, I know I am not entitled. Whatever rights I've had up to now, they aren't available to me any more. So Jean and the kids head for Nailsea with Conchita in tow and I'm alone in the house and I can't stand it. So I do something really original — I head for the boozer.

Later that evening I come out of a memory lapse in the Sun Inn at Barnes. I come into the present as I arrive back at the bar, somehow knowing the empty space in front of me is mine. I guess I've been to the loo. This guy I know is laughing his head off like an orang-utan in good humour. He indicates to the barmaid to give me another. This tells me I've been drinking with him before I went into the blackout.

'I should probably belt you in the teeth for what you just said.' His Cockney accent is the nicest thing about him. 'You Mick bastard, it was so funny I can't take umbrage.'

I'm glad he's got a sense of humour. He's a big guy, I couldn't handle him in the whole of my health, let alone legless on Merrydown straight from the barrel. 'What was it I said?' I ask him.

'You told me, you said: "You're such a pain in the arse you make piles seem like a gift from fucking heaven!"' He goes ape again and his whinnying laugh sounds ugly. I nip back to the loo to write down the line, since my memory is largely missing at that moment. While I'm in the toilet, I wash my face under the cold tap. As the water runs on my hands, my wayward mind is back in Jervis Street hospital as Da lies dying. I can't believe the game my head is playing. I've come to the pub to get stinking, just to get away from the *poor me's*, and I'm wallowing in self-pity because Da never saw my picture on my novel. 'You are some sad arsehole!' I tell your man in the mirror.

I get out of the pub on dodgy legs, taking a walk around Barnes Common. Anything to stop me feeling so sorry for myself. But the days of Da's dying won't quit. They hold me and I'm back in Dublin trying to keep the bruises on my heart from climbing onto my sleeve. I know I am a fuck-up, I accept I am not making it in the important areas of my life, but I love Da and he's a goner, and there's nothing I can do.

I find a pinpoint of refuge in the memory of walking and talking, between the hospital visits, with Kevin Hall, a neighbour who was all too aware that Da was dying. Walking back from the pub together after a drinking session with the little poet-painter, glad to hear his hearty laugh, both of us jarred enough to listen to old stories heard a hundred times over. Kevin, in his drunken decency, was eager to give me a lift, knowing the weight of Da's upcoming exit was an iron wreath around my spirit. He was sharp-featured with coal-black eyes that shone from the madness hidden until the drink gave it a walk around the block. He was telling me a chestnut and I didn't care how many times I'd heard it before:

Mary says: 'I hear May Burns is getting married.'

Bridie says: 'I didn't know she was pregnant!'

Mary says: 'She's not.'

'Well,' says Bridie, 'there's swank for ye!'

That particular day I went with Kevin up to his flat to have a bottle of stout with him, seeing he was nearly as lonely as I was myself. It's no lie to say that he and I fell about laughing at a lot of old jokes, and I was glad of his company. The laughing and the repartee, whatever passed between us in the short time together was a very welcome respite, one that I needed in the worst way.

Ma launched into a verbal attack on me when I came downstairs, and not just because she had food going cold. 'Why would you want to be listenin' to that eejit, half-mad when he gets the jar into him?' I didn't tell Ma I needed a half-mad man just then. Any more than I gave a damn about how she was feeling about me, or Kevin Hall, or even Da. If she was glad my father was dying, I didn't want to know. If she was sorry, so what! It was too fucking late for sorry, for Ma and for me.

About two weeks after this, Kevin came home from the pub of an afternoon, found he had left his door key upstairs in the flat. He had some drink taken, why the hell wouldn't he. So he decided he'd climb up the drainpipe and get into his flat through the lavatory window. He didn't make it, though he got to the three-quarter mark. Some of the neighbours, a few kids, gathered below to make encouraging noises while they laughed at his madness. When he fell down to his death outside the hallway he had shared with the rest of us, the laughing stopped.

When I read Ma's letter about the passing of another little man nobody knew, I felt very sad. As I thought of Ma sitting alone to write the letter, I lost the anger I'd stored up since the day I hurt her by preferring Kevin's company to her own. Putting pen to paper she had paid her dues for the put-down over my fraternising with 'that eejit, half-mad when he gets the jar into him'. Lucky Kevin to die half-mad, to have survived the seeming determination of the world to drive all of us fucking nuts.

While Jean and the children are away in Somerset, I get an out of the blue phone call from a fella who's in trouble with a movie. I can't help smiling. It's as if I'm becoming the Seventh Cavalry of movie rewrites.

'I heard you can write fast.'

Can I come and see him? Does a fish swim? He will pay me well. I go to the guy's studio-home, a magnificent set-up in the West End. He gives me a whiskey and shows me his movie. A love story with a motor racing background, most of the budget coming from tobacco companies if you judge by the product placement, all the cars carrying specific logos to help sell cigarettes. When the movie ends he asks me what is wrong with it.

'For openers it's about forty minutes short. Not forty you can tack on at the end,' I suggest. 'You need inserts, three minutes here, one there, a couple somewhere else.'

The guy offers me the job, I take it, he needs the script like last week. He pays me up front in cash, gives me a room of my own, an office space, with freedom to drink what I need to get the job done. In three days I leave him a happy camper. The additions are dovetailed into his original script and he's more than grateful. As I say goodbye he tells me that some day he'll hire me to write an original story.

I forget about him, even now I don't remember his name, and though Jean is happy with the very good money earned while she's been in Somerset, we are further apart than ever before. Sadly, I don't even mind that she doesn't care for me any more. We have our kids in common, nothing more, that I might be forced to leave them gives me a gut wrench that ought to be a one-time-only experience.

Three months later the Formula One guy calls me. He is to make a feature film and he wants me to write it. His producers want him to see a private showing of a certain new movie later that day. He'll call me back, tell me where to meet him, so we can see this movie they're all so crazy about together. He hangs up, I open *Variety*, the showbiz paper, and I'm reading a wonderful review for the movie I wrote for Phil Krasne — *Wedding Night* — when the guy rings me back. He tells me the movie we're going to see is *Wedding Night*.

'The review in *Variety*'s sensational,' he tells me. 'Talk about lucky timing.' He hangs up again, to call me back later with details about the viewing theatre. I practically reel in glee in my study. Somebody wants another film like the last one I did. Was it possible a god somewhere was gone laughing at my good luck?

In actual fact, I never hear from the guy again. He doesn't call me back in minutes as he said he would, he doesn't call me that evening or the next day, he never calls me again. I am so stunned that it takes days to stop waiting for the phone to ring. Then I know it isn't going to happen and I wonder is that god gone laughing at me and not with me. Either way he has a funny fucking sense of humour.

As we head halfway into October I wake up one morning with a lovely black girl I don't know. We are naked in bed together. This is a bad one, the worst amnesia yet, because this girl is so stunning, nobody should ever forget having sex with her. And I don't even remember how we met, how we got to where we are.

Somehow I get myself out of her home without waking her up. As I step out the door I have no idea where I am, but as soon as I hit the street I realise I'm in Hampstead. And just for a change my car is right there in front of me. Thank God. I'm so tired of wandering about to find the car, I'm so tired trying to find my life.

Meanwhile, I can't find my car keys. They are not in any of my pockets. I feel like weeping, like crying out loud, needing to yell out for somebody to please help me. I lean against the car, my eyes on my feet, and there beside my shoe are the car keys, lying where they have been all night.

I bend down, dying a couple of times before I can straighten up again. I'm too shaky to move, I go on leaning against the car. Then a very strange thing happens. I'm suddenly looking down from a great height at this pathetic guy leaning against this motor car. I can see he's in bits. In the same moment, in the subjective position, I hear this voice that belongs to me, saying in disbelief: 'Dunne, this is fucking ridiculous.'

That is the moment when I see for the first time what drink and I have achieved. The first glimpse of how pathetic I am. I begin to weep there by the car, a shaking, aching, sweaty, smelly, fiercely frightened little boy that many people mistook for a man. 'Oh my God' I hear this bit of a prayer coming out of my mouth. 'I am heartily sorry, so sorry, for being such a fuck-up!'

I am in such a bad way that I have to stop for a drink on the way home. It is about noon, so I am definitely in the doghouse with Jean, having deprived her of the car to take the children to school. So much for wanting to be a good father.

Alone in the pub, drinking to steady myself, I'm not going to get drunk. Not today, like so many of those days when I went in just for the one and got lost again without leaving the bar. Such bullshit! I'd never been interested in one drink, just as I couldn't stand people who could settle for one drink. They were such fucking bores!

When I get home Jean isn't there. I make coffee, glad to be free of the shakes. Sipping the hot drink, willing the caffeine into my veins, I am remembering John Dolan back in Dublin. The shirt cuffs always showing at his wrists, his slow smile as he tells me how he quit drinking, how he had found AA when he was quite literally lying in the gutter in New York City.

This memory helps me lift the phone. A voice tells me there's an AA meeting in Redcliffe Gardens that same evening at seven o'clock. I leave Jean a note with the car keys. I just write I've got something to do, that I'll see her later. On Upper Richmond Road I grab a cab, going to Finch's for my final drink. Jack Connell is away so I leave the pub without having a jar. And I go walkabout till the early evening, walking, munching candy bars, and more walking, until finally, it's time to go to the meeting. In the AA house I meet a guy called Pat. I had soldiered with him in the trenches that pubs are to the dedicated drunk. He is acting chairman to the meeting and I am stunned. This is a fella who could foul himself while you were drinking with him. And he looks wonderful, though he still sounds as if he doesn't trust anybody. I say to him that first night: 'I don't want to lose my missus, my kids. That's why I'm here.' He passes me a cup of tea and suggests that I just listen. I sit down with about twenty other people, men and women, and Pat gets the meeting under way. He identifies himself as an alcoholic, five years sobriety, one day at a time. So he had been off the juice while some know-alls like me felt sure the demon had got him, that he was dead and gone.

Pat enumerates the symptoms of alcoholism as he had come to recognise them in himself. This being a beginners' meeting he is keeping it all very simple. I'm ticking off the symptoms I can identify, I feel tears on my face. A guy beside me passes me a couple of tissues, somebody else gives me a lighted cigarette. A few minutes later, I hear myself very quietly, my head down between my knees: 'Jesus Christ. That's all that's wrong, I'm an alcoholic.' Now the tears really flow, one eye dumping fear, the other pouring out relief. I learn that alcoholism is a disease, recognised by the World Health Organization as the third biggest killer of mankind. I'm stunned by this news, almost weak with relief, guzzling a fresh cigarette, a taste of hope inhaled with the smoke.

When I get home. I tell Jean about AA, that I've found a way to beat the booze. She's glad I feel so confident, but: 'I've heard this a hundred times, maybe five hundred. You with the tears and the sobs and the bullshit! I'll never, never drink again, Jean, I swear it, I'll never touch another drop.' She gets a cigarette going, her hands shaking, her anger fuelled by the truth in every word she's saying.

'This time is different, Jean. This time I just know.'

Smoke pours from her mouth: 'That's great. But I don't care any more. Really, I just want you to fuck off, get out of my life, stop fucking things up for me and the kids!' Her tears flow, she looks at me as though I'm completely lost to her. 'Will you do me one great favour and just go, please, just go.'

I want to reason with her, ask for time to show I'm sincere, that this time I really have found the answer. I can't ask this of her, not after all I've put her through. Whatever's gone down, she's entitled to a life free of my fucking up, no law saying she has to live with a man she no longer cares for. It's all so plain to see. She doesn't love me any more, she doesn't like me, and she does-n't want me around. It's hard to swallow, but no part of me can argue with her right to be free of me.

I'm not saying I was still in love with Jean. But I never wanted our marriage to come to an end. So what! What did this matter when I could go drinking, not come home for a week or ten days. How much was I worth to Jean that day in the Hammersmith VD clinic?

How long is a piece of string!

'All right,' I say without any anger or whatever, resigned to the fact that what was asked was fair, that it was over for us. 'Give me a week or two to get something together, okay? After that I'll be gone.'

I won't pretend I can remember the weeks that followed the end of my marriage to Jean. I was numb from shock a lot of the time, I was so sad about having to leave the children, the home we'd worked for. For all the reckless carry-on, all the broken promises, despite all the warnings that now seemed so obvious, I'd never dreamed it would come to this. All I could do was haunt AA meetings all over London, my gut warning me this was the only way for me to stay off the booze.

Jean and I told the children I was going away to work on another movie, that I'd be on the phone, bringing presents when I came home again. My tears wouldn't have surprised the kids, they were used to me being a marshmallow.

I have fourteen hundred quid in the world and I give Jean nine hundred of it the day I leave. She takes the money without mentioning the twenty-five grand she has inherited a few weeks before. When she asks me what about the house, I tell her that my half belongs to her and the kids. I leave, trying to be cool in front of the children, act as though I am just going to be away for a few weeks.

At the same time this desperate need is screaming in my brain as I say good-bye to Sarah, Peter and Jonathan. It's a tearing urgency that I need them to understand: I want to assure them that nothing will ever change my feelings towards them; that there isn't anything they can do that will ever come between us in a serious way.

I keep this bottled up inside because there is just no way I can lay this stuff on them. It sounds like a guy who's dying, or at least like someone who knows he's not going to be seeing them for a long time.

Pat Glasser, my fellow dreamer from County Clare, drives me to Heathrow to take the plane to Ireland. He is sad to see me go, that I have had to go, really, from my own home. At the same time he envies me going to Ireland a free man. He has troubles in his own marriage, another fella with a great wife who took him before he grew up, just as Jean accepted me.

Glasser and I were two of a kind. Our problems erupted out of the behaviour we felt entitled to indulge in because we dreamed big dreams, and we needed many women and oceans of booze, and a wife who would have to be a saint to hang in there. Not much to ask when you say it fast!

Always one of the best to me, Pat knew me pretty well, so he had been more than surprised when I told him I was heading to Dublin. For years I'd been saying I'd never go back home, and now, out of the blue, I feel that there is nowhere else for me to go. All the anger I brought out of Ireland with me when I left for ever, it was all faded and gone, or so it seemed to me.

'If I can stay sober in Ireland, I'll be safe anywhere on earth.' I know I'm scared enough that I'm trying to reassure myself. But this is how I'm saying goodbye to Glasser, giving him a hug, telling him I'll see him when he comes home to Kilrush, where his mother was born.

'You'll be fine, baby. They broke the mould when they made you.' Pat was always willing to take the high road, help you stay up.

'At times I think they broke the mould, then they made me anyway!' I'm aiming to make him laugh but it doesn't work. He can hear the bit of self-pity there, just as I can, but he lets it go. And I leave him there at Heathrow, one friend who will always be there for me, regardless.

Climbing up the stairway to the plane, I realise I'm taking the first step, what the Yanks call 'the irreducible minimum' to some kind of fresh start. I'm nervous at the idea, and I'm scared white inside to be going flying without booze in me. This will be the first time in too many years, maybe the first time ever.

I want to get my life together, and I can, I know I can. I have to make it work, for the first time, really. I'm longing to be a father again to my children, and who knows, some day, maybe even a friend to Jean?

When the plane takes off I know I'm facing a large agenda. Thirty-four years old, some kind of big kid hauling around the reckless heart of a teenager.

Thank God that I found AA. I've hurt myself enough that I want no more of it. I know I have to listen to what the recovery programme recommends. And AA suggest that you Keep It Simple, which suits me down to the ground.

They tell you to go to the AA meetings, ninety meetings in ninety days being the ideal. I have been going, believe me, haunting AA rooms all over London, and it's going to be a meeting a day for me in Dublin, no matter what else is going on.

The other major message is to stay away from One Drink for One Day. They say that if you don't take that first one, things will stop getting any worse. In other words, your life will get better. I'd love some of that so I've hit fourteen meetings in a row, and so far, so good. I'm also turning on to the One Day at a Time philosophy. I've been giving it a run around the block. At this minute, it's working. I'll settle for that, just for today.

Longford Library

3 0015 00086600 6